WILLIAM MASON

The First New Zealand Architect

William Mason was born in 1810 at Ipswich. His early mentors were Telford, Nicholson, and Blore. He practised architecture in his native town and then emigrated in 1838 to New South Wales where he took employment with the Colonial Architect. From Sydney he sailed for New Zealand as a member of Governor Hobson's staff and became the first architect to live and work in this country.

Mason stayed twenty-two years in Auckland sampling the many occupations of a colonist – auctioneering, farming, and politics, as well as architecture. While a member of Parliament he moved south to Dunedin to enjoy the prosperity of a province suddenly enriched by the discovery of gold. He became Dunedin's first mayor and then, in 1877, withdrew to the seclusion of Lake Wakatipu.

Among Mason's well-known buildings are the former Government House at Auckland and St Matthew's Church, Dunedin. This book tells much about early building in New Zealand and, because it approaches colonial history from a new angle, provides some unexpected insights to New Zealand's formative years.

There are ninety-nine illustrations. The book has been designed by Hamish Keith.

John Stacpoole grew up in Auckland and attended university there. From the school of architecture he went to M. K. Draffin's office for two years before visiting England and Europe. He worked briefly with Professor Basil Ward in London, returned to Auckland and the Draffin office, and then moved to the Ministry of Works. In 1965 he was appointed architectural adviser to the New Zealand Historic Places Trust and in 1970 was co-opted to membership of the Trust.

He has lectured on the early history of Auckland for university extension courses and has published a number of articles on subjects germane to this book, has written a guide to the Waimate Mission House, and has in preparation (with Peter Beaven) an introduction to New Zealand architecture.

D1116873

WILLIAM MASON
The First New Zealand Architect

OUR PORTRAIT GALLERY.—No. 11. William Mason Esq., Mayor of Dunedin, J.P., and late M.H.R.

1. *William Mason Esq., Mayor of Dunedin.*

WILLIAM MASON
The First New Zealand Architect

John Stacpoole

1971
Auckland University Press
Oxford University Press

© 1971 John Stacpoole

PRINTED IN NEW ZEALAND
by Whitcombe & Tombs Limited,
Auckland, in 10 point and 8 point
Monotype Series 7, set by Monoset
Trade Services.

CONTENTS

ILLUSTRATIONS IN THE TEXT

(Illustrations of buildings designed by Mason, or by his office, are listed at the end of the text.)

ACKNOWLEDGEMENTS

This study of the life of New Zealand's first architect has been written over several years during which I have met with remarkable kindness and co-operation from so many people in this country and in England that it would require a chapter in itself to name them all. I hope they realize my gratitude. I cannot, however, fail to acknowledge my debt to Mr N. Y. A. Wales senior and Mr N. Y. A. Wales junior, of Dunedin, and to the New Zealand Government Architect, Mr F. G. F. Sheppard, each of whom has made his wide knowledge readily available, to the Librarians of the Auckland Public Library, the Auckland Institute and Museum, the Alexander Turnbull Library, the General Assembly Library, the Hocken Library, the Mitchell Library (Sydney), the Westminster Library (Marylebone), and the Royal Institute of British Architects, to Miss Pryde of the Otago Early Settlers' Association, Miss Mercer of the Dunedin Public Library, Miss Cocks, Miss Hornabrook and the late Michael Standish of New Zealand National Archives, to the Archives Offices of Greater London, Gloucestershire, Suffolk, and Surrey, to Mr Edward F. Mason of Woodbridge (Suffolk), the late G. P. King of Rowhedge, the Rev. A. H. Gosney of Colchester, Mr J. Townshend Smith of Epsom and Dr Denys Harding of Bedford College.

I would like to thank Lady Fergusson, Miss Una Platts, the Misses Hodgkinson, Mrs. R. M. Ross, and Mrs Una Smith of Auckland and Mrs A. Devenish-Meares of Hastings. I have had particular help from the Rt Rev. G. R. Monteith, Assistant Bishop of Auckland, Vice-Admiral Sir Maxwell Richmond of Whangarei, Mr K. C. McDonald of Oamaru, Mr Lloyd Veint of Diamond Lake, Dr E. H. McCormick, Dr M. P. K. Sorrenson, Dr G. A. Wood, Messrs T. C. Kissling, W. A. Laxon, C. J. Parr, R. C. J. Stone, and. H. Wyatt of Auckland, Dr R. K. Dell and Mr Hector of the Dominion Museum, Wellington, and Messrs O. E. Macfie, J. O. Aimers, C. T. Morgan, E. B. C. Murray, J. F. G. Stark, and R. A. King of Dunedin, and Mr Athol Preece of Palmerston North.

Photographs and drawings have come from the office of Messrs Mason and Wales of Dunedin and from various public collections. Messrs Clifton Firth of Auckland, A. T. D. Frost of Gloucester, and Michael Cornell of Ipswich have been most helpful in photographing particular buildings.

No one has helped more than Mrs Brenda Gamble who not only typed the manuscript but offered, also, many valuable suggestions and Mrs R. M. Ross who brought her encyclopedic knowledge to bear upon the proofs.

—J. S.

The publishers gratefully acknowledge grants to aid the publication of this book from the Dunedin City Council; Mason and Wales, Architects, Dunedin; the New Zealand Institute of Architects; and the Winstone Limited Centenary Educational Trust, Auckland.

ABBREVIATIONS

The following abbreviations have been used in footnotes:

A.D.	Army Department
A.I.M.	Auckland Institute and Museum Library.
A.P.L.	Auckland Public Library.
A.T.L.	Alexander Turnbull Library.
D.P.L.	Dunedin Public Library.
G.B.P.P.	Great Britain Parliamentary Papers.
H.L.	Hocken Library.
I.A.	Internal Affairs.
M.H.R.	Member House of Representatives.
M.P.C.	Member Provincial Council.
N.Z.F.A.	New Zealand Field Artillery.
O.P.	Otago Province.

I INTRODUCTION

The meanest artisan contributes more to the accommodation of life than the profound scholar. – Samuel Johnson.

The first necessity of settlement in a new land is the provision of food and fresh water and the second necessity the provision of shelter. Whatever the settler's ambitions he must attend to these primary needs before indulging any inclination for better things. In the provision of food and drink the connoisseur must wait, though travellers there were in the nineteenth century, who gladly made do with claret when water seemed less safe. In the other basic need – for a roof – the building artisan, whether such by training or by amateur necessity, is likely to precede the architect; but not for long. As the settlement begins to take organized shape the artisan is overtaken and the planner steps in. Appropriately enough, New Zealand's first architect was appointed by her first Governor.

The settlement of New Zealand by Europeans began, of course, on the shores of those drowned valleys of the North which open as harbours, able, as the saying goes, to shelter the whole British Fleet, and peter out like the Hokianga into pink and brown swamps full of mangroves and tea tree. It was among the settlers themselves, the motley collection of missionaries, traders, timberworkers and runaway seamen, that the first artisans were to be found. Among the missionaries, William Fairburn was a carpenter, as were William Hall, William Puckey and James Bean. John Bedggood was a wheelwright, James Kemp a blacksmith, John King a ropemaker and John Edmonds a stonemason. They put up their dwellings, stores and schoolhouses using whatever materials were to hand, laboriously pit-sawing timber, experimenting in the making of bricks or the burning of lime, or very sensibly adapting the *raupo* huts which were native to the country.

But after a while they became more ambitious. As early as 1820 William Hall was writing to the secretary of the Church Missionary Society that Mr Butler, the head of the mission at the Bay of Islands, drove him and his fellow tradesmen like 'a parcel of porters or bargemen'. 'I went into Mr Butler's house and he & Mrs Butler were quite in a fret, saying that they lived in a pigsty, and that everyone could get a house but them . . .

'Mr Butler wants a house built 40 feet long, 16 feet wide and 20 feet high, with a verandah at the back part of it, supported with columns and enclosed with palisading, and a room of 8 feet square under each end of the verandah. The house is to be two storeys high, with a hall and staircase in the centre of the building, and a circular fanlight, and pilasters at the front door.'[1]

All through the journals of Archdeacon Henry Williams there is constant reference to the labour of building. 'My brother and myself', he writes in December 1827, 'engaged the whole of this day and yesterday plastering and repairing some of the cells of the Beehive, as the school for the female children of the Mission is to commence next week in it. Our performance has been fair and may prove a valuable discovery for future housebuilders and repairers in this land for years to come.'[2] And six months later he writes: 'Mr Hobbs and I commenced the ceiling of the kitchen with plaister, being the first experiment made in this land: at first the mortar was too thin, then too stiff, however after much time and patience we made it stick up, and as we proceeded we accomplished our work more to satisfaction.'[3]

Other men were doing likewise. Over on the Hokianga, Thomas McDonnell had a considerable establishment. At the Bay of Islands men like Clendon, Mair, and Polack accommodated themselves with a surprising degree of civilization. Their buildings, we may assume, were either brought ready-framed from Port Jackson or were built on the spot according to their own ideas or whim, helped no doubt by the use of carpenters' pattern books and whatever experience the carpenters might themselves command.

So far as we know, James Busby's residence at Waitangi was the first New Zealand building planned by an architect. Before leaving Sydney to take up his appointment he went to John Verge, the architect of Elisabeth Bay House, for the design of a house which long remained the envy of other settlers. Verge wrote to Busby as follows:

'Sydney, 8th Novr., 1832.
'Sir,

'I have sent you a Design for a house intended for your residence in New Zealand, which I hope will meet with your approbation. It is to be framed in Sydney, weatherboarded outside, and lath and plaster inside.

'In this Plan I have studied economy as much as convenience, as everything will be very plain; the rooms, Stores, and closets may appear numerous, but they are small; and I think you could not dispense with any of those conveniences in a Country like New Zealand.

'The whole expense of Erecting and completing the same (if by Contract in Sydney) I estimate at £592 15s 4d, Five hundred and Ninety two Pounds 15s 4d.

'With a view to reduce this Estimate, I have enquired of several Gentlemen who have establishments in New Zealand, if it would be possible to get a portion of the Materials there at a cheaper rate than in Sydney; the result of that enquiry is that you cannot depend on getting any part of them there, unless you take men with you to procure them.

'Under these circumstances, I think it would be better to procure all materials here, more especially as the Building Timbers which are used here, are more durable than any Timber I have seen from that Country.

'I am &c
'J. Verge.'[4]

A few years later, when the first church at Waimate North was found to be inadequate, the Rev. William Yate of the Church Missionary Society commissioned Sampson Kempthorne, one of the first members of the Royal

[1]J. R. Elder (ed.), *Marsden's Lieutenants.* Dunedin, 1934. p. 243.
[2]Lawrence M. Rogers (ed.), *The Early Journals of Henry Williams.* Christchurch, 1961. p. 90.
[3]*Journals*, p. 137.
[4]*Historical Records of Australia.* Series I, Vol. XVII. Sydney, 1923.

Institute of British Architects, to design a new building. This he did and exhibited the drawings at the Royal Academy. The church was begun in 1838.[5] Its form is best discoverable in the drawings contained in the diaries of the Rev. W. C. Cotton who shows it as more Georgian than Gothic, a squarish wooden building with hipped roof and overhanging eaves, pointed windows whose glazing bars scarcely qualified as tracery, and a low tower and steeple. This building was itself replaced in 1871.

Busby's residency gave way to Hobson's government and life at the Bay of Islands was never quite the same. Captain William Hobson, R.N., arrived at Kororareka in H.M.S. *Herald* on 29 January 1840 and made his curiously flawed proclamation of sovereignty on 21 May, claiming the 'Northern Island' by treaty and the 'Middle Island' and 'Stewart's Island' by right of discovery. He had shown reasonable forethought in his choice of the 'officers' he brought with him. Most of these had been engaged by Governor Gipps at Port Jackson but some he interviewed himself. His suite in the *Herald* consisted of Willoughby Shortland, Police Magistrate; Felton Mathew, Acting Surveyor; George Cooper, Collector of Customs and Treasurer; James Stuart Freeman, Private Secretary; Samuel Edward Grimstone, Clerk; four policemen of the New South Wales Mounted Police, and three menservants.

On 17 March, the storeship *Westminster* arrived with Sarah Mathew, wife to the Acting Surveyor, various other females, private passengers, and mechanics, as well as John Johnson, Colonial Surgeon; J. J. Galloway, Assistant Surveyor; and William Mason, Acting Superintendent of Works.

It is William Mason's career which we will attempt to follow in these pages, not only as the first architect to settle in New Zealand but also as an exemplary colonist, a man of many parts deserving whatever praise we may at this late hour give him. He left few statements to illumine his personal life: his surviving letters are official rather than personal, his diaries matter of fact: he nowhere theorizes about his architectural intentions. But his apparent reticence is no more than the natural condition of a well-balanced man of his time, adventurous but conformist, ambitious but not self-seeking, self-respecting but courteous to others. His stated choice of virtues – strict integrity, punctuality and assiduity – when he sought the patronage of the first settlers of Auckland, may have represented his ideals more closely than such claims usually do. He chose, however, to follow his career in circumstances where such virtues were continually tested and it is intended here to let those circumstances frame his life, avoiding such conjectures as cannot be sustained by facts.

[5]It has been assumed (Colvin: *A Biographical Dictionary of English Architects, 1660-1840*) that the Waimate Church was built to Kempthorne's design. But Yate, by the scandal of his dismissal, had so roused the hatred of the missionaries in New Zealand that they may have refused the design he commissioned and have drawn their inspiration, instead, from Francis Greenway's church at Liverpool, New South Wales, which it certainly resembled. Richard Taylor writing about Waimate to his wife, 26 March 1839, describes 'the outline of a larger church of the same dimensions of that at Liverpool but if anything rather loftier . . . .' (Grey Papers, A.P.L.)

II ENGLAND

In the coach yesterday, coming from Suffolk, were two gentlemen and myself, all strangers to each other. In passing the vale of Dedham, one of them remarked, on my saying it was beautiful, 'Yes, sir, this is Constable's country.' I then told him who I was, lest he should spoil it. – Constable to Lucas, 14 November 1832. *Memoirs of the Life of John Constable Esq., R.A.* by C. R. Leslie, R.A.

William Mason was born in Ipswich, Suffolk, on 24 February 1810, the eldest child of George and Elisabeth Mason. The family, in the person of his grandfather (another William who was possibly the builder of Dagenham Church in Essex – the name, as architect, appears on its tower), had gone to Suffolk from Leicestershire in 1775. This elder William married Susan Seaman of Mendlesham, of a family which counted two deaths by martyrdom, and died in 1820. His fifth son, George, was born at Wickham Market on 12 December 1782, married on 18 April 1809, Elizabeth Forty, the daughter of Richard Forty of Stow-on-the-Wold, Gloucestershire, and died at Ipswich on 2 January 1865.

George Mason is described as being singularly absent-minded and far from astute. In his younger days he worked in London and there met his wife, seven years his junior, who had been brought up at Ewell in Surrey and later lived with her aunt, the wife of a London brassfounder named Bowen. On his marriage George returned to Ipswich and apparently practised as an architect-builder. Later he became Borough Surveyor and one of the original Ipswich Dock Commissioners under the Act of 1837, but whatever success he had in life was attributed by his family to the superior intelligence of his wife, a remarkable woman, shrewd, thrifty and handsome, who raised a large family and died in 1884, at the age of ninety-seven, after falling downstairs on a visit to Felixstowe, and to the ability of their second son, another George.[1]

The year 1810, when the first child, William, was born, was the last reigning year of George III before the Prince of Wales became Regent. The Peninsular Campaign occupied England abroad while at home the Whigs waited expectantly for their call to power. In five years time Waterloo was fought. It was the period of Wellington's triumph. Ipswich would have suffered like other ports from the interruptions to trade and, facing the North Sea, it certainly had its share of alarms, with militiamen in the streets and warships in the harbour, but William Mason is unlikely to have

[1]Family information from Mr E. F. Mason of Woodbridge, Suffolk.

remembered much of this. His youth was conditioned more by peace and the long convalescence from war.

He was sent to a private school and afterwards articled to his father. Ipswich is an old town of the kind called 'quaint' but it is not without architectural splendours – many churches, surpassed perhaps by those of the surrounding villages; the gateway of Wolsey's Cardinal College of St Mary; the Tudor mansion called Christchurch; and numbers of fine seventeenth-century timber houses of which the most famous is Sparrowe's house. This gaily ornate house is three-storeyed on a corner site, so that it shows one short and one long side to the street. The first floor oversails the ground floor and the second floor is under a steeply gabled roof with four gabled dormers down the long side. Under each of these dormers and under the gable-end window, but separated from them by a heavy cornice, is a large oriel window. These oriels are flanked by pilasters with richly pargetted garlands and mythological figures between them. Beneath the cill of each oriel is a plaster panel which, in the case of each side window, represents one of the four continents – for America an Indian with a bow and arrow, for Asia a figure and a camel's head, for Africa a rider on a crocodile, and for Europe the sceptre of authority. Under the fifth window where symbols of Australia, the fifth continent, might have gone, is a representation of Atlas, for Australia, the country for which William Mason was to leave England, was unknown when Sparrowe's house was built.

All these buildings and many others in the surrounding countryside were certainly familiar to the young Mason, who might well have become an architect by the obligation of his name if the tradition of building had not already been there. After the initial training with his father, he went to London, well versed in architectural principles but wanting the wider experience which only London could give. He was lucky. He eventually took employment with Edward Blore, 'special architect' to William the Fourth and to Queen Victoria in the early part of her reign, though he seems to have worked before that with Thomas Telford (1757-1834), the most eminent engineer of his generation but the designer also, between 1824 and 1834, of some thirty churches in the highlands of Scotland, and to have studied under Peter Nicholson (1765-1844),[2] at one time Telford's associate, who undertook the teaching of mathematics, land surveying, geography, navigation, mechanical drawing, fortification and particularly the building sciences, in which subject he was the most prolific, inventive and influential writer of his generation.

Blore was one of the busiest architects in England during the eighteen-twenties, thirties and forties but his work is generally undistinguished. His father was the historian of Rutland and perhaps under this influence he developed an enthusiasm for Gothic architecture and throughout his career worked for its revival. In 1816 he had met Sir Walter Scott and delighted him with rough sketches for his house, Abbotsford, which he was then commissioned to carry out. Scott writing to Daniel Terry thought him 'a very fine young man, modest, simple, and unaffected in his manners, as well as a most capital artist.'[3] Nearly twenty years after his employment with Blore, Mason wrote of it (and himself) in these terms: ' . . . whose early days were exclusively devoted to the study and practise of his profession under circumstances of rare advantage, who at the age of nineteen years superintended the erection of Carlton Hall,[4] a building covering more than an acre of ground, and who, at a subsequent period under Sir Edward

[2] *Dunedin Punch*, 1 December 1865.
[3] J. G. Lockhart, *Life of Sir Walter Scott*. Edinburgh edition, 1902, Vol. V, p. 150.
[4] It is not clear what building is indicated by Carlton Hall but it is just possible that Mason referred to Carlton House Terrace which was finished in 1829 when he was certainly nineteen. It was, however, supervised by James Pennethorne. Its architect, John Nash, was also engaged on Buckingham Palace until his disgrace, and Mason's employment with Blore may have followed the latter's appointment in Nash's place. The several country houses called Carlton Hall, in different parts of England, all seem to belong to periods other than that to which Mason refers.

Blore, superintended the improvements at Buckingham and Lambeth palaces besides designing and completing many other public and private buildings in various parts of Europe . . . .'[5]

Blore was never knighted but is said to have refused the honour. His practice certainly extended to the mainland of Europe, one well known commission being that house, shadowed by cypresses planted by Catherine the Great and Potemkin, where Churchill, Roosevelt and Stalin met for the Yalta conference – Aloupka, the fabulous Crimean palace of Prince Michael Voronzov, Viceroy of the Caucasus, who had grown up in England during his father's ambassadorship and had once been a member of the Prince Regent's circle. But which of these foreign commissions were carried out by Mason we do not know. Aloupka dates from 1837 so that drawings may well have been done during his time in Blore's office and he seems to have enjoyed his employer's favour sufficiently for such work to be given to him.

Young men making their way in architecture at that time had first to find a master from whom to learn their profession and then a patron to supply the practice. One of the recognized means of catching a patron's eye was to exhibit at the Royal Academy, but such old hands as Blore, with an extensive practice at home and abroad, rarely bothered with the Academy, and Mason, working in his office, exhibited only once. This was in 1832 as the sculptor of a 'Design for a Monument'. Blore thereupon presented him with a copy of his own book, *The Monumental Remains of Noble and Eminent Persons*, inscribed 'Wm Mason Esqr presented by the Author'. Mason's draughtsmanship and his presentation of designs in beautifully finished oil sketches, of which several from a slightly later period have survived (Plate 29), would anyway have entitled him to a place in those august halls. Blore's most famous pupil was William Burges, the architect of Cork Cathedral and Cardiff Castle, but Burges was seventeen years Mason's junior. Benjamin Ferrey was his exact contemporary, Gilbert Scott was one year, A. W. N. Pugin two years and William Butterfield four years younger.

In 1832 Mason was living at 12 Milton Street, Dorset Square, later to be called Balcombe Street, in a house owned by another architect, Charles Hacker. In the previous year he had married Sarah Nichols, a Berkshire woman apparently fifteen years older than himself. Nothing is known of the circumstances of the marriage. Sarah is nowhere described as beautiful nor, apparently, was she either particularly talented or rich, so it can only be a matter for speculation whether the young husband was deceived, carried away by his first love-making, or merely following an inclination for older women. Five years after this marriage he returned to Suffolk, the lowland county of Constable and Crabbe, to practise in his home town of Ipswich. His work at Lambeth Palace had earned him the approval of the Bishop of London who proceeded to employ him independently in the construction of a number of churches and parsonages in his diocese which then spread further north than it does today. To this period belong the three Essex churches of St Lawrence, East Donyland; St Botolph, Colchester; and St James, Brightlingsea. Soon after the passing of the Poor Law Act of 1834, he submitted plans of a poorhouse to the Poor Law Commissioners, 'the principal object kept in view being the better classification and inspection of the inmates', and was instructed to build union houses at Ipswich and Eye in Suffolk, Kingston-upon-Thames and Epsom

[5]*New-Zealander*, Auckland, 21 September 1853.

2. *Thomas Telford, Engineer and Architect.*

3. *Peter Nicholson, Architect.*

in Surrey, and Stroud in Gloucestershire. These plans were published. What else he did from Ipswich – apart from designs for vicarages at Brightlingsea, Essex, and Bedingfield, Suffolk – is unknown, but a competition drawing survives[6] for a new customs house (Plate 23), a building given, in the event, to J. M. Clark whose very satisfactory design, quite unlike Mason's proposed Greek temple, was completed in 1844. The drawings for the vicarages are almost identical. Their Gothic form, common enough in the Suffolk countryside, was considered advanced for the eighteen-thirties and showed, perhaps, an awareness of Pugin's St Marie's Grange though the Gothic sham is made apparent by the blocking-in of windows on one wall where they were not required internally, however effective externally. (Plate 36). It is interesting to find an affidavit by John E. Sparrowe on the drawing for Bedingfield.[7]

The poorhouses were each built to similar plans which seem fairly standard today but may have been less usual when they were accepted. Generally they are based on a system of radiating wings left and right of a central block with the main circulation and public rooms at the crossing of opposed wings. It is a familiar pattern for hospitals – and gaols. Eye, Epsom (Plate 31) and Stroud (Plate 33) have survived, the first in mutilated form.

Of the churches, the truly remarkable St Botolph's (1838), in white brick, was built in Norman style close to the old priory. It is bigger than the priory and has 'the curious assertiveness that belongs to the Victorian age.'[8] Despite the Norman overlay linking it to the adjacent ruins, it remains an essentially Georgian building in plan and interior decoration (Plates 24-27). Medievalism prevails outside and enlightenment inside, yielding only to the plain cushion capitals seeming to await the hand of a carver and to the interlacing arches of the balustrades. Yet the incongruities have been skilfully resolved. The roofs over the side galleries are cross-vaulted and the main roof barrel-vaulted. East Donyland (1837) in the same material was intended to be a copy of the octagonal chapter house at York. The adaptation of the octagonal form to the purposes of a church, to aid a weak-voiced vicar, was carried out with marked success and produced a most original building. Preceding both of these churches was St James, Brightlingsea, white brick in the lancet style, rather like some of Blore's London parish churches and lacking any of the personal features apparent in St Botolph's or East Donyland. The interest lies in the fact that it provided an almost exact pattern for St Paul's Church, Auckland, built by Mason four years later.

In the year 1838 Mason was still only twenty-eight years old. He appears as a well-made confident man, with strong, fair hair and a broad Saxon face. His eyes were good, his chin determined, his mouth straight, full, and smiling. He was resourceful and energetic, a good horseman and a first-class shot. He decided to emigrate to New South Wales. His reasons may have been partly economic, for the great period of Georgian building was drawing to a close and there were more finely trained craftsmen than England could now find work for, but there is no cause on the other hand, to doubt the statement made in later years that he had 'a strong desire to assist in building up the Colonial Empire of Great Britain.'[9] The fury of expansion which swept England was one of the major influences in nineteenth century colonization, though the word Empire in those days had yet to acquire its later particular meaning.

[6]In the possession of Mr E. F. Mason of Woodbridge, Suffolk.

[7]In the County Archives Office, Ipswich.

[8]Nikolaus Pevsner, *The Buildings of England: Essex.* London, 1954. pp. 118-9.

[9]*Evening Star*, Dunedin, 24 June 1897. Compare Sir George Grey speaking in 1890, in the House of Representatives, about ' . . . the fervour which existed in Great Britain in the time of my youth to found a New World differing greatly from the Old World.'

Whatever their reasons, the Masons, with a six-year-old son born in the first year of their marriage, sailed from England in the late winter of 1838 and arrived at Port Jackson in June. But the long adventure of sailing across the world did not end at Port Jackson for less than two years later Mason reached still further out to New Zealand.

III AUSTRALIA

A race so tenacious of its immemorial village life that in 1830 a Sussex family could hardly be persuaded to seek its fortune in Staffordshire, or a Dorset family that Lancashire existed, was flocking by the hundred thousand in quest of the Golden Fleece. . . . By 1860 the whole world was the Englishman's home . . . – G. M. Young, Victorian England: Portrait of an Age. London, 1953.

The England left behind was the England of Oliver Twist and Nicholas Nickleby, suffering at once the social upheaval of the Industrial Revolution and the economic back-lash of speculation and over-production, an England where men who could remember the arrival of refugees from the violence in France wondered if the same violence might yet erupt at home.

New South Wales, on the other hand, had begun to discard her role of convict settlement and to receive attention, in the nineteenth-century phrase, as a good field for immigration. Sydney was fast becoming known as the capital of a new world, full of hope for the optimistic free settler prepared to make use of the peculiar if sometimes distasteful advantages of a penal colony. Her neat Georgian streets of town houses and cottages, barracks, churches and warehouses had taken shape in the days of Governor Macquarie and the architect, Francis Greenway. Under subsequent governors the construction of public buildings, highways and bridges continued.

As if to underline the difference between the two countries, the year 1838 brought a great drought to New South Wales, with consequent agricultural distress and shortages of food. To Mason, the parched paddocks must have seemed a poor substitute for Suffolk. While sheep could be bought for sixpence each, a loaf of bread cost five times that amount, butter was five shillings a pound and flour £130 a ton. Water piped from the Botany swamp cost sixpence a bucket at the distribution point, near St James's Church, and then had to be strained before it could be drunk.

The prospects for new arrivals were scarcely inviting but Mason was lucky enough to find immediate employment in the Colonial Architect's office, 'a long narrow building attached to the east wall of Greenway's barracks in Hyde Park, Sydney.'[1] Mortimer Lewis, who held the office from 1835 to 1849, lived on the premises during a part of that time and was once to complain that men from the barracks used to climb the wall and get over his house by crawling along the valley of the double roof, thus

[1] Morton Herman, *The Early Australian Architects and their Work*. Sydney, 1954. p. 200.

taking unofficial leave. The staff included a man of patently better education and greater skill than the rest, probably to be identified with James
Tucker, who became Australia's first novelist and playwright. Mason was
disconcerted on sympathizing with him, returning haggard after several
days' absence, to be told that he was a convict on ticket of leave and had
just received twenty-five lashes for drunkenness.

Such contacts with the criminal element were unavoidably common-
place but seem to have taken Mason by surprise: on another occasion he
went parrot-shooting to Cook's river with his younger friend George Eliott
(before this articled to a London army surgeon) and ended up in a sly-grog
den with fifteen or twenty convicts dancing to the music of a fiddle.

Architecturally he had a personal triumph when a committee raised
money for the Mechanics' Institute and called for competitive designs for a
new building to house it. From the dozen or so entries submitted the
committee selected two – one 'Gothic' and the other 'Ionic' – both of which
were found, on reference to the keys to the accompanying mottoes, to be
Mason's work. That one man should carry off both first and second prizes,
of fifty and twenty-five pounds, naturally produced an outcry from the
other competitors. A public exhibition was demanded and given and 'So
manifest was the superiority of Mr Mason's designs that the judges'
decision was unanimously approved and all opposition silenced.'[2] Then, in
1839, Governor Gipps decided on the use of storage silos for wheat, to
prevent a recurrence of the recent shortage. These were planned by Mason
and built with convict labour, on an island in Darling Harbour. It would
appear that they were the 'bottles', twenty in number and each twenty
feet deep, which were cut out of the solid rock of Cockatoo Island, a task
which required engineering rather than architectural skill.

Lewis, the Colonial Architect, was most notable in the early period of his
appointment for his love of Greek architecture and his sponsorship of the
Greek revival in Australia. Later he showed himself much influenced by
the eclecticism of succeeding decades and designed as readily in Gothic
style or in a mixture of Georgian and Regency motifs. Some early signs of a
similar approach already appear in William Mason's submission of two
designs, stylistically at variance, for the Sydney Mechanics' Institute.
This may have been Lewis's influence but it is certain that Mason had
already tried his hand at all these styles. His old master, Blore, and others
for whom he worked in London, had their preferences for Gothic or Classic
style but always claimed sufficient versatility to deliver either.

What Mason did make use of in later years was the verandah, a feature
which had been much used in the early colonial houses of Australia though
it was in no way exclusive to them. It had been demanded by the first
official class of army men who had learnt of its virtues in other tropical
stations and who similarly introduced it to Regency England.

In 1838, in the month following Mason's arrival in Sydney, Governor
Gipps reported to Lord Glenelg that: 'There are at present in progress in
the Colony in the Department of the Colonial Architect: 1 Government
House, 11 Churches, 4 Gaols, 1 Lunatic Asylum, 1 Watchhouse, 3 Courthouses, 1 National School, 1 Signal House, 1 Police Office, and numerous
other places of separate confinement; also in a few weeks there will be
another Gaol, 3 or 4 more Courthouses, 2 Watchhouses, a Police Station,
and another Church commenced, independent of the Custom House, Police
Office, and other buildings at Port Phillip, and they are all under the

[2]This passage and much of
the information preceding it
is taken from the *Otago
Daily Times*, 26 June 1897.
The article is anonymous
but if not based on inter-
views with Mason may well
have been written by G. E.
Eliott who was then living
in Dunedin in retirement.

superintendence of one Architect, Mr Lewis, of whose talent and assiduity I cannot speak too highly; but he has in his office only one Clerk of Works, one writing clerk and one Draftsman, whereas, for the preparation of plans and estimates alone . . . I am confident that five times this number would not suffice . . . .'[3]

Mason, added to this establishment, had no need to be idle. If he was distressed by the importance of goals, courthouses and police stations in the community – not to mention treadmills – he could turn his attention to Government House then in the course of building above Sydney Cove. Indeed it is not at all improbable that he had already worked on the drawings, for Lewis's responsibility was purely supervisory and the designs had in fact been prepared by Edward Blore who received this commission in 1835 when Mason was presumably still on his staff. This well-known building is very typical of Blore – the crenellated parapet with clasping buttresses taken well above it, the tower and immensely high pointed archway (later to be obscured by the addition of a covered carriage entrance) all illustrate his medieval attachments.

It was a time of change in Sydney as elsewhere. Free institutions and free settlers had altered the character of the town. The transportation of prisoners, except to Tasmania, ended in the following year. But with all classes, the tales of returning travellers of the land across the Tasman, a country already sending cargoes of flax and timber and buying largely in return, found ready audience. The fertile cannibal islands of New Zealand fired many Sydney imaginations and William Mason's among them.

[3]*Historical Records of Australia.* Series I, Vol. XIX.

IV KORORAREKA AND OLD RUSSELL

New Zealand may well be called a beautiful island, as lovely in its details as it is wonderful in its formation .– Robert W. Kenny (ed.), *The New Zealand Journal, 1842-1844, of John B. Williams.* Salem, 1956.

The horrific descriptions habitually given of the degradations of life at old Kororareka, and the calm beauty of the scene as it presents itself today, tend to produce an image of biblical wantonness and retribution. Hone Heke's men running through the town, bent on their work of selective destruction, while striking terror into the hearts of the citizens of Auckland, might have been as well regarded as the instrument of a savage Jehovah. Bishop Selwyn was able righteously but inaccurately to declare: ' . . . all that had been devoted to Mammon, was gone; but heathen vengeance had spared the patrimony of God.'[1]

When William Mason arrived in the Bay of Islands in the storeship *Westminster* on 17 March 1840, the Treaty of Waitangi was five weeks old and the destruction of Kororareka – by then to be called Russell – was still five years off. He found the Governor absent at Waimate where he had gone a week previously, on 9 March, to convalesce from the stroke he had suffered while reconnoitring the Waitemata. This absence must have been awkward. Mason had not been included among the original party of Government officers but had been appointed personally by Hobson before the latter's departure from Sydney. Hobson confirmed the position in a letter dated 20 April from Waimate: 'It having been intimated to Mr Mason previous to my departure from Sydney that he was to consider himself attached to this Government as Superintendent of Works, with Salary from the date of Embarkation (1st March) let the passage money paid by that Gentleman be returned to him and Mr Mason's name be entered in the list of Authorised Passengers by the Westminster.'[2] The passage money which was then refunded amounted to ten pounds.

Mason, however, had not waited for this clarification and in the midst of the confusion caused by the Governor's absence and the departure of George Cooper, the acting Colonial Treasurer, for Sydney, he went about his job, as different as it could be from the practice he had known in London or Ipswich or even Sydney.

On 23 March he made his first requisition for stores. It included 147 pounds of beef, 550 pounds of flour, 4 gallons 3 pints of rum, 2 pounds

[1] A Letter from the Bishop of New Zealand etc., *Church in the Colonies No XII New Zealand Part IV.* 2nd ed. London, 1847. p. 32.
[2] National Archives, I.A.1, 44/2323.

4½ ounces of tobacco, 1 portable forge, 20 felling axes, 4 crosscut saws and, ominously, 2 pairs of handcuffs. His first task, evidently, was to cut timber and he was taking no chances with his men. Some indication of the scale of rations is given in a later requisition when his party of twenty-six 'mechanics' at Auckland, had, as dependents, seventeen women, fourteen children over the age of ten years and twenty-seven children under the age of ten years. For each of these, except the children under ten years, he claimed 1 pound of beef per day, ½ ounce of tea, 3 ounces of sugar and 1 ounce of soap. For the men he claimed 1½ pounds of flour, 1 gill of rum and half an ounce of tobacco. The women were to have only 1 pound of flour and no rum or tobacco and the children under ten years were to have half the women's ration, except soap of which they were, realistically, to have the full adult ration. The Governor, whose consent was required on even the most trifling matters, agreed to this ration for 'those who pay' but informed Mason that the gratis ration was 1 pound of meat and 1 pound of flour to male adults, half to women and a quarter to children.[3]

Until his visit to the Waitemata and his subsequent stroke, Hobson had lived on board the *Herald* while his officers found accommodation wherever they could round the shores of the bay.[4] Willoughby Shortland had taken a house in Kororareka and his fellow officers, Mathew and Freeman, lived there 'in a dog kennel of a cock loft' with him.[5] Mason made do with a tent and shared it with a fellow passenger from the *Westminster*, Thomas Paton, who had been disappointed in his intention to begin sheep farming in New South Wales. Mathew set about finding a temporary site for the capital in the Bay of Islands and on 23 March reported his good opinion of Okiato, the property of James Reddy Clendon, an Englishman who acted as American consul. 'The Buildings', he wrote, 'would afford accommodation for the residence of a Police Magistrate, a Store, Barracks, Hospital, Mechanics Workshop and indeed every convenience which can be for some time required.' Clendon later claimed before the Land Commissioners that these buildings had cost him £3,600 to erect. On 23 April, Mason in conjunction with Willoughby Shortland, made a valuation of the property amounting to £1,300 annual rental for buildings alone. This appeared to take no account of the three hundred acres which Felton Mathew deemed the most level land in the Bay but which Edward Jerningham Wakefield considered so steep that he was soon able to note with malign pleasure that the Lieutenant Governor's cow had fallen down a slope and broken her neck.[6] Felton Mathew had not waited for his fellow officials' valuation but had already given Clendon an undertaking to purchase the property outright for £15,000 and had obtained the Governor's approval.[7] This figure was finally agreed on – £13,000 for the buildings, to bear interest at ten percent per annum, thus tallying with the Mason-Shortland estimate of rental, and £2,000 for land – with possession promised at the beginning of May.

The provision of a home no doubt relieved the Government of many of the uncertainties of its position. Hobson himself had somewhere to take his family who had already arrived on 16 April in the *Buffalo*, the officials had headquarters, and the problem of storage was relieved. Even stores from the *Westminster* had proved an embarrassment and, more than a month after her arrival, John Israel Montefiore, later to be associated with Mason in Auckland, wrote to him to offer space in the holds of the *Tuscan* which he had bought and which was then lying in the Bay.[8]

[3]National Archives, I.A.1, 40/121.
[4]William Colenso, *Fifty Years in New Zealand*. Napier, 1888. p. 31.
[5]Felton Mathew, Journals in *The Founding of New Zealand*, ed. J. Rutherford. Auckland, 1940. p. 77.
[6]Edward Jerningham Wakefield, *Adventure in New Zealand*. London, 1845. Vol. 1, p. 361.
[7]Ruth Ross, *New Zealand's First Capital*. Wellington, 1946.
[8]National Archives, I.A.1, 40/115.

Clendon began to sell allotments at Okiato, which was now renamed Russell with a town plan drawn by Mathew. For convenience, because the name Russell was later given to Kororareka, it is referred to as Old Russell. Another township to be named Churchill was projected at Hokianga while Busby's plan for Victoria, the settlement he hoped to establish at Waitangi, had not yet been abandoned. All this while Auckland was looked to as the site of the permanent capital and the present population was easily contained in the houses of Kororareka and the other existing settlements.

Had William Mason shown himself as visionary as these others he might well have been overwhelmed at the thought of so much building to be undertaken. In fact building seems to have been confined to kitchens and outhouses, a gaol, a mess house or bakehouse, and some barracks at Old Russell, and the conversion of existing buildings for a courthouse, post office, and general offices. He also put up houses for himself and for schools and boats' crews.[9] While Clendon's buildings had been quite substantial, the new additions seem to have been little more than shacks, providing much-needed temporary accommodation for those who, in spite of Mathew's over-sanguine earlier assessments, could not be found a place in the existing establishment. In Kororareka, in the first week of October, a customs house was built, thereby acknowledging the pre-eminence of Kororareka over Russell as a place of trade, and was immediately pulled down when it was found to be on tapu ground.[10] Gaols seem to have been always a first consideration. With a letter from the Colonial Architect's Office, Russell, dated 18 July 1840, Mason enclosed a design and specifications for the lock-up proposed to be erected at Port Nicholson. This would have pleased Jerningham Wakefield had he known of it, but the lock-up was not immediately built, for Wakefield wrote of Shortland's sanctioning a new building to replace the Maori *whare* gaol when he visited Wellington as Acting Governor after Hobson's death.[11]

But Mason's letter on the subject establishes two points. Firstly that he had moved to Russell with the Government rather than continue living at Kororareka as might have been more convenient to him, and secondly that he had assumed the position of Colonial Architect rather than Superintendent of Works. This was short-lived. A gazette notice published on 21 July in the *New Zealand Advertiser* gave the date of appointment of various officers as 19 June. This of course confirmed appointments (with the remaining exception of the Colonial Secretary) which had previously been held in an acting capacity. They were:

'Major Bunbury	Magistrate
Willoughby Shortland Esq.	Acting Colonial Secretary
Felton Mathew Esq.	Surveyor General
J. Johnson Esq.	Colonial Surgeon
Wm Davies M.D. Esq.	Health Officer
W. C. Symonds Esq.	Police Magistrate
Michael Murphy Esq.	Police Magistrate
H. D. Smart Lieut.	Magistrate
J. R. Clendon Esq.	Magistrate of the Territory
Mr William Mason	Superintendent of Public Works
Mr Charles Logie	Colonial Storekeeper'.

The distinction drawn between those dignified as *Esquire* and those called *Mr* must have infuriated Mason. He wrote at once to the Acting

[9]*New Zealand Journal*, London, 20 August 1842. 'Explanatory Statement of Expenditure in the department of Public Works for 1840.'
[10]*New Zealand Advertiser and Bay of Islands Gazette*, 8 October 1840.
[11]*Adventure in New Zealand.* Vol. II, p. 325.

Colonial Secretary who appears at the moment to have been not Shortland but the Private Secretary, J. S. Freeman.

'Russell
'July 22nd 1840

'Sir,

'In consequence of seeing myself styled Superintendent of Public Works in an Abstract brought before me on the 21st instant [I must ask] for some explanation.

'I have the honor to inform you my appointment of Colonial Architect was intimated to me verbally by the Lieutenant Governor on the 17th of May from which day it was considered I had the whole charge of that department.

'The reason assigned by His Excellency for my being placed in the first instance under the Surveyor General was that my capability to discharge the duties of Colonial Architect was then unknown.

'Although I have received no direct communication on this subject but having seen myself called in an official document of a late date Superintendent of Public Work I have to request that you will inform me if any alteration has taken place in my appointment and the nature of such alteration.

'I have the honor to be Sir
'Your most obdt Servt

'J. S. Freeman Esq   'Wm Mason
'Acting Colonial Secretary'[12]

This letter was referred to Hobson who, recovered in health, had just returned from another expedition to the Waitemata. He directed that Mr Mason be informed that 'His Excellency in sanctioning his appointment to the Head of a Department never contemplated creating the office of Colonial Architect for the present at least.'[13] Mason had no alternative but to capitulate. His superiority over the majority of those now ranked above him, particularly Freeman whose pretensions were shortly to bring him public disgrace, showed itself quite soon and became more manifest as the years advanced. That he had some reason to assume the title of Colonial Architect is made plain by a letter of 15 May 1840[14] in which Freeman, for the Colonial Secretary and at the Lieutenant Governor's direction, informed him that the offices of Surveyor General and Public Works were quite separate and he need have no feeling of constraint. As head of his department he had sole management of the artificers, labourers and boatmen employed by the Government and, from the date of the letter, of the superintendent of stock also. It seems legitimate to read into this letter some earlier interference by Felton Mathew whose assumptions of superiority annoyed others beside Mason, but he assumed too much from his newly independent status. He headed his letter book 'Colonial Architect's Book' and so it remained without change of title for years to come. From May to July other Government officers, including the Colonial Secretary, addressed him as Colonial Architect in all correspondence. Hobson, however, aware of the extreme limitations of his exchequer, may well have foreseen his inability to commission any buildings of consequence over the next few years and he must be given credit for avoiding the absurdity of having a Colonial Architect without any architecture.

In the meantime the Lieutenant Governor's return from the Waitemata

[12]National Archives, I.A.1, 40/293.
[13]ibid.
[14]National Archives, I.A.4, 260.

must have put preparations in train for the establishment of Auckland. Plans had to be laid and stores brought together. Mason evidently had a house prefabricated for himself and had timbers prepared for the store which was to be the first building to be erected in the new capital. Into the barque *Anna Watson*, which had been chartered for the expedition, he loaded 33,000 shingles, 12,607 feet of scantling running measure, 4,700 superficial feet of planking, 8 tons of coal, 8 tons of bricks and 1 ton of iron. In addition there were 83 tons of luggage, tents, tarpaulins and sundry goods which could not be measured.[15] The official party comprised the Surveyor General and Mrs Mathew, Dr Johnson, Mr Mason, Mr Edward Marsh Williams (the missionary Henry Williams's eldest son who was to act as interpreter and postmaster), Captain Rough (the new harbourmaster), and Captain William Cornwallis Symonds. There were also four supernumeraries in the cabin and thirty men, fifteen women and thirty children travelling steerage.[16]

On 13 September the *Anna Watson* sailed out of the Bay of Islands bound for the site of the new capital.

[15]National Archives, I.A.1, 40/587.
[16]Rutherford, *The Founding of New Zealand*, p. 185.

4. *Mason's cottage, Official Bay.*

V AUCKLAND

At the commencement . . . we must be content with what is useful, plain, and solid, remitting to a future day what is merely ornamental. – Lord John Russell to Governor Hobson, 9 December 1840.

It is not given to many men to found the capital of a new country. If Australia builds a Canberra, Brazil a Brasilia, or the State of Punjab a Chandigarh, the thing is done on a large scale backed by public funds which are limited only by the magnitude of the impression which it is desired to make. Auckland, however, founded with the country of which it was to be capital, began on the slenderest of budgets. Jerningham Wakefield, fulminating at Port Nicholson, described the whole thing as burlesque. But those who took part – men and women in the flush of youth, idealistic or self-interested – responded with imagination to the challenge it set them, eager to turn their visions into fact.

It was spring and clematis was in flower. The sun shone fitfully on sea and bracken-clad volcanic hills and on the *Anna Watson* as she sailed up Prince Regent Channel and rounded North Head to enter the Waitemata river where the *Platina*, with disaffected settlers from the south and the prefabricated sections of a house for the Lieutenant Governor, already lay at anchor.

The story of those first few days is too well known to tell again. On 16 September, the day after their arrival, Felton Mathew and Dr Johnson went ashore and climbed to the top of a high hill from which the country could be seen in every direction. William Mason, in his capacity of Superintendent of Works, 'brought down' a spar for a flagstaff from the banks of the upper harbour then referred to as the river. This was set up, on a promontory later to be called Point Britomart or Soldiers' Point, and the flag was raised there on the 18th in the rather protestful presence of almost a hundred Maoris who were dissatisfied with the sale of their land by the chief Rewiti Tamaki on the previous day. Healths were drunk and salutes of guns were fired and the day finished with an impromptu regatta with the mollified natives taking part for a prize of half a pound of tobacco each.

With the help of Apihau Te Kawau and his tribe from Orakei,[1] two neighbourhoods – of settlers at Commercial or 'Store' Bay, and officers at Official or 'Exclusion' Bay – were soon established. The government-

[1] [John Logan Campbell], *Poenamo*. London, 1881. p. 307.

employed mechanics were afterwards planted in the next bay naturally called Mechanics Bay. The officials were housed in tents or comfortable double-lined *raupo* huts, far warmer than the unlined weatherboard houses which were to follow. Mason himself, with Edward Marsh Williams, is said to have been the first to sleep under a roof,[2] having brought a pre-fabricated house from the Bay of Islands and set it up in Official Bay.

A month later Hobson came down from Russell for the first time since the founding and during a visit of ten days chose a site for his own house. Up to the present Mason's tasks had been largely exploratory. Down on the beach at Commercial Bay he had set up the Government store for the reception of public property and he had investigated the possibilities of brickmaking and lime burning, of timber felling and milling. He reported as follows:

'Wai te Mata
'September 21 1840

'Sir,

'In conformity with my instructions, I have the honor to report to you for the information of His Excellency the Lieutenant Governor, that immediately the 'Anna Watson' came to an anchor in this harbour which was on the 18th Inst [*sic*] I proceeded on shore for the purpose of examining the most desirable spots for collecting Sand, Burning lime, and forming a Brickyard, I found an abundance of Sand, on every part of the South shores.

'The best spot for collecting shells is on the point of the South shore opposite the Sentinel rock, but it will be desirable to remove them before they are burnt, to the spot on which they may be required.

'I have not yet seen a desirable place for forming a brickyard.

'On the morning of the 16th at sun rise I proceeded in the Harbour Masters boat, up the river to ascertain the best spot for falling timber. I selected that point immediately opposite the Ranger Rock, which affords every facility, the "Kauri" timber growing to the waters edge, the expense of procuring timber will not be in proportion one half that incurred for the Public works at Russell. I cut two small spars for flag staffs one for the settlement here the other for the island of "Motu Koria" which I towed down with the boat and had them barked and prepared on board the ship for erection.

'The Surveyor General having selected a spot for the store, and encamping the mechanics I began to prepare on the 17th for its commencement by clearing away the brush and fern, and leveling the ground, I had two tents pitched and four families sent on shore in the evening.

'On the following day Friday the 18th the Mechanics were employed erecting the Flagstaff discharging ships, sorting the timber and preparing for the erection of the store, and clearing site for Superintendent of Works house.

'On the 19th all hands were employed erecting the store, the framed sides and ends were completed today, the ridge set up and five pairs of Rafters. I sent two more Families, and two single men on shore this evening which are all our tents will accommodate. We are put to considerable inconvenience because we have not sufficient accommodation on shore for the Mechanics it is desirable that the Marquee should be sent the first opportunity unless the tents from the Buffalo arrive.

'Today two men have been sent to Motu koria to erect the Flag staff, one

[2] J. J. Craig, *Historical Record of Jubilee Reunion of Old Colonists*. Auckland, 1893. pp. 9-10.

man is aboard the ship to attend to the discharging of the Store, and Superintendent of Works house. All the others are employed on the Store which I hope to have completed by Thursday night.

'I have the honor to be

'Sir

'Your Most Obedt Servt

'Wm Mason

'Supt of Public Works

'J. S. Freeman Esqr
'Acting Colonial Secretary
'& & &'[3]

On 10 October he reported that he had the 'Store ready for the reception of dry goods on the evening of Thursday 24th Sept and on the 25th Platina and Anna Watson began discharging cases. . . . On Monday 26th commenced the 4 rmd house with 7 men & having completed the framed sides on the evening of the 29th divided force & commenced Capt Symonds' house on morning of 29th, Dr Johnson's on Monday the 5th of October & Capt Rough's on the 7th inst all of which I hope to have completed as far as can be without boards tonight.

'On the 26th Sept I selected a site for the Brick yard combining all the advantages that could possibly be expected in one spot. It is situated on the East side of the proposed town and abounds with fine earth for all purposes, a stream of fresh water, on the opposite side of which there is pit sand, at the head of the stream about a half mile distant is a gully full of wood suitable for burning bricks, the men named in the Register employed in the Brickyard have been clearing the ground, building house for Brick maker & preparing hake grounds.'[4]

On 16 November, after the Governor's visit, he reported that four trees had been brought down the river and sawyers were sawing timber for stringers but the principal employment of the men was in cutting a road to Government House and clearing the ridges for the Surveyor General, 'which I hope will be completed this week that the mechanics may build their houses and commence with G.H.' He had about 7,000 bricks on hand but the weather was against them in building up stocks.[5]

Other settlers had by now come in. Among them was a James George who had spent seven and a half months at Coromandel after coming from Tasmania and who wrote his memoirs in 1875, calling them 'A Few Odds and Ends 1823-1876'[6], and adding the note: 'If I was rich enough I would print it after it was revised a bit.' Printed they never were nor, happily, were their misspelt pages revised.

On 14 October 'as I wanted employment at my trade' George went 'to the Superintendent of Public Works Mr Wm Mason and Mr C. W. Symonds C.P.M.,[7] I wished them to let me have a small piece of land for two years, to put an oven and House upon . . . but they decided that I could not be accommodated, But that they would engage me as Baker at £2 2. 0 per week . . . . Poor George was unable to get his oven until the completion of Government House, even though, in January, he tackled Hobson himself as he walked up Shortland Crescent with Felton Mathew. 'I was surprised at his [Mathew's] pomposity I thought he made himself greater than his Excellency. . . . But I despised F. Mathews Esq he was well named Cobweb after laying out Auckland, as it was a disgrace to any Surveyor, for even a School Boy, would lay a Town much better, I guess.'

[3]National Archives, I.A.1, 40/492.
[4]National Archives, I.A.1, 40/589.
[5]National Archives, I.A.1, 40/706.
[6]Typescript, A.P.L.
[7]Chief Police Magistrate. Symonds was the son of Rear-Admiral Sir William Symonds, Surveyor to the Navy.

For Mason and for William Cornwallis Symonds, whose manly personality was everywhere acknowledged, George seems to have had more than usual respect. But his friend Hellyer who had an estate up the river with Captain Clayton, in going from Auckland, met Mr Mason 'who had been at his estate with a Government boat's crew and had measured and marked the Kauri trees with the broad arrow, all that was near the Waters Edge, or the most convenient for the Government use, when Mr Hellyer asked him why he had done so, he Mason (it was reported that he went shore with the contractor) said that he had an Act of Parliament to do so.'

Mason's authority in the settlement was obviously growing. Over the summer his chief task was the erection of the house sent out for the Governor. This had been prefabricated by the London firm which had supplied Napoleon's house at St Helena but it is described as larger, more convenient and more substantial than Napoleon's. The conveniences did not include a kitchen, which was at first provided in a *raupo* hut. The building was 120 feet by 50 feet and 24 feet high, and had a terrace verandah supported on iron columns. It was built of Norway deal, contained sixteen rooms and cost £2,000.[8] James George tells us, 'When the frame was put up the workmen had a jollification it was in the month of March 1841 I went up and the dinner was laid out in front of the frame or building the Chairman a Mr Davey foreman of works hailed me to take his place he let me know how matters stood – he had taken a sup too much – and he got me to write a note to Mr Mason the Superintendent of Public Works that her Most Gracious Majesty the Queens health had been duly honored also the Govrs health, and ladys, and all the officials, there was plenty of Ki Ki and Grog such as it was, of pork and potatoes and lots of beer and waiperou the first land sale was held in the House on the 19th & 20th April 1841. Mr Mason was the Auctioneer.'

When the Hobsons moved to Auckland in the following March, the house was still unfinished and Mrs Hobson had to entertain Lady Franklin, the wife of the Governor of Van Diemen's Land and her first important visitor, by lodging her in the new house while the Hobsons themselves dwelt in a cottage close by. This would no doubt have pleased Lord John Russell who had written counselling the utmost possible parsimony. 'The governor of an infant colony should aim at nothing beyond the decencies of a private and moderate establishment, and his ambition should be not to outshine, but to guide, befriend, and protect those who are living under his authority.'[9] As late as 14 May tenders were being received for a laundry, fittings in the butler's pantry and flooring to bedrooms. It was a pleasant house, grand enough to have a marble fireplace in each room and, until Mason put up St Paul's Church, it was the major architectural feature of the new town. It served until the night of 23 June 1848, when it was burnt to the ground, the fire having started in the housekeeper's room in timbers used to support the brickwork of the chimney. Many of Auckland's first houses were influenced by its design (Plate 5), which owed much to the additions Mason made to its otherwise bald elevations.

Building was not all in Mason's hands. Major Bunbury proceeded with the stone barracks at Fort Britomart with his soldiers as tradesmen and George Graham, Clerk of Works under the Board of Ordnance, as his supervisor. John Logan Campbell, on a visit to Kororareka, saw the whole beach lined with carpenters all busy preparing skeleton houses to be shipped down to the capital as soon as the first sale of town land should

[8]*New-Zealander*, 2 August 1848. *Bell's Weekly Messenger*, London, 28 December 1839.
[9]G.B.P.P. 1841 XVII (311): Lord John Russell to Governor Hobson, 9 December 1840.

5. *First Government House, north front.*

6.   *First Government House, south front.*

take place.[10] But the public offices, post office, customs house and the courthouse and gaol compound, all temporary, certainly came within the province of the Superintendent of Works. These, with a powder magazine, a bridge to Hobson's Creek, gates to the Government Domain, and similar works, were Mason's next major task. On 6 May a plan for the courthouse was submitted to His Excellency and a fortnight later Mason estimated the cost of the centre portion at £390, with further provision of £600 for its completion. There is a later note on this estimate that the plans are supposed to have been burnt when the Works Office was destroyed in January 1842. The building, put up by John Swanson and Archibald Cochrane, was not impressive even though Mason pleaded for and was eventually permitted to add a classical portico. It fronted Queen Street on what is now the southern corner of Victoria Street West with the gaol compound running up behind to Albert Street. (Plate 37.)

Before it was finished Mason tendered his resignation on the grounds that his office gave little scope for architectural practice and with the hope, no doubt, that he could make his fortune independently – by architecture or not. 'Sir', he wrote to the Colonial Secretary, 'I have the honor to communicate to you for the information of His Excellency the Governor my intention to resign the situation I now hold under the Government.

'I wish to give up my appointment the 31st July but if at that period no person offers to fill the situation I will do the duties of the Office I now hold until His Excellency can fill it up.

'But at the same time I beg it may be done as speedily as possible.'[11]

His resignation was accepted and after a brief trial under his care, H. C. Holman was appointed to the post at the same salary, which was £180 – twice the salary of his clerk and superintendent of stock but barely ten shillings a week more than his foreman.[12] Mason's last action was to ask for a rise for his clerk. It was refused.

He went immediately into partnership with Thomas Paton (who at the same time resigned his office of postmaster), as auctioneers and architects. Paton, with whom he had formed a friendship at Kororareka, was five years his junior and, through Mason's influence,[13] had been appointed postmaster at Port Nicholson, but had stayed only till a similar position was available at Auckland.

[10]J. L. Campbell, Journal, A.I.M. Typescript, p. 271.
[11]National Archives, I.A.1, 41/677.
[12]G.B.P.P. 1843 XXXIII (134): 'Estimate of the probable Expenditure of the Government of New Zealand.' The Colonial Architect's Book (National Archives, I.A.4, p. 24) gives a 'Schedule for the Estabt. Public Works', under the date 16 April 1841. It lists '1 Superintendent, 1 Clerk, 1 working Foreman, 12 Carpenters, 5 Masons and bricklayers, 18 Sawyers, 2 Painters and glaziers, 2 Quarrymen, 7 Labourers, 1 Superintendent of Stock, 2 Carters; and, for the Government Domain, 1 Superintendent, 1 Gardener, 1 Keeper and 7 Labourers.'
[13]Thomas Paton to George Brown, 15 June 1840. Correspondence printed in the *Mail Coach.* Vol. 1, No 10. Auckland, 1965.

VI THE MAN OF AFFAIRS

We were all young in those days . . . Enid Evans (ed.) *Reminiscences of Mrs. S. H. Selwyn.* Auckland, 1961.

Three months after the April land sale, with 200 houses built and independence from New South Wales achieved, Auckland was an established fact. Mason had been joined by his wife and son from the Bay of Islands, where they had arrived in October aboard the ship *Earl of Lonsdale*, with Colonel Godfrey, Captain Mathew Richmond and William Grahame among their fellow passengers, and life began to take a regular pattern. Captain Rough, the harbourmaster, tells us of their occupations: 'The cultivation of our gardens in Official Bay was a source of great enjoyment. Clearing ground, planting fruit trees and shrubs imported from Australia and Tasmania and cuttings from the Bay of Islands, making roses bloom where no flowers grew before was comparatively an easy matter and afforded delightful exercise to all who were willing to work in the healthful and charming morning air of that very fine climate.'[1] Mason had bought two lots at the sale of town land at which he himself had acted as auctioneer. For the first, which was the Queen Street block running back to High Street on the northern side of Vulcan Lane, he paid £202. 18s. For the other, the site in Waterloo Quadrant now occupied by Newman Hall (the present house was built by David Nathan) and by the late Sir Ernest Davis's house, he paid £148. 7s. On this latter, naturally wooded and at the head of the fine spring from which the soldiers of Fort Britomart drew their water, he set to work. 'In the garden of our spirited townsman Mr. Mason of Mason and Paton', wrote a correspondent of the *New Zealand Herald and Auckland Gazette* at the end of 1841, 'is to be seen a second crop of potatoes appearing above ground.... This garden and a few others, viz:– Dr .Johnson's and Mr. Leach's[2] do certainly reflect much to the credit of their industrious proprietors.'

In the summer evenings he would sometimes go walking with his Sydney friend George Eliot Eliott (who named one of his sons William Mason), now in Auckland as a clerk in the Colonial Secretary's office. They would no doubt talk of their adventures in Australia, laugh over Eliott's rescue of the Treaty of Waitangi and the Seal of the Colony when the four-roomed offices in Official Bay were burnt, recount his struggle with a Maori robber in a swamp or this: 'One evening in the summer of 1841 we were sitting

[1] *New Zealand Herald,* 18 January 1896. 'Early Days of Auckland.'
[2] William Leech, 1799-1860, later Postmaster and Collector of Customs at New Plymouth.

on the cliff overlooking the harbour close to Point Britomart where the barracks were then, smoking "the pipe of peace" . . . M and I were chatting away about all sorts of things, from a recipe for making sugar beer to defining an isosceles triangle, settling the affairs of the nation in general and of New Zealand in particular. We were both Government officers then. Amongst other things, of course, we wondered how long the Home Government would stand the racket of paying for the Government of the Colony, and, as all colonies were very small potatoes then in the eyes of the British Parliament, what we should do when we were thrown on our own resources. We might import goods, but how were we to pay for them? If with cash, we should precious soon come to our bottom dollar. We had nothing to export. The Governor (Hobson) had a cow in the Domain, Constable[3] had a pair of working bullocks, and Felton Mathew had a horse – these were all the cattle and there were no sheep in the country. It is true we had maize and potatoes and pigs but we wanted them for home consumption.'[4]

In the midst of this discussion the sound of an eruption was heard and, assuming it to be volcanic, they decided they would not 'stay to be burnt to a cinder. Then we began to talk about where we should go to – America, North and South, Canada, India. At last we settled we would go back to Sydney first and then determine where we would ultimately pitch our tent.' The 'eruption' turned out to be the noise of an empty tank being rolled up to his store by Israel Joseph the little Jewish auctioneer.

The Auckland Book Society was formed with twelve members consisting of the Governor and eleven 'officers', Mason among them. No doubt they exchanged among themselves the few books they had and surely they were among the purchasers at what James George tells us was the first book sale in New Zealand. 'I remember a schooner named the "*Sisters*" from Hobart Town via Wellington . . . brought . . . a Jakey Moses who set up as an auctioneer on the Beach he had several usefull articles of Crockery and Iron Pots and among others several Folio Volumes of Books, Rapins History of England, Howards Encyclopeadia of 1788 or 9 they were offered for sale, I purchased the Encyclopeadia for 14/6 per Vol 3 vols, Rapin was sold also, I purchased it afterwards for £4. 10. 0.' On 1 September 1841, the Book Society held a meeting at which they determined to extend the plan of their original society and form an institution called the 'Auckland Library and Museum'. The twelve members became the committee but there is no evidence that they advanced the project any further.

Travellers began to arrive in Auckland though no emigrant ships had yet come. Lady Franklin made an expedition into the interior with Captain Symonds and Dr Dieffenbach. That attractive early settler, John Charles Blacket,[5] sailed his splendid clipper yacht, *Albatross*, (Mr S. Doudle, master), into the harbour and entertained His Excellency the Governor and Mrs Hobson and a large party to a *déjeuner à la fourchette*, marking His Excellency's going ashore with a salute of nineteen guns. A fortnight later upwards of fifty of the principal gentlemen of the town entertained His Excellency to dinner at Wood's Royal Hotel, each paying thirty shillings for the privilege and a six course dinner. The only goose in the colony was placed upon the table. Among the score of toasts honoured as the Chairman called for repeated bumpers, William Mason, in the absence of Captain England, proposed the health of the Land Claims Commissioners who were Colonel Godfrey and Captain Richmond, Mrs Mason's fellow passengers in the *Earl of Lonsdale*.

[3]Edward Constable, a prominent settler who eventually lived at Waiuku.
[4]*New Zealand Herald*, 17 December 1892.
[5]Second son of Sir William Blacket, Bt., he established himself at St George's Bay.

It was a busy time. Within a few days, on 28 July 1841, the foundation stone of the Metropolitan Church of St Paul was laid with considerable ceremony. Mason's appointment as architect by the church trustees had no doubt influenced his resignation from government office. The church had been first proposed at a meeting at Government House in April. By 17 July, over a subscription list including five pounds from Mason, the *New Zealand Herald and Auckland Gazette* was able to announce that the proposed edifice 'will be of brick in the old English style of architecture and will contain 600 sittings, of which one third will be free.' In the same issue Mason called for tenders from limeburners, bricklayers and builders, excavators, fencers and brickmakers. One thousand bushels of lime were estimated to be needed and three hundred thousand bricks. The procession for the laying of the foundation stone started from Government House at noon, led by Charles Terry,[6] Auckland's first settler, as Master of Ceremonies, with a guard of honour from the 80th Regiment in Garrison, a party of Freemasons with decorations and insignia with the architect among them bearing the plans,[7] followed by the Chaplain, the Rev J. F. Churton, His Excellency and the Government officers and a 'large body of the more respectable citizens and natives.' A temporary platform had been set up for Mrs Hobson and the ladies and proceedings were opened by George Clarke, Protector of Aborigines, addressing himself in Maori to the natives present, promising them the benefits of Christian civilization and peace where previously their only pleasure had been in killing each other. A sealed bottle containing coins of three reigns, a newspaper, and the names of those principally concerned, was placed in a cavity of the foundation stone and a further stone laid by the Governor on top. Several speeches later the whole party repaired to Wood's Royal Hotel to restore themselves with a 'cold collation'.

On 10 July 1841 William Mason and Thomas Paton had advertised in the *New Zealand Herald and Auckland Gazette* that they 'avail themselves of this opportunity to inform the Public, that their engagements with the Government will terminate on the 31st of July current, when they intend commencing Business at this place as AUCTIONEERS Commission and Shipping Agents and ARCHITECTS under the Firm of Mason and Paton, and hope by strict integrity, punctuality and assiduity, to merit a share of public patronage.' Three weeks later they announced that they would open for business on the Monday following. 'Mr. Mason having had several years experience, both in England and the colonies, as an Architect, they will be happy to prepare Plans, give Estimates, and superintend the erection of Buildings; until the Auction Mart, now being erected in Lower Queen Street, is complete, they will feel pleasure in executing any commission with which they may be entrusted, that can be effected without the use of their Auction Mart.'

Their auction rooms and store were built on the northern corner of Queen Street and Vulcan Lane on part of Mason's land. This piece of land, running through to High Street, he divided into six lots – two on High Street, two on Queen Street and four with extremely narrow frontages to Vulcan Lane. These four, on two of which the Queen's Ferry and Occidental hotels were eventually built, were served by a four foot lane giving access to the backs of the properties, the whole thus forming one of those pocket-handkerchief subdivisions for which the purchasers at the early land sales are now much criticized. The subdivision failed to make Mason's

[6]Charles Terry, F.R.S., F.S.A., editor, at different times, of the *New Zealand Herald and Auckland Gazette* and of the *New-Zealander*, had already landed at the site of Auckland when the Government party arrived.

[7]As one of three signatories to a request for a 'dispensation' from a Sydney lodge, Mason was a founder of Freemasonry in Auckland, but he subsequently took little part in the affairs of the Order. In Ipswich he had been initiated into a local lodge in 1836, sponsored by the Master and secretary who, six weeks before, had assisted with Masonic ceremony at the laying of the foundation stone at St Botolph's Church. The Sydney lodge, No 260, had some years before listed the architect, Francis Greenway, among its members.

fortune. From 1844 to 1862 he sold the various sections, including any buildings on them, for prices ranging from £38 to £220.

The organization of work on St Paul's (nearly two years would pass before its consecration) was a major task in itself; but before the end of August Mason was calling for tenders for a strongroom to be built for the New Zealand Banking Company in Bank Street and for a house. From now on the advertising columns of the newly formed newspaper, the *New Zealand Herald and Auckland Gazette*, would reflect the name of Mason and Paton more than any other firm as they called attention to their sales of the finest land, of livestock, 'capital' houses, hogsheads of London porter, puncheons of whiskey, casks of sherry wine, of Van Diemen's Land timber and shingles, iron pots, grindstones, Cavendish tobacco, prints, calicoes, muslins, muskets, powder, planes, and Liverpool soap. Goods were usually straight from the ship but like almost all men of substance who were not engaged in one of the professions or in farming, Mason and Paton were at times storekeepers. On 5 May 1842, David Nathan, William Mason, and John Logan Campbell were gazetted as licensed auctioneers. They were the three most notable businessmen of the infant town.

The Auckland Newspaper and General Printing Company, which published the first *Herald*, included among its major shareholders virtually all the Government officers and a slightly weaker representation numerically of the leading merchants. On 10 August 1841, for various reasons, it became necessary to elect a new board of five trustees from among the twenty shareholders eligible. Those elected were Captain Mathew Richmond, Land Claims Commissioner, Captain W. C. Symonds, Police Magistrate and Member of the Legislative Council, Dr Johnson, Colonial Surgeon, J. I. Montefiore, a much respected merchant, and William Mason. These trustees thereafter became involved in a violent dispute with the man they appointed as editor at the end of 1841, Dr S. M. D. Martin, who vigorously espoused the cause of the land claimants against the Government. Mr G. M. Meiklejohn, who has written an absorbing history[8] of the first *Herald*, sees the constitution of the board as infinitely sinister because four of its five members were Government officers. He neglects anywhere to notice that Mason had resigned his post some time before and he neglects also to notice that Mason, Symonds, Richmond, and Johnson were everywhere admitted to be the most honourable and just members of the Government party, and were themselves at variance with the Shortland-Mathew-Cooper faction which was ultimately saddled with the *Herald*'s demise. Martin's editorship was short-lived and soon after his dismissal the board found itself forced into the appearance of doing the right thing for the wrong reason when finally in March 1842 it recommended the dissolution of the company. Its troubles were not only editorial but financial also. By the time the end came, death had removed Symonds from the scene and, of the other trustees, only Richmond, apparently, was named by Martin in his case for damages for breach of contract. Considering the cause of all the hullabaloo it is significant, and also unnoted by Mr Meiklejohn, that Martin and Mason, within a few days of Martin's final dismissal, both became members of a committee of eight (which also included Montefiore but no Government officers) formed at a public meeting at Wood's Hotel to urge the Government to reduce the price of land. The figure of ten shillings per acre included in the original motion was reduced to five shillings on Mason's amendment.

[8] G. M. Meiklejohn, *Early Conflicts of Press and Government*. Auckland, 1953.

But months before this newspaper scandal reached it stormy conclusion, the Masons suffered a personal tragedy which influenced all their later lives. On the afternoon of Saturday 14 September, at five o'clock, young William Mason, their son, then nine years old and a remarkably promising and intelligent boy, was missed at home. At nine o'clock his father and Thomas Paton went in search of him but without success. On Sunday morning they resumed their search when Paton found the boy's body in four feet of water head first down a well which had been sunk on William Mason's own orders to supply the building of the new church. 'His parents,' stated the *Herald*, 'thus bereaved of their only hope, are plunged into the deepest distress.' No evidence of foul play was brought at the inquest but many must have found the accident strange and seven years later an explanation was found for it.

A clue to the tragedy is to be found in the unpublished memoirs of the widow of H. C. Holman, Mason's successor as Superintendent of Works. Mrs Holman states unequivocally that the nine-year-old William Mason was murdered by one of his father's mechanics, a man named Joseph Burns who bore Mason a grudge. The charge is repeated by Robert Mair and in the reminiscences of 'Kaumatua'[9] published many years later in the *New Zealand Herald*. It was believed that Burns, who was said to be a veteran of Trafalgar, knocked the boy senseless and threw his body into the well.

Young William Mason died – or was killed – in 1841. Early in 1848 Joseph Burns was brought to trial for attempting to murder a woman, Margaret Reardon, who had borne him two children though not his wife. This fine pair had separated some weeks before and the woman had gone to live with her sister. Burns, in the meantime, heard of the death of her husband in Sydney and came to ask her to marry him or, if she would not, to let him say goodbye to the children. An extraordinary scene ensued. Reardon refused his offer of marriage and Burns begged her sister, who was using a carving knife to spread bread for the children, to turn the knife on him and put an end to him; but being refused this favour, he suddenly whipped out a razor, attacked his former consort who was kneeling on the floor, and slashed her five times on the throat while he vowed he would drink her heart's blood and she would tell no more tales. Her sister drove him off with a chair.

Burns was imprisoned and sentenced to transportation. On 2 March he asked the gaoler to send for the magistrate, Mr Beckham, that he might make a confession. To the astonishment of everyone he gave a detailed account of how he and two other men, Duder and Oliver, both one-time shipmates, had murdered Lieutenant Snow, a half-pay naval officer, and his wife and child at their house on the North Shore four months previously. The savage death of the Snows had till then been thought to be the work of disaffected Maoris. Their charred and mutilated bodies had been found by officers of H.M.S. *Dido* who had rowed ashore in darkness when they saw the house burning in the early hours of 23 October 1847.

Duder was charged with murder and was acquitted when it became obvious that neither he nor Oliver could have been party to it. Burns retracted his confession and even attempted suicide in prison, but evidence was so strong for his own responsibility for the murder of the Snows that on 3 June he was solely charged with the crime.

Margaret Reardon now testified that she had known of Burns's intention to rob Snow on the night of the murder, that Burns had said to her, rowing

9 Probably William Field Porter, junior.

back from Auckland to their house at O'Neill's Point on the afternoon previously, that he had 'done lots of jobs for the Queen and now intended to do something for himself', that he had set out with a tomahawk and a bayonet in the night and had returned wearing only his undershirt. He had given her a pound.

Burns was convicted and sentenced to be hanged from a gibbet set up on the North Shore at the scene of the crime. When asked by the Registrar of the Court 'What say you, Joseph Burns, that the sentence of the Court should not be passed upon you?' he replied 'The best of all things, that I am innocent. You, civilians, know that I am as innocent as the child unborn.' But once more he confessed and, when about to be launched into eternity, asked the chaplain to warn the people against the vices of drunkenness and uncleanness that brought him to an untimely end. He was hanged on 17 June at noon. Eighty years later, an old Maori woman, Heni Pore, step-daughter of that Thomas Russell who had been a ship's chandler and mast maker in Fort Street, told James Cowan of her childhood memory of an old man riding in a cart on his own coffin, on his way from the gaol in Queen Street, up Shortland Crescent to Official Bay where a boat waited to take him to the North Shore for his execution. This was Burns accompanied by the chaplain, J. F. Churton. His crime for which unknown Maoris had been blamed, had indeed been attended, in the words of the Judge, 'by circumstances so aggravated, that men could not for a season bring themselves to believe that this land contained a man of our race capable of committing it.' Margaret Reardon, however, had put the record straight. In giving evidence she had addressed the prisoner: '. . . even the Natives told you you were no good and when they saw me labouring hard to support the little children they offered to assist me to sow my potatoes if I would leave you.'[10]

Burns had been Mason's employee and had been dismissed by him, in what circumstances we do not know. Though there is no official evidence, it is entirely credible that he killed Mason's son in revenge and that this deed was added to the final catalogue of his crimes. Certainly many people believed it was so. Mason's sorrow lasted a lifetime and his retirement many years later into mountain seclusion was to be attributed to this one cause.

Death by drowning was a not uncommon hazard throughout the colony in the first years of settlement. Ten weeks to the day after young William Mason's death, his father's friend and one of the most loved and respected men in the community, William Cornwallis Symonds, was drowned in the Manukau harbour. The committee appointed to raise up a monument to his memory provided Mason with an office which must have been doubly hard to bear.

It was November. In England two curates of Windsor, George Augustus Selwyn and William Charles Cotton, were making preparations for their journey across the world, one to be bishop and the other his chaplain. Auckland, to which their minds turned, was beginning to expand – the village of Epsom on the 'Manakao' road had been planned and now the first suburban farms were sold there. Mason and Paton advertised the sale in terms of extravagant praise for the advantages of the land offered. (Plate 7.) We may believe that their praise was honest for Mason bought one nineteen-acre lot on his own account and three more lots of the same size in partnership with Paton. These occupied the land between the

[10]The facts of this case may be found in the following: Elisabeth A. Holman, 'Reminiscences', typescript, A.I.M.; James Cowan, *The Story of Auckland* (collected from *New Zealand Herald*), A.P.L.; *Southern Cross*, 3, 24 June 1848; *New-Zealander*, 4 March, 3, 7, 14, 17, 24 June, 2 September 1848; *New Zealand Herald*, 24 December 1897 (Supplement), 'Reminiscences of Kaumatua'. See also Mundy, *Our Antipodes*. London, 1852. Vol. II, p. 90.

SUPPLEMENT
TO THE
New Zealand Herald
AND AUCKLAND GAZETTE.

No. 10. Vol. I.]   AUCKLAND, SATURDAY, SEPTEMBER 11, 1841.   [PRICE ONE SHILLING.

SALES BY AUCTION.

TOWNSHIP OF ANNA·
SITUATED HALF WAY

Between AUCKLAND and MANUKAO

WHICH, IN A SHORT TIME, WILL BECOME THE

SECOND TOWN OF IMPORTANCE

IN THE COLONY!!

Mason and Paton

BEG to inform their Friends and Constituents that the above Township will be brought to the hammer on MONDAY, the 13th Sept, at Twelve o'clock precisely.

The Proprietor of this splendid Property, purchased it regardless of expense, knowing, from its peculiar situation, that Nature had marked it out for a

TOWNSHIP.

Those who have access to the Surveyor-General's Plan, may find its locality, by referring to Sections 33, 34, and 50, forming a block of 42 acres, and those who enjoy the delightful walk on the Manukao Road, may know it by its being

PLEASANTLY SITUATED

IN THE

VALE OF EDEN.

Its Acropolis commanding a view of the waters of Waitemata, Maeakao, and the Thames.

IN THE IMMEDIATE VICINITY

OF

THE RACE COURSE,

AND

MOUNT EDEN,

It is also close to the celebrated

ONE TREE HILL,

AND OTHER VARIED AND ROMANTIC SCENERY

In fact, the site of this Township, for its beauty and eligible situation, cannot be surpassed by any in the vicinity of this City, while the richness and fertility of the Valley of Eden are too well known to the Public to require any comment.

In the immediate vicinity of the Township, there is plenty of scoria available for Building purposes; adjoining, a never-failing supply of pure water, and firewood in abundance.

The Allotments in this Township are well worthy the attention of all classes, as they hold out great advantages.

A plan will be ready for public inspection at the Rooms of the Auctioneers.

. Terms very liberal.

Sept. 10, 1841.

ANNA.
Mason and Paton

WILL SELL BY AUCTION,

On WEDNESDAY next, September 15th, at 12 o'clock, at their Temporary Rooms,

THE REMAINING PORTION OF THIS TOWNSHIP.

Terms,—20 per cent. Cash deposit, and the residue by a Bill at Twelve Months.

Without Reserve.

TO BE SOLD BY AUCTION,

By Mason and Paton,

On MONDAY, September 20th, 1841, at Eleven o'clock, at the Risk of the former Purchaser, who has failed to comply with the conditions of sale,

ALL that piece or parcel of Ground, part of allotment No. 1 of No. 4 of the Township of Auckland, numbered 3 on a plan of the subdivisions into which that allotment has been divided for sale.

This allotment being sold at the risk of the former purchaser, will be re-sold without reserve on the same terms and conditions as at the previous sale.

Mason and Paton,

AT an early date, will put up to Auction, several well situated Allotments in Victoria street and Prince Albert-street of which full particulars will be hereafter communicated.

☞ *It now being proved by the Sale effected by Mason and Paton on the 7th instant, that EPSOM is considered one of the most delightful situations imaginable, and certain to become a place of importance, the Proprietor is induced to offer Section 2, for Public Competition on TUESDAY, 14th September, by Mason and Paton, at their temporary Rooms, at One o'Clock.*

IMPORTANT NEWS!!!

THREE SHIPS are daily expected from England, with Emigrants for the

MANUKAO COMPANY.

One of them has arrived at Port Phillip, and may therefore be HOURLY looked for.

SEVEN SAIL OF EMIGRANT SHIPS

Have been laid on in England and Scotland for

AUCKLAND AND MANUKAO,

and will bring out the Judge, the Attorney General and the Surveyor General, who will, doubtless, on his arrival commence surveying the

New Township of Manukao,

and therefore enhance the value of Land situated half way between Manukao and the Metropolis; and private communications have reached Auckland that several

THOROUGH-BRED HORSES

are on their way here from England, consigned to parties in this Town, therefore we may expect

RACES NEXT YEAR,
AT
EPSOM.

Mason and Paton

Have the honor to submit to Public Competition, on TUESDAY next the 14th instant, at their Rooms, at One o'clock precisely,

THE CONTINUATION of the universally and much sought after

VILLAGE OF EPSOM!!!

So delightfully situated half-way between Auckland and Manukao, and may justly be termed

THE GARDEN OF EDEN,

The above forms section 2 of the Village of Epsom, and is subdivided into beautiful allotments which have been carefully laid out in such a manner as to suit the views and convenience of all classes of purchasers.

The site of this Village is so felicitously chosen, that it commands a considerable frontage to the

GREAT MANUKAO ROAD,

And it is well known that this will be the direct line of communication with Manukao, which will be the

Second Town of Importance

in this rising colony, and on this very spot which Nature has pointed out for a

Race Course,

Thereby affording a certainty of Business combined with amusement.

It is well known, that Parties who have once visited this enchanting spot, have expressed their anxiety to return, therefore to live there will evince judgment. There is not in the whole of the Islands of New Zealand, a place so rich in romantic scenery as this—It "stands alone in its Glory."

This delightful valley is sheltered from the winds, and in the Summer season the cool breezes are felt from

THE SEA.

With these peculiar advantages, how would our Friends in Old England envy us, could they but see this delightful spot, which may well be said to outrival the celebrated

VALLEY OF CHALON.

The soil of it is too well known to comment on. Suffice it to say, that it is peculiarly situated, alike for the Private Gentleman, as

A Quiet Retreat from the noisy World,

And for the Market Gardener, as the richness of the soil cannot be outvied in the

WHOLE WORLD!

The Auctioneers feel convinced that any further comment, on their part, would be useless, therefore they solicit intending purchasers who have not already visited the above Property, to view it previous to the day of sale.

Terms.—20 per cent. cash deposit, and the residue by bills at six months.

Village of Eden.

Mason and Paton

Have received instructions to sell by Public Competition, on TUESDAY next, September 14th, at One o'clock, at their temporary Rooms, Shortland Crescent.

TWENTY allotments suited for Market Gardens, small Farms, and Private Residences, in this delightfully situated Village

Terms.—Ten per cent Cash deposit; the residue by a Bill at Twelve Months.

Mason and Paton

Beg to direct the attention of the Public to the

MOST EXTENSIVE

SALE OF MERCHANDISE

Ever offered to the Inhabitants of Auckland, on THURSDAY, the Sixteenth Instant, at Twelve o'clock, at their Rooms, Shortland Crescent, consisting of—

BLANKETS and WELSH FLANNELS.
Biscuit
Dungaree
Striped S hirts
Frocks
Soap (Liverpool)
Pit Saws
Paint, in colors
Iron Pots
Nails
Brown Drill
Shirting
Silk Handkerchiefs
Trucks, with wheels complete
Doors
French Window-sashes
Gunpowder
Tobacco
Dutch Clover
Perennial ditto
Lucerne ditto
Evergreen Fiscal
Asparagus ditto
Rhubarb ditto
Hollands Gin, white and straw color, in half pipes
Brandy in half pipes
Rum in ditto
Porter and Ale bottled
Taylor and Trueman's stout, in wood
Porter and Wine Corks

And other Articles too numerous to mention.

List of Books.

Popular Encyclopædia, 13 volumes
Johnson's Works, 12 vols.
Goldsmith's Citizen of the World
Young's Night Thoughts
Devil's Elixer, 2 vols.
Fatal Follies, 4 vols.
Plays, 2 vols.
Tales of an Evening
New Zealanders
Beauties of Blair
Hume's Essays
Miscellaneous Works, 20 vols.

Auckland, September 10, 1841.

THIS DAY, AT TWELVE O'CLOCK,

Dalziel and Co.

SOLICIT THE PRESENCE OF THEIR FRIENDS TO A

LUNCH

AT WATSON'S LARGE ROOMS,

EXCHANGE HOTEL.

AFTER WHICH, they will submit to Public Competition—

8 Working Bullocks
7 Close-pole and open Drays
Bullock Harness
A quantity of Hay and Bran
2 Hogsheads Ale
2 Pipes and 1 Hogshead Brandy
1 Hogshead Red Wine
3 Hogsheads Gin
1 Quarter-cask Rum
15 Dozen very superior Port Wine
15 Ditto Sherry
4 Casks Sydney corned Beef
1 Hogshead Tobacco
2 Casks Sydney Flour
2 Bushels Split Pease
1 Bale superfine Clothing
An invoice of Drugs
And various other Articles.

Shares in the Auckland Printing Company.

TO BE SOLD BY AUCTION,

By Brown & Campbell,

At their Rooms, on TUESDAY, the 14th Instant, at Twelve o'clock,

SHARES in the above Company, Four Pounds paid up on each Share.

Terms—Cash.

Brown and Campbell

WILL SELL BY AUCTION,

On TUESDAY Next, at 12 o'clock, at their Rooms in Shortland Crescent,

GENERAL MERCHANDISE,

AFTER WHICH

A SELECTION OF BOOKS,

Among which will be found Chambers' Edinburgh Journal, Penny Magazine, Library of Useful Knowledge, Sheep, Cattle, British Husbandry, Spectator, Tait's Edinburgh Magazine, London and Westminster Review, Park's Travels, Cottagers of Glenburnie, Park's Anology of Religion, Vicar of Wakefield, Shakespeare, Palmyra, Pamela, Robertson's Charles V., Wolstoncraft's Rights of Woman, Alexander's History of Women, Candid, or All for the Best, an 8-Keyed Accordion, &c. &c.

Sept. 20th, 1841.

SALE BY AUCTION,
OF WRECK OF

FIVE TON BOAT,

Brown and Campbell

Postponed till TUESDAY Next, the 14 inst., at 12 o'clock, at the request of parties wishing to inspect the Boat.

TO BE SOLD BY AUCTION,

By Mr. I. Joseph,

On MONDAY next, the 13th instant, at his Rooms, Shortland Crescent, at Eleven o'clock precisely,

THE fine fast-sailing Schooner ELLEN, 23 Tons Burthen, as she now lies off Commercial Bay, 8 Months old, together with all her Masts, Sails, Running Rigging, &c.

The Ellen was built at Mangainui, under inspection, of the best and most approved materials.

Terms.—One half Cash, the residue by approved Bills at 6 Months.

IMMEDIATELY AFTER THE ABOVE,

Mr. I. Joseph

Will offer for Sale, 40,000 SHINGLES, and a quantiy of TIMBER.

Also,

THE UNDERMENTIONED GOODS:

Rum, Gin, Brandy, Claret and Champagne, Sherry (in three dozen casks), Vinegar, bottled Porter, Arrack, Corks, Biscuit, Pickles, Prints, Blankets, Tools, Razors, Mustard, Soap, Butter, Rice, Rope, Flour, Window Glass, Gunpowder, Salt, Molasses, Tobacco, Raisins, Cigars (superior quality), Looking Glasses, Mattrasses, Regatta Shirts, Moleskin and fancy Coats and Trowsers, and sundry other Articles.

MR. MANTON,

BEGS to inform the Inhabitants of Auckland, that he intends opening an Academy for the Tuition of Youth, on Monday, next at his temporary residence,

CHANCERY STREET,

Mr. M. assures those Parents who may intrust him with the Education of their Children that no exertion shall be spared on his part to render their studies as complete as possible.

TERMS, (WEEKLY.)

	s.	d.
Entrance Fee	2	6
Children seven years and under	2	0 per week.
Above that age	3	0

Open from 9 a. m. to 5 p. m.

TRESPASS.

IN consequence of a Robbery having been committed on my premises, on Sunday or Monday last, Notice is hereby given, that all persons found trespassing within my Fence, during the day, will be prosecuted according to Law, and all persons entering my grounds, after Nightfall, will be summarily treated as felonious trespassers.

HENRY TUCKER

Shortland Crescent, } 9th Sept., 1841 }

present Mount Eden Road and St Andrew's Road and from Windmill Road in the north to Glenalmond Road in the south.

In January 1842 fashionable Auckland (but not the ailing Governor) flocked to Epsom to enjoy the first race meeting. The few horses seem all to have competed in each race but even then no field was greater than six. The Garrison won their laurels early. In both the Town Plate of thirty sovereigns and the Consolation Handicap Stakes, Mr Mason's chestnut gelding *New Zealander* bolted, but in the last race, the 'Little Go Beaten Stakes', betting on him was six to four and he justified the confidence and won cleverly by a length.[11] This great horse afterwards belonged to Sir George Grey and was repurchased from him by Mason when Grey left for Cape Colony in 1853. We are told that Mr Berry, the Sheriff at Auckland, then wanted to buy the animal but was not prepared to pay Mason's price. Asked if the horse could jump, 'Mr Mason who was on the horse's back said he would try. Thereupon he set the horse at a five barred gate which was in front and cleared it beautifully and brought him back over it.'[12]

It seems clear at this time that the auctioneering business of Mason and Paton flourished tolerably well but the architecture did not. Edward Ashworth, an architect from Exeter who arrived at Auckland in October 1842 and left again, disappointed, in January 1844, found in that space only two or three overtures were made to him to undertake buildings or survey lands 'but the offers in the article "payment" were so miserable that I reluctantly rejected them.'[13] He, however, was a man who had attributed his little success in England to 'want of the patronage of the great' and appropriately enough in Auckland he became drawing master to the Governor's children. It is difficult to visualize Mason in such a role. Ashworth found the drawing room at Government House superb (though this was no doubt attributable partly to the aura of Mrs Hobson) and St Paul's Church a rather pretty design. But the Grecian Doric facade to the Courthouse was, in his eyes, ridiculous and ' . . . the flimsy but not inelegant dwellings of weatherboard so quickly constructed seemed to mock and deride the profession of an architect . . . .'

[11] *New Zealand Herald and Auckland Gazette*, 12 January 1842.
[12] *Otago Daily Times*, 26 June 1897.
[13] Edward Ashworth, 'Journal'. Manuscript, A.T.L. Ashworth had been articled to Robert Cornish, Cathedral Architect of Exeter, then to the better-known Charles Fowler. He left New Zealand for Hong Kong but soon returned to Devonshire where, and in Somerset, he designed or restored a number of churches.

VII   EPSOM FARMS AND CHURCH AND CHURCHMEN

The land around Auckland being flat and naturally clear of timber, except in clumps and in gulleys, a horseman might suppose he could speed with loose rein across it in any direction. Level as it looks, however, this champaign is only passable by the roads; for the surface is thickly strewed, by the vomiting of past eruptions, with rough and sharp atoms destructive of hoof or boot. – Lt. Colonel Godfrey Charles Mundy, *Our Antipodes.* London, 1852.

Any man of Mason's background, in mid-nineteenth century England, was likely to have had some experience of farming, gained from cousins still on the land. Yet, one of the odder things about Mason's subsequent career was the alternating periods he spent in the practice of architecture and of farming. It is too simple to suppose that he retired to farming only when building activity fell away. It is more likely that, initially, the distress caused by the death of his son, which he had apparently surmounted at the time, returned with full force some months after the event and brought about his withdrawal from the affairs of the town. Moreover, the humble nature of the few buildings being commissioned gave little play for talents trained on palaces and there were already several other architects in competition.[1] Understandably his thoughts turned to the borough lands now mapped out by Felton Mathew's surveyors.

The official policy of cutting up the more easily available land round Auckland into suburban allotments and small farms, seldom exceeding twenty acres, had already met severe criticism. The growth of small settlements along the 'Manakao' road was castigated by the *Herald and Gazette,* 25 September 1841, in no uncertain terms: 'If towns and Villages are allowed to be established in the early stages of the Colony, on every ten acre allotment which is sold by the Government, the country will be very soon covered with roadside inns and grog-houses of the lowest description, surrounded by a few dirty hovels, inhabited by the worst characters, and called a *Village,* by the name of "Paradise," "Ascot," &/c., and serving as a rendezvous for all agrarian idlers and reprobates.' The firm of Mason and Paton was naturally involved in all this, acting as it did as agents to the Government and to the various speculators concerned in setting up the villages of Parnell, Windsor Terrace, Epsom, and Anna, and both partners had bought small farms at Epsom after the sales of September 1841.

[1] Sampson Kempthorne, James Baber, Edward Ashworth, Frederick Thatcher, and Reader Gilson Wood all arrived within the first four years of settlement. Ashworth, who was in the same ship as Baber, has already been quoted in witness to the little architectural work available and it is a fact that none of these men was then able to make a living in his profession. From September 1841, Louis Perret, the author of six great folios descriptive of the catacombs of Rome, spent eight months at Russell during which he supervised the building of the *pisé* printing house for the French Catholic Mission and then returned to Europe.

Mason now began to cultivate an area of about forty acres forming the northern part of their holding, while Paton farmed the southern part, the line of division apparently being Balmoral Road. For Paton, Mason designed a house called Eden Hill which remained in the family, a reminder of colonial days, until the last part of the Paton property was sold in 1955 and the house demolished. It was a very attractive house admired by no less a person than the widowed Mrs Hobson who visited it a few days before she left New Zealand. Paton finished a large part of it with his own hands and described the appearance as 'perhaps stylish . . . it is built of wood, & mud, stone & brick chimney, and is considered the prettiest in the colony. . . It is well plastered and harled outside, and would be difficult to distinguish from a stone house.'[2] (Plates 41 and 42.) Mason's own house, on high land now bounded by Mt Eden and Penrhyn Roads, he called Eden Grove. It was described as a *cottage orné*, complete with thatched roof, and it must have been completed by November 1842 for in that month he sold his Waterloo Quadrant house and land to Dr Davies, the assistant Colonial-Surgeon, for £650 – a good price at a time when an extraordinarily high rental might be paid for houses but little for their purchase. Capital was short and interest was normally twelve or even fifteen percent.

Farming at Epsom was more concerned with cropping than with grazing. Soon Mason was able to lay on the table, at an after-dinner exhibition of the Agricultural Association, maize yielding seventy bushels to the acre. Much wheat was grown and Mason, with a return of his old enterprise, purchased in 1844 another two acres of land adjoining his own property and built Auckland's first flour windmill. (Plate 8.) In this he had the advice and assistance of Mr Low, later of Low and Motion's well-known mill at Western Springs. Mason's Mill became known in later years as Bycroft's Mill and gave its name to Windmill Road. It opened on 1 May 1844 and must have made a picturesque feature in the landscape as seen across the valley from Eden Grove. The *Southern Cross* in the previous January had commented, 'Mr. Mason . . . will by this undertaking confer a great benefit upon Epsom in particular, upon the colony in general; and we trust, upon himself individually. Mr. Lowe (the ingenious maker of the beautiful model of a flax-dressing machine which was exhibited at the Agricultural Show) is engaged to erect the mill for Mr. Mason.' By November 'Triptolemus' was writing from Tamaki, the one other major farming settlement, complaining of the difficulties of sending wheat through 'quagmire and swamps to the mill in the interior'. He called for a corn market and a granary, with a mill worked by steam, and stated that the charges at the Epsom mill of one shilling per bushel for grinding wheat, were greater than the cost of sending wheat to Hobart to be ground. This letter was the subject of an editorial which absolved Mason from any blame for his charges: ' . . . he has every right to demand his own prices, he has been at great expense in erecting his mill and he has built when no other person in the place would do so and for our part we sincerely hope it will pay him well.' The writer then appeared to infer the identity of 'Triptolemus' by adding, ' . . . a windmill about Mr. Kempthorne's farm, or on one of the headlands, might answer the purpose well.' Mason quickly replied, 'My object was simply this: finding there was no probability of a mill of any kind being erected I put myself to the greatest personal inconvenience, and solely as an inducement to encourage the culture of wheat, that we might not be another year dependent on the neighbouring colonies for supplies;

[2]Thomas Paton to George Brown, 12 June 1843. The *Mail Coach*. Vol. I, No 12. Also note by Thomas Paton, 1 July 1899, '. . . built 1842 wood on scoria foundation 3 feet in height, the architect Mr Wm Mason the builders George McVae and Bros the timber best Kaurie from the Manukau forest.' A.P.L. postcard photograph of the house.

8. *Mason's mill, from Eden Grove.*

and not with the selfish motive attributed to me. I have done my part, my object is gained, a mill is erected. I shall now be most happy to produce my accounts and give the mill to any person that will work it for the exact cost, and I shall be happy to hand it over on the same terms tomorrow to Triptolemus.'

A year later on 29 November 1845, an advertisement appeared in the *New-Zealander*.

'Eligible Investment.

'Mr. Hart,

'Begs to announce that he has received instructions from Mr. William Mason to put up to Public competition on Monday the 8th of December next at the mart at 12 o'clock precisely,

'EDEN MILL,

'EPSOM.

'This mill is built of Scoria,[3] and every part is of the best material. The proprietor having spared neither time nor expense to render it the most complete thing of its kind in the Colony. It contains one pair of French Burr Stones; Smutting and Dressing Machines; and all that would be necessary to carry on the lucrative business of a Miller. The Mill has ground and cleared in the day 100 bushels of Wheat. There is also attached, a Weather-board store and Miller's House. It is hardly necessary for the Auctioneer to point out that the extensive Districts of the Tamaki and Epsom are almost entirely dependent on this Mill for getting their Wheat ground. To an industrious Man this presents the opportunity of realising in an incredibly short time, a handsome competency.

'Terms will be most liberal. . . .'

The terms of the advertisement are less altruistic than Mason's year-old offer to hand the mill over at cost and his purchaser two years later was certainly unexpected. It was the Rev. Walter Lawry, the General Superintendent for the Wesleyan Church, who bought the mill for his personal estate. Lawry held the property for five years and then sold to John Bycroft who retained it for another seventeen years. The ivy-covered stone tower was taken down in 1929 and the last remains removed in 1952.

The partnership of Mason and Paton had been dissolved in September 1844 and soon afterwards both partners branched out in their farming, Mason moving to East Tamaki, and Paton, while remaining at Eden Hill, buying some hundreds of acres at Papatoetoe. Mason's last task as an auctioneer was probably his attendance at the Government land sales of 28 June and 30 September 1844. 'His charge', wrote the Colonial Treasurer, 'is very moderate being only one guinea for his attendance at each sale.'

All this time, combined with the affairs of Mason and Paton and with his new interest in farming, Mason had continued his architectural activities such as they were. St Paul's Church, his *chef d'oeuvre* in Auckland, (Plates 38-39) was first preached in by Bishop Selwyn on the morning of 7 May 1843,[4] when he took for his text, 'I will not suffer mine eyes to sleep till I find out a place for the temple of the Lord', but it was not consecrated until St Patrick's Day, 1844. Its design, seeming moderately impressive in contrast to other Auckland buildings of the forties, was an almost exact parallel with Mason's St James's Church, Brightlingsea.

Selwyn was evidently pleased with the church and impressed by the magnitude of the committee's undertaking in building it. He was about to transfer St John's College and his own seat from Waimate to Tamaki and

[3] i.e. bluestone – not the red lava stone which we call scoria today.
[4] Selwyn, 'Journal'. Typescript, A.I.M., p. 19.

in his extreme displeasure with Sampson Kempthorne, who had previously acted as his architect, wished to employ Mason on the work at Tamaki. W. C. Cotton, writing at Waimate in September 1844, tells us: 'The Bishop hard at work as tho he had been bred an architect planning St John's College, Bishop's Auckland. For that was the name he wrote below it when he had done. I went into the Palace in the evening and by 11½ he had not only drawn the ground plan assigning to each department its proper situation but had sketched a most beautiful general view of the whole. He is going to send this down to Auckland immediately & will have the kitchens Hall & boys dormitories commenced immediately. Oh! how I wish master M.R.H. you were here for the next three years to carry these glorious plans into effect. He is going to send down Pugin's works, and other books of architectural detail, together with his plan, that the architects may get correct details. He fancies Mr Mason who built the Ch. is quite competent for the task, but as he has hitherto employed Mr Kempthorne he thinks it necessary to throw the work open to competition.'[5]

Sampson Kempthorne, whom the Bishop had employed previously, was the architect son-in-law of the Rev. Josiah Pratt, secretary of the Church Missionary Society. He came to New Zealand with some reputation in 1842 but, by assuming an unwarranted authority for the Society's affairs in New Zealand, fell foul of the Bishop and eventually of the Society. In this matter he believed so strongly in the rights of his case that he travelled to England in 1847 to argue it with the Society.

Cotton's own opinion of St Paul's had been guarded. 'Auckland Church is much better than I expected – very well proportioned inside: but disfigured by horrible tie beams and a still more horrible beam, quite too low down at the West end, intended to support a Gallery at some future time. The Brick walls are rough inside and not well built all open v[erti]cals. Outside one or two pieces of mud coloured stone (wrought) inserted here and there among the honest red brick has a most unhappy appearance.'[6] He apparently did not realize that the roughness of the brick afforded a key for its subsequent plastering (carried out in 1850), nor could he visualize the final effect of the steeple, surmounted by a ball and cross, which was eventually completed in July 1844. The church retained this form until 1863 when it was ingeniously enlarged to the designs of Colonel T. R. Mould, R.E., by building a new nave across the existing structure which then formed transepts to the whole. In 1885 the whole building was demolished to make way for the reduction of Point Britomart and the improvement of the roading pattern about Emily Place.

The total cost of St Paul's as built by Mason, but before the erection of the steeple, was £2917 17s 9d. On this amount he received a fee of five per cent and gave back £61 8s 0d as a donation to the none too prosperous building fund.

Mason made one more offer to the Church at this time. A meeting was held at the Prince Albert Hotel to discuss the erection of a church to be called St Peter's, Windsor. 'Mr. Mason in addition to his offer of an allotment of land for the purpose, was kind enough to lay before the meeting a plan and specification of a pretty little church – in the old English village style – towards which upon the first glance the approbation of the meeting appeared to be secured – nor did the subsequent rational investigation of the matter draw forth any suggestion of improvement on it – on the contrary, it appeared to be the general opinion that the well earned

[5]'Journals', Vol. VIII, p. 31. Manuscript, Dixson Library. W. C. Cotton, 1813-1879, one of a family notable through several generations, was a younger schoolfellow of Bishop Selwyn at Eton and his fellow curate at Windsor. He graduated from Christ Church, Oxford, in 1836, with a first in Classics and a second in Mathematics, and two years later had published at Oxford two 'Short and Simple Letters to Cottagers from a Bee Preserver', which were afterwards expanded into an illustrated volume, *My Bee Book* (London, 1842). He published also a volume of poems and a single long poem called *New Zealand*, descriptive of Selwyn's mission. From his lifelong devotion to the study of bees and his extraordinary familiarity with them, he was known as 'Bee' Cotton. He came to New Zealand as Selwyn's domestic chaplain and taught Greek and kept bees at both Waimate North and St John's College, Tamaki, compiling all the time the voluminous diaries which, illustrated with hundreds of drawings, are in the Dixson Library, Sydney. He returned to England in 1847 in fulfilment of a promise made to his father who was Governor of the Bank of England, a considerable philanthropist and a compulsive builder of churches. He it was who gave Selwyn the huge tent he called his 'canvas cathedral'. W. C. Cotton had hoped to marry Mary Eliza Hawkins, daughter of the antiquary Edward Hawkins. It was evidently her architect brother, Major Rhode Hawkins, whom Cotton apostrophized as 'master M.R.H.'.

[6]ibid, Vol. V, p. 64.

reputation of Mr. Mason, the architect and designer of St. Paul's – was, if possible, enhanced by this projected one. Mr. Mason technically designated his design as of the MONASTIC BARN style, and said that with judicious management the cost would not excede £400, built with scoria.'[7]

In the event, Mason's offer of land was passed over, possibly through the scrupulosity of the Bishop but also in point of the suitability and aspect of the site of which he was always extremely careful, in favour of land advanced by Edward Rich. The church built on it (not to Mason's design) also underwent a change of name and was called St Andrew's, Epsom. The same newspaper report, already quoted, continued with praise of the Epsom farmlands: 'We cannot pass over the opportunity thus afforded of reporting that the valley lands between the Mounts Eden, St. John, Albert and One Tree Hill are in a state of forward cultivation – beyond what the dwellers of Auckland are accustomed to dream of . . . . We almost envy Mr. Mason his place . . . .'

The extent of Mason's association with St John's College, Tamaki, is uncertain. We have Cotton's suggestion (4 September 1844) that the work was to be put out to competition and a drawing survives (Plate 43)[8] of Mason's design for a schoolhouse, bearing a remarkable resemblance to Selwyn's own sketches copied into Cotton's journal. This drawing by Mason is dated 4 May 1845 and was probably intended for St Paul's and not St John's for, in October 1844, the *Southern Cross* announced that the architectural work at St John's was to be entrusted to Sampson Kempthorne whose homely design for the stone house there was in strong contrast to the more ambitious Puginesque design Mason produced. Commenting on Kempthorne's appointment, the *Auckland Times*, 15 October 1844, informed its readers that 'We should have been better pleased if, after his services to St. Paul's church and other public purposes, Mr. Mason had been employed on this work also; but we daresay Mr. Kempthorne will be energetic under the supervising eye of His Lordship.' We must therefore assume that, in referring to Mason as the Bishop's architect in charge, J. King Davis in his *History of S. John's College* was no more than strictly correct and that his work was supervisory, though it would probably have included the temporary establishment at Purewa occupied during the main building operations. Selwyn's whole plans had to be modified on the score of cost and even the supervisory work may not have lasted long, for Cotton notes in September 1845 that Mr Thatcher 'is now Superintendent of Works', and expresses a hope that building will be speeded up in consequence. The works referred to were public works but from May 1846 Frederick Thatcher and fellow architect Reader Wood, who was described as Civic Bursar, shared what had been the homestead of R. C. Barstow's farm, by then incorporated in the College property, and were each paid a quarterly retainer by the College for architectural services.[9] Wood's fee was nominal and two years later Thatcher became resident architect and a candidate for holy orders.

Bishop Selwyn's tremendous influence upon the architectural style of ecclesiastical building in Auckland should not be allowed to obscure the fact that he had several able men to interpret his ideas and the advice of others like Arthur Guyon Purchas, that remarkable amalgam of talents, surgeon, priest, musician, scientist and inventor who, the brother of an architect, was himself responsible for the design of St Bride's Church, Mauku.[10] His variety of accomplishments was almost matched by That-

[7] *Auckland Times*, 2 February 1843.
[8] In the possession of the Dean of Auckland.
[9] See Bishop Selwyn's Ledger and the Senior Bursar's Abstract Book 1844, both in Auckland Diocesan Office.
[10] E. H. Roche, 'Arthur Guyon Purchas – A New Zealand Pioneer', *New Zealand Medical Journal*, June 1954.

cher, who was for some time private secretary to Sir George Grey during both his Governorships and later to Bishop Selwyn at Lichfield. Reader Wood remained at St John's for only a short time before taking a Government appointment, but he subsequently designed the Melanesian Mission buildings in Auckland, very much in the Selwyn manner. He entered Parliament in 1861 and became Colonial Treasurer, a role to which he brought considerable financial acumen.

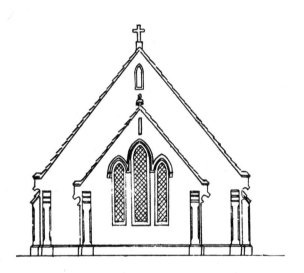

EAST   FRONT.

9.   St. Paul's Church, Auckland, east end.

VIII   EAST TAMAKI AND HOWICK

Fix'd in his farm, he soon display'd his skill
In small-boned lambs, the horse-hoe, and the drill;
—George Crabbe, *Tales*, Tale III, The Gentleman Farmer.

From the sack of Kororareka in March 1845 till the capture of Kawiti's Ruapekapeka pa – the Bat's Nest – ten months later, Auckland trembled at the threat of Heke's war in the North. The Britomart barracks were entrenched, blockhouses built, earthworks thrown up near the Roman Catholic Chapel, and the windows of St Paul's barricaded. William Mason was gazetted a lieutenant in the Auckland Battalion, New Zealand Militia, a force of three hundred civilians enlisted under a hasty enactment of the Legislative Council. Remarkably enough, all four subalterns were architects, but only Reader Wood among them took part in the fighting.

Though the attack on Auckland never came, its threat drove many of the outlying settlers into town and the lands they abandoned were to be bought for a few pounds. Already in 1845, Mason had applied through Edward Rich[1] for the waiver of Crown rights of pre-emption over a block of 1,000 acres near Henderson on the upper Waitemata.[2] Rich claimed for an equal area, their earlier joint claim for 4,000 acres having been rejected, and then the claims were withdrawn altogether on Rich's statement that the land was of poor quality and would not suit either his or Mason's purposes.

On 6 December 1845, misfortune struck again and Mason's house, the pretty *cottage orné* at Eden Grove, was completely destroyed. A piece of paper thrown on a fire was carried up the chimney by a strong draught and, landing on the thatch, set fire to it. The house was quickly reduced to ashes and virtually nothing was saved. He decided to sell this farm as well as the adjacent mill property and in the following May the *New-Zealander* was able to publish a report of the sale: 'We understand the beautiful estate of Mr. Mason, at Eden Grove, within three miles of the capital, and comprising, only, Fifty acres, without dwelling-house, that having been recently destroyed by fire, has been disposed of, by him, for the large sum of Four Hundred Pounds. This transfer to an intended resident settler, well acquainted with the adjacent colonies, as well as the Southern Districts is evidence of the opinion and estimation, of persons competent to decide, of the comparative advantages of the

[1] Edward Rich was a son of George Rich, a considerable farmer at Mount Eden. He imported stud cattle and sheep, including the first merinos, and exported to Australia. Another son was Francis Dyer Rich who developed the famous Bushey Park estate in Otago, and Matapiro in Hawkes Bay. In 1881 he formed with others the New Zealand Thames Valley Land Company in London.
[2] National Archives, I.A.315, 45/51 and 45/107.

Northern and Southern Division of this Island. As our Southern Contemporaries are so zealous, in their vituperation and depreciation of the lands of the Waitemata, in the neighbourhood of the capital, we would very much wish to know what Fifty acres of Land, without any house, would realise, at the present time, within three miles of the blockaded town of Wellington.'

With this money to his account, Mason now planned to farm on a larger scale and applied for an area of 1,817 acres[3] of volcanic country between Smales Mount (Matangi-nui) and the Tamaki river, about twelve miles from Auckland on the south side of the river and three miles from the village of Otahuhu. The land was advertised for sale in the *Gazette* of 15 December 1846 but, lacking a purchaser, was leased to Mason for ten pounds yearly rental. He occupied this land at once but appears to have held it for a comparatively short time when he was able to purchase an adjacent area of 125 acres forming the western headland of the Pakuranga stream where it flows into the Tamaki, from Henry Richard Oakes[4] of McLeay River, New South Wales. This farm, which remains intact to this day, is said to have been the site of a mission station called Te Wairau. It was obtained by Oakes as a Crown Grant for the sum of £125 in December 1844, so he lost money on the sale to Mason four years later for £81 2s.[5] The tidal river, which tends to muddiness in its upper reaches, sweeps into this headland to provide navigable waters close to shore. The property was bounded on the Pakuranga arm by a farm of 95 acres which Oakes sold in 1851 to the troublesome Major John Gray (half brother to Sir George Grey's father[6]), who had recently been dismissed from command of the Fencibles at Panmure. Gray sold the property in 1853 to Albin Martin, one of the founders of the Auckland Society of Arts and the friend of John Linnell, Samuel Palmer, Sir George Richmond, and other painters of the period.[7] On the southern boundary, up the Tamaki river, Fairburn's grant began. The story of William Thomas Fairburn's claims to 40,000 acres, traditionally purchased from Maoris who allowed him all the land he could see from Mount Richmond when facing south, is well known, but it is worthy of note that the last piece still belonging to the Fairburn family, of more than 5,000 acres finally granted him. is an area of 20 acres on Mason's old boundary. It is part of the Fairburn farm once known as Otara Grove.

Mason remained on his new property no more than two years when he saw further opportunity for improvement and bought from Fairburn 350 acres at the East Head of the Tamaki. For this he paid £500 and sold his Pakuranga farm to Fairburn for £250.[8] No doubt the arrangement suited Fairburn who was thus able to consolidate his property in one area and make a tidy profit also. The price he paid reflected not only the improvements Mason had made but also the more settled conditions and the greater confidence of the settlers in freedom from attack by hostile Maoris.

The East Head property justified once more Mason's unerring eye for a fine site. The East Head is formed by a narrow peninsula of great natural beauty with long sandy beaches on either side and high cliff faces at the northern end. Sir John Logan Campbell had looked at this headland from the island of Motukorea: 'As you gazed on this plumed headland of exquisite beauty you now and again laboured under the optical illusion that it was moving; you thought at one time it was nearer the island,

[3]Lots 32, 33, 34, 37, 39, 40, 41, 44, 45, 47-52. Lot 2 Pakuranga. It included the area later bought by Rev. Gideon Smales and called by him Hampton Park.

[4]See Edward Markham, *New Zealand or Recollections of it*. Wellington, 1963. Oakes went from Van Diemen's Land to the Hokianga with his father in 1834. Markham predicted he would be 'a sad scamp' and in fact he and his father became so detested at Hokianga that they returned to Australia in January 1837.

[5]Major Matson of the 58th Regt., who had recently married Isabel, the daughter of Baron Charles de Thierry, gave Mason brief accommodation with the sum of £80.

[6]Neither Sir George Grey nor Major John Gray chose to recognize the relationship, a circumstance less odd than it would otherwise appear, if it is remembered that Grey was a posthumous child brought up in England while his father's brothers remained in Ireland.

[7]Una Platts, Auckland City Art Gallery Catalogue, *Early Identities*, 1955.

[8]Lands and Deeds Office, Auckland. Vols. A2/46 and 1D/452. Also C.T. 32/81. Though the conveyance is dated January 1853 there is little doubt that Mason moved to East Head at least two years earlier.

and then again farther off. You imagined it was making obeisances to the
little island, and endeavouring, with the most graceful and quiet move-
ments, to attract attention towards its pretty plumed head, and command
admiration.'⁹ Even when Mason bought this land the plumed head, which
is now called Musick Point and is the site of a radio station for aviation
control, was reserved to the Crown. But Mason's farm contained all the
remaining land of the peninsula and the whole of the two beach frontages.
Today, houses and a golf course cover its gentle hills and the great pines
and gum trees Mason planted have only recently been felled. The gabled
wooden house he built, plain, substantial and well proportioned but
otherwise no different from many early farm houses, stood for a hundred
years overlooking the western beach, now called Buckland's to Rangitoto
and the islands of the Gulf beyond. Eastern Beach was for many years
called Mason's Beach. In this landscape there was no need to build a mill
tower either for use or ornament. Was this the dream for which Mason,
now forty years of age, had left England twelve years before, the typical
English ambition to own land, to exercise a modest kind of authority
through local government, to live within the law and the reasonableness
of the Church of England? Architecture seemed temporarily forgotten.
He was even guilty occasionally of mild pomposity for the young men of
the previous decade were growing older.

There was much hard work to be done. The land which was later to
ripple with cocksfoot and fine English grasses was covered in scrub. It
was surprisingly remote and no doubt lonely, though travellers from
Howick came three miles by track to the western beach to be ferried
across the river and landed at Sandy Point, whence they walked or rode
past the now thriving St John's College to Auckland. It was also a different
working proposition from the East Tamaki farm where a dairy herd had
been soon supplanted by barley growing. East Head was run as a mixed
farm but with a preponderance of sheep.

Yet Mason was never one to cut himself off for long. He had been
appointed a Warden for the Hundred of Howick in 1849 and now, in 1851,
he was elected to the Common Council of Auckland as the representative
for Tamaki East. This gave him the dignity of an Alderman and invested
him automatically with the duties of a magistrate. Evidently liking this
taste of politics he next announced himself, in July 1852, as a candidate
for the Legislative Council of New Ulster, for the Pensioner Settlements
electorate. 'Personally,' he announced rather grandly but inaccurately,
'I will say nothing of the gentleman – Lieutenant Symonds – already in
the field as my opponent, who desires to add to his duties as a Pensioner
officer, and a *paid* magistrate, the responsibilities of an *independent*
legislator. . . . Will the Pensioners exercise their privilege of voters, as
citizens or as *soldiers*. . . . Your fellow colonists are looking to see whether
they can rely on you as fellow labourers in the duties of a representative
government; – or whether habits of obedience, – admirable in a soldier –
have become so inveterate as to destroy your independence as citizens,
and therefore to unfit you for the duties of electors . . ..'¹⁰

His suggestion that pressure might be brought to bear on the soldier
pensioners drew a reply from the Colonial Secretary. The campaign lasted
two months and before it was over Mason was himself accused of using the
influence of his old friend Captain Salmon.¹¹ Salmon denied it in an
advertisement on 1 September: 'A Report having been circulated in

⁹*Poenamo*, p. 229.
¹⁰*New-Zealander*, 7 July
1852. John Jermyn Sym-
onds was a younger brother
of Mason's old friend, W. C.
Symonds. He had relieved
Mason as executor of his
brother's estate.
¹¹John Salmon came to New
Zealand in 1842 on the
death of his brother David
who had been a merchant
at Kororareka and for
whose estate Mason appa-
rently acted as executor
(*New Zealand Government
Gazette*, 31 August 1842).
Both brothers had been
ship's masters and it was
probably in association with
John Salmon that Mason
made the venture into shipping which is mentioned in
several contemporary ac-
counts: that he was one of
the founders of the first
steam navigation company
in New Zealand. (*Evening
Star*, Dunedin, 24 June
1897). Salmon was a mem-
ber of the Legislative Council from 1853 to 1868.
(Chapter VIII East Tamaki
and Howick).

Auckland that Captain Salmon has been using his influence unfairly to assist Mr. Mason in his canvass for the Pensioner Settlements and such report being altogether untrue, Captain Salmon takes this opportunity of publicly contradicting it. Mr. Mason is an old and valued friend of Captain Salmon's and as such has lately been very frequently at his committee room. . . . '

In the event Mason lost the election, as his new friend Vicesimus Lush recorded in his diary, by the narrow margin of nine votes.[12]

The Reverend Vicesimus Lush, M.A., later Archdeacon of Waikato, went as vicar to All Saints' Church, Howick, in 1850. His diary first mentions the Masons on 5 July 1851 when he 'Rode to a Mr Mason a settler a few miles from Howick to render to him an account of the collection in the weekly offertory since Easter Day – Mr Mason having consented to act as a sort of Church warden.' The following April Mason sent the Lushes a very fine turkey which was no doubt eaten five days later, after he had acted as godfather at the christening of Henry Alfred Lush by Bishop Selwyn. As he was leaving the vicarage after the service, he promised to make his godson a present of a heifer calf and to take care of all her increase for him – 'truly a Colonial present.'

Lush records something of the Mason household and of their occupations and diversions and for the first time Mrs Mason emerges from the shadows. 13 May 1852: 'Shortly after breakfast we all started in the cart for Mr Masons farm – an exceeding romantic estate of some three hundred acres. . . . Mr & Mrs Mason are very partial to children . . . & Mrs Mason took great notice of my little boy though the tears often came into her eyes as she stooped to speak to him. . . . ' 16 June 1852: 'Mr Mason came to dinner: gave him six young blue gum trees and a few Cape of Good Hope silver trees with seed of the Black Acacia: all these very valuable & beautiful trees which I have been most fortunate in rearing . . . ' 20 October 1852: 'Blanche rode over to Mrs Mason's: heard that the excitement in Auckland was increasing and provisions were likely to rise to famine price . . . .' The excitement had been caused by the discovery of gold at Coromandel which Mason thought, and Lush hoped, would not prove very productive.

When the Lay Secretary of the Church Missionary Society came to inspect land for a Native Training School, Mason joined them and greatly influenced their choice. Some months later Lush congratulated himself on Mason's favourable judgement of the quality of the soil on the farm he had bought for himself. Always Mason's opinion was sought. Lush rode out to consult him how best he could mend a font sent from England by his brother and badly damaged in transit, and on the following Sunday Mason stayed after the service to examine the font and gave it 'most unqualified praise and thought it, in point of style, the best, as yet, in the Colony . . . .' A few months later it was the new altar service which earned praise: 'They [Mr and Mrs Mason and the church warden and schoolmaster] thought it superb, and much admired the shape of the flagon and cup.'

Mrs Mason's servant troubles are related with great seriousness. A young lady staying in the house read to them until midnight. Several times Mr and Mrs Mason laughed aloud at the reading and next morning their maid complained she could not stay in such a riotous house where master and mistress kept their servant awake till after midnight with their laughter.

[12]Vicesimus Lush, Diary. Microfilm, A.P.L.

Another account tells us, at least, that it was Mrs Mason's habit to have hot water brought her at six in the morning and breakfast at seven. Troubles with colonial servants were proverbial. 25 November 1853: 'This was the third week of our having mutton in Howick – Mr Mason sent up 10 carcases . . . & found a ready sale. . . . ' 26 November 1853: 'Mr Mason brought over his two plough horses which I had promised to purchase the price is frightfully high £60 each: but when they have done my ploughing and so saved me some £150 I shall sell them again. . . .' 3 January 1854: 'A great moving today in the village – Mr & Mrs Hill[13] and family go to Mr Mason's farm at the Tamaki Heads – Mr & Mrs Mason come to Captain Macdonalds cottage, while the Captain and his wife leave for their large house vacated by the Hills. Mr Hill gives Mr Mason 300£ a year for his farm of 320 acres – There is not more than a third of it as yet reclaimed from the bush: but then he has the horses (2) oxen (4) cows (15) sheep (250) goats (15) fowls (200) carts, ploughs, harrow &c for his *use* – being bound to leave the same number of cattle &c on the farm when he leaves it – i.e. – (so report says) at the end of 5 years. Mr Mason gives the Captain £50 a year for his cottage and 5 acres: what extravagant rates of payment. It makes me wish to build a house on my own farm that I too might have a tenant at a good price. The Captains cottage cost him 200£.'

The great moving is unexplained but it is reasonable to connect it with Mason's recent activity in submitting an entry for a competition for a new Government House. He had engrossed himself in farming for nearly ten years and now, perhaps, felt the time ripe, after the discovery of gold and the elation it had produced in Auckland, to return to the practice of architecture.

10. East Head homestead.

[13]Hill's son founded a well-known Auckland firm of customs agents, Shirley W. Hill & Co.

IX GOVERNMENT HOUSE

*What is true of human polity seems to me not less so of the distinctly political
art of architecture.* – John Ruskin, *The Seven Lamps of Architecture*, 1849.

[1]Minutes of Executive
Council, 25 May 1853, National Archives.
[2]ibid., 18 August 1853.
[3]Charles Heaphy, V.C.
(1822-1881) is known as a
water-colourist, surveyor,
and soldier, rather than as
an architect, and it is possible that his entry for the
competition for a design for
Government House was the
only incursion he made into
this field. His versatility
may have been inherited
from his father, Thomas
Heaphy, Court Painter to
the Princess of Wales, a
protégé of the Duke of
Wellington, and founder of
the Society of British Art-
ists. His paintings once
fetched much higher prices
than those of his contemporary, Goya. Stanley's 1853
edition of Bryan's *Dictionary of Painters and Engravers* tells us that the father
was intractable and volatile,
equally expert at quarrying
for stone, constructing a
pleasure boat, building a
house, devising an improved
axle or laying down a railway.' Peter Nicholson's portrait (Plate 3) is engraved
from a painting by Thomas
Heaphy.
   James Baber (1821-1898)
came to New Zealand in the
ship *Tuscan* in 1842 and
was soon employed in the
Survey department where
he made the acquaintance
not only of Charles Heaphy

Several months before leaving East Head to the Hill family, William
Mason had entered a competition promoted among architects for the
design of a Government House at Auckland to replace Hobson's house,
gutted by fire five years before. Two prizes were offered, of £30 and £20,
for the design of a building to cost £8,000, with walls of scoria stone,
mouldings of Matakana stone, brick partitions and slated roof.[1]

When the awards were made[2] it was found that the winning design was
the work of the Deputy Surveyor-General, Reader Wood, and the runner
up was jointly the entry of two of his staff, Charles Heaphy and James
Baber.[3]

It would appear that the Executive had immediate doubts about Wood's
entry, for a memorandum of 25 August requested Heaphy and Baber to
prepare detailed estimates and specifications of their plans, 'for the
information of His Excellency', with as little delay as possible.

Whatever the Executive Council thought of the two winning designs,
William Mason wrote at once to the *New-Zealander* (3 September 1853)
criticizing both for inadequacies of construction. Hostilities thus opened,
Wood replied that Mr Mason was mistaken in supposing joists were to
span 70 feet, that a span of only 31 feet was called for, while Heaphy and
Baber took war into the other camp and after defending their own drawings pointed out that if *working* drawings had been called for, 'Mr. Mason
would not in his design marked *Ad referendum* have shown two 9 inch
partitions *unsupported* over his drawing room; in the design *Conge D'Elire*,
two unsupported partitions over his kitchen; have forgotten to take his
kitchen, dining room and drawing room chimneys through the first floor
and roof, and have arranged a 24 inch brick wall, entirely unsupported,
over his dining-room.' On 23 September, Mason, writing from Tamaki
obviously shaken, made his defence to these charges against his professional competence and added for good measure, that recountal of his early
experience which has already been noted: 'whose early days were exclusively devoted to the study and practice of his profession, under circumstances
of rare advantage . . .' and so on. He claimed also that it was only his
concern for public expenditure which led him to write in the first place.

Just what happened then is not at all clear. Whether as a result of Mason's protests or more probably for other reasons, nothing definite was done for more than a year. Mason's action in leasing his farm would seem to indicate that some sort of promise had been made him but he may on the other hand have been simply unable to resist the high rental he had been offered, and the freedom it gave him once more to practise his profession. He continued to live at Howick and received there a letter written on 28 December 1854, from Colonel Wynyard in his capacity of Superintendent of the Province of Auckland. 'It having been found necessary to employ an Architect to build the proposed Government House and the Public Offices I have to request that you will inform me whether you would be disposed to undertake that duty at a Salary of £300 per annum. It being understood that that sum shall cover the Salary of a Clerk if you find it necessary to employ one.'[4] Mason's acceptance was immediate and the Treasury Clerk was informed that his appointment as Architect for the Government House and Provincial Building should bear the date 28 December 1854 and that his salary of £300 per annum would be a charge against the vote of £10,000 for the Government House.[5]

The whole question of governmental authority at this time was extremely confused. Though the first Provincial Council was elected in August 1853, Governor Grey had left the Colony at the end of that year, before the General Assembly required by the Constitution Act was convened. When finally it met in May 1854, Colonel Wynyard, who was not only Superintendent of the Province of Auckland but also Acting Governor and Commander of the Forces in New Zealand, withheld representative government from the Assembly while awaiting approval from London and provision for the members of the existing Executive Council. In the absence of any directive from the Imperial Government, and finding Wynyard adamant, the Assembly soon acknowledged the continuing authority of the Executive Council and settled down to law-making. This left administrative affairs in the hands of the Executive and of the Provincial Councils for the time being. Within a very few weeks of its meeting, however, the Assembly had to deal with a strong move from Wellington members to hold the session of 1855 in a more central position in the Colony. This nearly successful move considerably frightened the Aucklanders and it may be assumed that the urgency then accorded to the Government House project by the Provincial Council of Auckland was partly the result – a satisfactory residence would at least endear Auckland to the Governor and where he lived the capital would be. The whole affair was brought to a head by James Busby, representative for the Bay of Islands and once Resident there, who moved for action.[6]

Mason's letter of acceptance of Wynyard's offer had rather disengenuously assumed that he was receiving the appointment of Provincial Architect and in fact that is what he became. 'As you have done me the honor of offering for my acceptance the appointment of Provincial Architect,' he wrote on 3 January, 'and as I have felt it my duty to respond to this mark of your Honor's confidence by intimating my willingness to undertake the duties of the office, I would with your permission beg leave to offer a few suggestions relative to the erection of a Government House which I believe to be the first work I shall be called upon to superintend.' He proceeded to argue the virtues of a building in scoria stone in preference to wood, assuming that wood had been stipulated because of the

but also of Reader Wood. When Wood, in the capacity of Colonial Treasurer, left for England in 1864 to raise a loan for Colonial Defence, Baber took charge of his architectural practice and worked from Wood's Shortland Street office under the style of Wood and Baber. Baber himself appears as Deputy Waste Land Commissioner in 1858 and as Inspector of Buildings in 1861. On 31 May 1854 Baber wrote to the Superintendent asking for an increase in pay. As draftsman he was receiving £225, Heaphy as district surveyor £300, Wood £300, and Ligar, the Surveyor-General, £720.

4 Provincial Council Papers, A.P.L.
5 ibid.
6 *New-Zealander*, 11 November 1854, Supplement.

greater speed of erection. He pointed out that circumstances had changed with the decision of the Home Government to confirm for the present 'His Excellency Colonel Wynyard in the office of Acting Governor as notified in the Gazette on the 27th December.' Maintenance, insurance and fire risk would all be greater with a wooden building. Stone would be available from Mount Eden. 'My only object is to call your Honor's attention to the fact that in my opinion there are ways and means presenting no serious practical difficulties of decreasing to such an extent the cost of a permanent Government House to be built with scoria as would justify you with the approbation of the Executive in instructing me to prepare plans and specifications for a work of this character.' A fortnight later Wynyard resigned the Superintendency on instructions from the Colonial Office, which found his dual roles of His Honour and His Excellency incompatible, and Brown[7] was elected in his place.

Evidently the terms of a report by a special sub-committee presented to the Provincial Council on 12 December 1854 had by now been communicated to Mason. 'The Committee appointed by the Council yesterday to enquire and report this day whether a stone or wooden building should be erected as a Government House, and also recommend which tender[8] should be accepted by His Honor the Superintendent, find that time has been so short that the Architect could not prepare all necessary details and estimates and that the tenders vary considerably in consequence.' They proposed that 'present plans etc. should not be adopted,' that 'the proposed erection should be of wood and that new plans, specifications etc. complete with working drawings should be prepared.' They further recommended that the accommodation should be as before and that the work be commenced as speedily as possible at a total cost of £10,000 including furniture. This report was adopted by the Council on 15 December.[9]

The *New-Zealander* reporting on these proceedings noted that it was understood that the buildings, being of a temporary character, might afterwards be converted into public offices 'whenever a permanent mansion should be thought advisable.'[10] This accorded with Governor Hobson's original intentions that the site would prove too valuable for a residence and should be given over to other purposes.[11]

Mason lost no time in getting down to work and tenders were called for 28 February.[12] He had other concerns also: a female lunatic destroyed herself by passing her arm through the bars of her ward window, breaking a pane of glass, and cutting her throat with a piece of it. Mason reported (11 March) that the building was completely unsatisfactory. A month later, on Easter Sunday, he visited the old slaughterhouse near Hobson's Bridge and informed the Superintendent: 'I cannot find terms sufficiently strong to express my disgust at this hothouse of filth and pestilence.' The following week he presented a report on the Provincial Government Offices which called for new buildings for the accommodation of the Superintendent, the Registrar, the Land and Survey Office, the Law Officer, the Provincial Architect and the Provincial Road Surveyor. The gaol would require replacement on a new site. For the Registrar, offices would have to be fireproof and while waiting for cast iron work to be sent from England an 'iron house' might be bought as a temporary measure.[13]

He moved from Howick into town and took or built a house called Bleak House which remains unidentified but was situated in Symonds

[7]William Brown of Brown and Campbell.
[8]Tenders on the earlier plans, presumably Heaphy and Baber's, were actually called in November. They were for alternative buildings in stone or wood.
[9]Provincial Council Papers, A.P.L.
[10]13 December 1854.
[11]G.B.P.P. 1842 XXVIII (569). Hobson to Lord John Russell, 5 August 1841. The building was transferred to the University of Auckland in 1969, when another house was provided at Epsom.
[12]*New-Zealander*, 31 January 1855.
[13]Provincial Council Papers, A.P.L.

Street.[14] (Dickens's novel, with its foggy evocation of the city he and Sarah knew so well, had reached Auckland the previous year.) At Bleak House their Howick friends visited and stayed – the Lushes, Every McLean[15] and his sister Ellen, and the Hills. Mason took up some of his old interests; he rejoined the Freemasons and was elected vice-president of the Farmers' Club which had rooms in the Exchange Hotel and had Major Greenwood for President and Joseph Crispe, W. T. Buckland, Joseph May, Every McLean and Major Matson as its other committee members.[16] He was once more active as a lieutenant in the Auckland Battalion of the Militia. Recollecting his pioneer efforts to establish sea communication with the coastal settlements he purchased shares in the newly formed Auckland Local Steam Navigation Company which had begun a service north as far as Mangonui and back to Coromandel, Waiheke, and Howick, with a brand new vessel called the *Wongawonga*. Its counterpart, the Auckland Steam Navigation Company, traded to Australia with the *William Denny*. Auckland in the fifteen years since her foundation had thriven apace. It is true that mud still formed her streets in winter and there were few buildings of consequence, but the Wesleyans, the Presbyterians and the Roman Catholics, as well as the Anglicans with St Paul's, all boasted stone or brick churches,[17] the two forts made a substantial contribution both in buildings and in social amenity, there was an elegant theatre, two rival newspapers, numerous good shops and warehouses and many attractive villas in the vicinity. For her townsmen it seemed just cause for pride. If there was no water except from wells, there was the long new wharf at the foot of Queen Street to boast about; if no state or council school system yet existed, several private schools provided education for those who wanted it; and there was good English written in the newspapers, acceptable oratory at the hustings, and the Choral Society could muster fifty vocalists with the backing of a military band.

In the middle of September, Lush rode into town to call on the new Governor, Colonel Gore Browne, and found him living in Captain Travers's house in Waterloo Quadrant but about to move into the house which, built for Frederick Whitaker in 1843, Colonel Hulme had bought from the bishop for £600. For this the Governor was required to pay £400 a year. Hulme Court as it is called today is one of the most beautiful of Auckland's early dwellings – a spreading stone-built house of one storey, with trellised verandahs on three sides – the kind of house which Mason might have designed at that time, fresh from New South Wales where many of these colonial Georgian houses occur. But no evidence can be found to connect him with its building. All that can be said is that if he was not its architect it is difficult to account for it at all. It was before Thatcher's time, who anyway was dedicated to the 'Old English' style, and before Wood, and neither Kempthorne nor Baber, the only other architects then practising, showed sufficient talent in their later work for an ascription to be made to either of them. There is of course the possibility that it was designed by an architect in Sydney where Whitaker's brother lived. It could even have brought Walter Robertson to Auckland, eventually to settle.[18]

Gore Browne and his wife, who were sometimes the subject of a joking reference to the firm of Browne and Campbell, she having been a Miss Campbell and the firm of (William) Brown and (John Logan) Campbell being the most influential in the town,[19] held their first levee in the new

[14]Jury List, *Southern Cross*, 10 February, 1857.
[15]Thomas Every McLean, Mason's nearest neighbour at East Head, became a considerable landowner and a breeder of bloodstock. He was called to the Legislative Council in 1873. McLean's own house near Howick was later called Bleak House and the name is preserved in Bleakhouse Road.
[16]*New-Zealander*, 11 April 1855.
[17]High Street Chapel, St Andrew's, and St Patrick's, all designed by Walter Robertson who came from Sydney at the end of 1846 and died at Auckland in 1851. None of them could yet match Mason's St Paul's.
[18]For a note on Walter Robertson see the final chapter.
[19]Lush, 14 September 1855.

Government House, still unfinished, in May 1856 on the Queen's birthday. Lush had already passed judgement on the building. 'It is far from a good design being too much pretence – the elevation showing columns, pilasters, architraves, a pediment etc as though it were a *stone* building in the Grecian style – instead of being but of wood – a good building could have been designed which would have manifested its materials and yet been an ornament to the place.'[20] Lush had obviously been talking to his friend Thatcher.

It is true that Mason's building had some unusual features now subdued – the segmental pediment has been replaced by a triangular one; the triple window beneath it has been hooded and a covered porch to the garden entrance has done away with the rather blank look the house once had. Detailing is often clumsy and the timber construction makes a pretence of being stonework by overlaying the corners with chamfered boards to represent quoins and by using great slabs of close-butted kauri timber on the central block; but these slabs are of such dimensions (eighteen inches by one and a half inches) that it is impossible to think of them as weatherboards. Construction is often ingenious, making use of a kind of prestressed beam over the big spans of drawing room and dining room, while the oddest feature, since removed, a partition between these rooms, which sank into the floor on some kind of mechanism, led to an hilarious *contretemps* at an early party.[21] It is said that the builder's men took umbrage that he had not been invited and rigged the partition in such a way that it stuck halfway at suppertime and left the guests peering over the top at the banquet set out in the dining room. Nothing would shift the mechanism and they had all to be led ignominiously through a back passage and in a side door.

It is impossible, now, to say who inspired the style of Government House, whether Mason, Heaphy and Baber, or even Reader Wood – or Wynyard himself who was a son of General William Wynyard, Equerry to George III, and could be expected to have had rather conservative architectural preferences. The central block (Plates 11, 44) is not specially like the country houses of the period and it is, of course, much too small and self-effacing, despite the vice-regal function, to claim kinship with any of the Queen's palaces. But it does strongly resemble, in scale and general feeling, some of the London clubhouses of Pall Mall and St James, which had a similar quasi-public character adapted to domestic purposes. Crockford's, the Travellers' and the old Carlton all had elements in common: balustrading, rusticated quoins or the break front. Other features like the three round-headed windows over the central doorway are reminiscent of the work of Robert Adam (who used them in almost exactly this form at Seton Castle), while the side wings seem to derive their bracketted overhanging eaves from some of Nash's Italian villas in Park Village East, and the arcades at the ends of the main block echo, however humbly, the same architect's famed Marble Arch which once stood in front of Buckingham Palace. To go still further back, a strong resemblance may be found between the centre block and the north front of Inigo Jones's Queen's House at Greenwich (Jones used the motif of three round-headed windows on the destroyed west front of St Paul's Cathedral), and to look abroad is to find a suggestion of France where the segmental pediment, rare in England though Mason was probably familiar with the Worcester Guildhall, was more commonly used. Blore's additions

[20] ibid, 12 November 1855.
[21] Probably at a ball given by the southern members of the General Assembly on 17 July 1856. For the first ball given by the Governor on 3 July, from which Mrs Gore Browne was absent because her carriage had overturned on the way there from Hulme Court, the whole of the ground floor was made into a ballroom 'presenting to the spectator a sight hardly to be expected in the Home country, much less in so young a colony as this.'

11. Second Government House, Auckland.

to Buckingham Palace had been in the French Renaissance style. Such diverse influences and consequent incongruities make it impossible to sustain the customary present-day description of Government House as Palladian, for it lacks entirely the rigid grammar of the orders applied by the English exponents of that manner. Its neo-classicism is, instead, free and picturesque, even a little uncouth like Adam's late Scottish castles.

The plan of the house is generally straightforward but unusual and convenient in the importance given to the side entrance and in the ingenious fitting of three floors in the side wings to the height of two floors in the main part of the house. These wings have the appearance of something added and it is quite possible that Mason had not intended them at all. Forward-standing pavilions linked to the main building by the arcades would have provided a much more satisfactory composition. Even so, they were better in Mason's treatment of them, before the insertion of windows in the north wall of the attics. The finely proportioned suite of rooms formed by the drawing room, dining room and intervening hall, with the wide gallery behind, remains the most pleasing of its kind in the country, a simple but successful handling of related spaces to give maximum flexibility of use while suggesting just the right degree of grandeur for the governor of a young colony.

The early history of the house was remarkably unfortunate. Already in March 1856 when it was far from complete, Mason was asking for £1,930 9s. 6d. over and above the £10,000 previously voted. By the time the province was seeking reimbursement from the Colonial Government, two and a half years later, the total cost was shown as £14,581 16s. 9d. with interest at 10 percent adding a further £5,000.[22] Into the bargain the Gore Brownes apparently disliked the house from the start and were so anxious to relinquish it for other uses that the Governor began to negotiate quite soon for another house to be built on the knoll overlooking the present Domain playing fields.[23] It would seem that Mason's building would then have been given over to the use of the General Assembly.

Such a role was evidently envisaged by a select committee under the chairmanship of John Logan Campbell which reported back to the House of Representatives in August 1856. The House, adopting its report, decided that 'in the opinion of this House, the building built by the Provincial Government of Auckland for the Government House, is not suitable for the residence of the Governor. That, in the opinion of this House, the building in question is suitable for the Houses of Assembly, and for the offices of the General Government, and that it is very desirable that it should be occupied for that purpose. That in order to repay the Province of Auckland for the cost of the building, the present Government offices and the building of the present Houses of Assembly, together with the lands on which these buildings are situated, be given up to the Province, if the Province will accept such a proposal. That in the opinion of this House, wholly independent of the question of the seat of Government, it is proper that a suitable building for the residence of the Governor should be built in the Government Domain.'

The Governor almost immediately set about implementing the final provision but in the confusion which ensued, in settling the rival claims of Auckland and Wellington to the title of capital, no more building was actually undertaken. The house does seem, however, to have been regarded as the probable Parliament House in some places and as late as 1861 a

[22]Provincial Council Papers, A.P.L.. See Appendix I. The Government, in the person of E. W. Stafford, offered to settle for £8,000.
[23]See memorandum from Colonel Mould, 9 October 1856, of the 'probable expense of cutting, forming and metalling a road from the NE angle of the Wall of Albert Barracks across the swamp and thence round the knoll on the left of the present track in the Demesne, up the hill crossing the small stream at the present bridge or Culvert and thence to the proposed site of the Government House . . . .' See also the letter from the Governor's Private Secretary to William Gisborne, 2 January 1857, commenting on the control and public access to the Government garden 'if the domain is let', and a minute signed C. W. Richmond, 2 September 1856, 're importing 3000 yards of the best description of Iron Hurdles for fencing that part of the Government Domain which it is intended to reserve for the use of his Excellency.' National Archives, I.A.1, 60/1708.

broadsheet printed in Christchurch, showing the portraits of all members of the third Parliament, reproduced a photograph of Mason's building as if it were the seat of Parliament. In 1872 there was no longer any doubt as to the capital and a new Government House had just been completed in Wellington. It is interesting therefore, in the light of later history, to find Mr Maurice O'Rorke proposing in the House on 25 September 'that . . . this House is of the opinion that a respectful Address should be presented to His Excellency the Governor, requesting him to recommend the dedication of the Government House and Grounds at Auckland as the seat of the New Zealand University, on the condition that, when a Government House shall be required at Auckland, the Province of Auckland shall expend not less than £10,000 in erecting a suitable residence in the Government demesne at Auckland.'

On 18 September 1856, F. G. Steward, the Governor's Secretary, wrote to the Christchurch architect B. W. Mountfort, inviting him to come to Auckland: 'The Governor's responsible advisers think the delay attendant on calling for designs for the new Government House would prevent its completion by the time it would be required. They have therefore determined to select a site, determine on the sort of building and commence at once. The Governor is, however, very anxious to have the advice and assistance of Mr Mountfort. If therefore Mr Mountfort can make it convenient to come to Auckland by the return of the steamer or if he can overtake her at Nelson where she may possibly be detained, the Governor's responsible advisers hereby promise him an equitable remuneration.'

By the second week of December, Mountfort was installed in a room at the old Survey office and was asking for a drawing-board, T-square and set-square to be made available to him. All this must have been extremely embarrassing to Mason and it is not difficult to detect resentment of Gore Browne's high-handed action in the various governmental memoranda and in the comments of Colonel Thomas Mould who commanded the detachment of Royal Engineers at Auckland and who now stepped into the picture. (Six years later he was to design the very sympathetic additions to Mason's St Paul's Church after the latter had settled in Dunedin.)

There exists a draft of conditions for a competition for a stone house, preferably in the medieval style of architecture, to cost £7,000.[24] These were not put into effect but, as a check on Mountfort, Colonel Mould was asked to submit a design also. Whether Mason was invited to compete does not appear.

Mountfort submitted his design in early January. He had chosen the 'middle pointed' style. 'I consider the style chosen as the best for any building for while admitting of any amount of ornamentation, it is also the least costly of any as it allows of no disguise of materials (always in building an expensive process) and also the absence of all cornices, strings and projections if not required . . . .' In forwarding these plans to the Government, together with Colonel Mould's, Steward makes no comment on the latter but refers to Mountfort's design 'which the Governor thinks affords the accommodation required in the most convenient form. He is perfectly satisfied with it but leaves the decision to his advisers . . . . Finally I am desired to say that the failure in the interior fixtures and fittings of the present Government House proves the necessity of sending to England for many of them, more especially those belonging to the Kitchens. By

[24] All this material on Mountfort's work for Gore Browne is contained in letters to the Colonial Secretary in the National Archives, I.A.1, 60/1708.

12. Colonel T. R. Mould, C.B.

this means good articles may be obtained at a less cost than the very inferior ones which can be procured here.'

Stafford, as Colonial Secretary and leader of the Government, quite cynically submitted Mountfort's designs to his rival, Mould, for comment. Mould bluntly pointed out what he considered to be a distressing lack of regularity, defects in construction, corbelled chimneys over openings which would be certain to fall, objectionable placing of water closets, faulty arrangements according to modern notions and a manifest weakness in the great weight of the roof coming on to slight pillars. He found the internal fittings barn-like and while he allowed that the design would no doubt be externally picturesque in its quaintness and irregularity he questioned whether it would be 'lastingly pleasing to the eye formed to observe regularities in outline.' He further estimated the cost at £12,850 (the allowance had finally been for £8,000) and stated flatly that the plans and drawings would be quite insufficient to put into the hands of a builder even to tender.

These comments were submitted to Mountfort who thereupon, with his partner Isaac Luck, drew up a fifteen-page answer. He advanced the opinion that the native historical architecture of England should have a prominent place accorded it in the new Colony. He took Mould's objections point by point and added for good measure the statement that 'A superior artizan may possibly produce a design for a building which would contain all the required accommodation; but the Architect is engaged for the purpose of giving the superadded graces, of *correct* design, *suitable* decoration and *convenience* of arrangement.'

More than two years later Mountfort plaintively wrote to the Colonial Secretary enquiring about the fate of his design as he had not been favoured with any communication. Stafford noted on the letter: 'Reply that it is not proposed at present to proceed with a new Govt. House even if the plans prepared by Mr Mountfort were suitable. Request him therefore to submit an account.' Mountfort's claim came in for £250 on an estimate of £10,000. Even here Mould had the last say and reported that the charge was excessive and suggested two percent on £8,000 'which would give him about £2. 2. 0 per day for the period from 5th Dec to 17th Feb during which he was in Auckland.' It was vastly more generous payment than Mason had received for his building.

In the meantime the Masons continued to live at Bleak House. Lush speaks of a visit in July: 'We went to Mr & Mrs Mason's where I left Blannie and Mr Wilson. I went into the town & did a large amount of shopping.' He himself stayed at Alexander Smith's in St George's Bay. Next day he took Blannie to the Museum and called on the Lloyds[25] and the Thatchers, then back to the Masons. There he found Maria Hill and soon after Ellen McLean and Mr Every McLean arrived. They all had dinner and then went off to the Choral Society concert at the Oddfellows' Hall. Six months later it was a performance of the Messiah they went to. 'It was not over till half past ten. Blannie went home with the Lloyds: while I went to Mr Smith's where I met Mr & Mrs Mason with whom I had a long talk about our neighbours the Hills & their truly unfortunate circumstances – Mr Mason attributed all their misfortunes to Mr Hill's ill-judged speculations & their want of plan in managing his farm – he is going to turn them out & he & Mrs Mason are going tomorrow to the East Tamaki to take possession once more of their old farm – now far the worse

[25]J. F. Lloyd, MA (T.C.D.), Vicar of St Paul's.

for being so long under Mr Hills bad management.'

Lush need not have felt sorry for his friend, that Hill's bad management should compel him to resume the farm. Contributing also to the decision were Mason's own troubles and disagreements in town. Early in 1856 it had been proposed to put all public works such as roads, bridges and building under a Board of Works and, though some opposition was encountered, the Board was finally set up in April 1856. All tenders advertisements were then signed by William Mason, President of the Board of Works, where previously he had signed as Provincial Architect. The Board seems to have consisted of four men but Mason and the late Harbour Works engineer, Daniel Simpson, were apparently the two executive members.

Soon after its inception the unfortunate Board became a target for the invective of 'Promising' John Williamson, the proprietor of the *New-Zealander*, in his attacks upon the Provincial Government and its mouth-piece the *Southern Cross*. The editor of the *Cross*, Hugh Carleton, who had gone from Eton to Trinity College, Cambridge, and who later married a daughter of Archdeacon Henry Williams, made no secret of his contempt for Williamson, risen as he said from the lowest ranks of a colonial printing office, and for the latter's political aspirations. For most Aucklanders the rivalry of the *New-Zealander*, known to them as the 'Spotted Cow' or 'My Grandmother's Review', and of the *Southern Cross* made first class sport; but for their victims it was less amusing. On 23 July the *New-Zealander* published an attack on 'The Works of the Board of Works' which they listed since March 1855, thereby including work supervised by Mason as Provincial Architect. The works listed include 29 bridges, 6,651 feet of causeway and 63 miles of trunk roads. They might have added that Mason, with Daniel Simpson and Cormack O'Rafferty, had explored three alternative lines of communication between Waiuku and the Waikato.[26] Mason had also taken part in the survey of the Waiuku block for subdivision. The implication of the attack was that certain works were done for political advantage. In August they published several remarkably literate letters from a workman named Henry Ashurst who had been engaged to build a fence round the public pound and who now accused Mason and Simpson of manipulating drawings and accounts in relation to it to cover up earlier mistakes. Next to their purpose was an equally literate workman, Thomas Murphy, who had been foreman on the Government House job. This trickster revealed himself further in the subsequent enquiry into the building of Government House. On 19 November the *New-Zealander* published a paragraph on 'Our Want of Practical Architecture' in which they characterized one entry in the competition for Government buildings at Wellington as 'a row of cottages with two Vandalised porticoes.'

All this was part of Williamson's campaign in running himself for the Superintendency. He was duly elected and began to reward his servants and to get rid, as far as possible, of his opponents in office. It is impossible not to surmise that his evident personal animus against Mason may have had its origins in his early employment with the printers of the *New Zealand Herald and Auckland Gazette* of which Mason had been a trustee. That this animus was not directed equally against all members of the Board is shown by his appointment, once Superintendent, of one of its members, Cormack O'Rafferty, to the office of Waste Lands Commissioner.

[26]Their five-page report, which declared itself against a canal, was published in the *Auckland Provincial Government Gazette*, 7 July 1855.

In defending this appointment he made the magnanimous statement that opportunity would be given 'to the parties in question to prove, if they can, that the faults which have for some time been charged against them in their official capacity were not attributable to them individually or collectively but to the system or policy – such as it was – pursued by the Government whose servants they then were.'[27] So much for what was already being termed in regretful retrospect the *educated* Government.

The opportunity given to Mason consisted of an enquiry into the building of Government House. Mason showed his contempt for the procedure by ignoring the summons to attend. The matter was discussed in the Provincial Council, generally hostile to Williamson, and members expressed their opinions that, at least, plans and specifications which were missing should be produced to the committee of enquiry. James O'Neill said that the architect would not come forward to give any information in the matter. Mr Robert Graham asked what steps had been taken to get information from Mr Mason. That gentleman was one who had always done his duty to the colony, and would not, he was sure, shrink from his duty in this instance. Mr Merriman thought there was some misunderstanding in the matter for the gentleman referred to was exceedingly unlikely to retain possession of documents the property of the public. The documents were mysteriously found[28] and soon afterwards Mason consented to appear before the committee. Nothing of moment came out of the enquiry. Substitutions of materials by the architect were shown always to be justified, extra costs were shown to be largely the result of ordering additional work, and Thomas Murphy, the foreman, emerged as a man proud to deceive both his employer and the architect.[29]

Mason appeared before the committee on 17 February 1857. On 6 February he had already gone out to Howick to resume possession of his farm so there was no longer any question of his continuing to work under Williamson and he could afford to laugh at the *contretemps* in which Williamson immediately became involved when he and the Council each appointed a member to fill a vacancy and so found themselves in a comic opera situation which required Speaker Bartley to sit through a whole day and night while no business was done and angry citizens pelted the building with stones.

Mason's two years in town had been productive, so far as he himself was concerned, of one major building. Other buildings were certainly carried out – the stockade at Mount Eden, a two-storeyed building eighty feet by twenty, the conversion of the old Colonial Secretary's Office in Princes Street to the uses of a post office, the even odder conversion of the new slaughterhouse into cells for hard labour men, a stone powder magazine in Barrack Square – but the pinchpenny and temporary nature of most of them, was not inducive to any great display of architectural merit.

Some months before, Hugh Carleton of the *Southern Cross* and David Burn of the *New-Zealander* had bandied between them a quotation from the Old Testament using it in reference to Sir George Grey and the burning of the first Government House. Mason might have thought it applied to Williamson's treatment of himself: 'let timber be pulled down from his house and being set up, let him be hanged thereon' (Ezra 6:11).

[27]*New-Zealander*, 26 November 1856.

[28]These documents, which have once more disappeared, cast some slight doubt on the completeness of Mason's responsibility for the Government House design. Several sheets (see note by Cunningham, Provincial Council Papers, A.P.L., 2 February 1857) were marked with a star in a manner similar to the marking of Heaphy and Baber's competition drawings. Almost certainly they were in addition to Mason's drawings.

[29]Provincial Council Papers, A.P.L.

X   EAST HEAD AGAIN

*Well, really our unfortunate distracted islands take a deal of government –
which is a costly article.* – C. W. Richmond to J. Atkinson, 27 February
1856. *The Richmond-Atkinson Papers.* Wellington, 1960.

The Hills had left East Head in sad disorder and both house and fields
needed a great deal of work to restore them. Mason was now a man of
forty-seven and his wife had reached her sixties. It is unlikely that either
still had to the same degree that enterprise and vigour for which they
were once known. But he gradually brought the farm back to its peak and
seemed still to spare energy for other things. In April 1858, having heard
from Captain Haultain, a fellow officer of Militia, that he intended resigning his appointment of Resident Magistrate for Howick, he offered himself
in Haultain's place[1] but was passed over in favour of Captain Montressor
Smith who had held the appointment previously. He became enthusiastic
for the project of a canal between the Manukau Harbour and the Tamaki
River and called on his old adversary, the Superintendent, to inform him
of the interest of the settlers of Otahuhu. Williamson, linking it with the
recent discovery of coal at Drury, ordered a survey by Thomas Mould and
John Lambert Tole,[2] and there the matter rested.

In the winter of 1859, though Lush tells us he was overspent and deeply
mortgaged, Mason joined with a group of leading Otahuhu and Tamaki
landowners (J. Hargreaves, William Goodfellow, John Grigg, Alfred
Buckland, Albin Martin, W. T. Buckland, Every McLean, Joseph Grigg,
Thomas Shipherd, Francis Dyer Rich, Samuel Clarke, Frederick E.
Braithwaite and Thomas Cawkwell) in petitioning the Government to
open up the Thames Valley for grazing.[3] They complained that they were
at present feeding stock on potatoes because of the lack of grazing, that
two months after harvest all wheat grown was consumed and that many
'capitalists', being unable to obtain land, had abandoned the province
entirely. It was a long standing complaint which in its ultimate solution
led to many abuses, affluence for some and financial disaster for others.
In particular Alfred Buckland, Every McLean and F. D. Rich were
eventually tangled up in the vast projects of men like Thomas Russell
and James Williamson, who opened up the Waikato with a too free use
of the resources of the Bank of New Zealand and earned the ultimate
censure of a Government committee of enquiry. On the other hand John

[1]National Archives, I.A.1,
59/667.
[2]Provincial Council Papers,
A.P.L.
[3]National Archives, I.A.1,
59/1647, 1656.

Grigg departed for Canterbury and founded Longbeach, 'the finest farm in the world', while Albin Martin is remembered only as a painter and for his friendships among painters. From the inner circle of those farming financiers Mason was happily excluded.

The old friendship with the Lush family was resumed and visitors from Auckland – the Elys[4], Warringtons,[5] and the Alexander Smiths[6] – came to stay. Then, in February 1860, the Masons once more moved into Howick village to a place called Springfield House and turned the farm over to a newly married couple Mr and Mrs Frederick Braithwiate.[7] This was apparently 'young Braithwaite' the assistant commissary-general with whom the Masons had been friendly in town and who had several years before been concerned in a scandalous episode at a Masonic ball when he, Major Bridge and Captain Marlow had kicked each other's shins and Dr Johnson and George Manners Mitford had attempted to pull each other's noses.[8]

The reason for the shift is not at all clear. That Mason was greatly concerned with the Maori situation in Taranaki we know from Lush's diary. On the outbreak of the war he was promoted Captain in the 3rd Battalion Auckland Regiment of Militia and doubtless went into camp with them at Otahuhu. This may have seemed to him sufficient cause, but what then of Braithwaite's commitments?

At the end of the year a public meeting held at Howick on Christmas Eve called on Mason to stand for Parliament and a month later he was returned unopposed without having made any public declarations on political or other issues. It was a situation unique in Auckland, though not in the South. It seems worth-while to comment on the remarkable quality of members of the Third Parliament, which this was, for it contained an array of talent, not necessarily political, with which any man might be proud to be associated. Members were called together in July 1861 by which time the Taranaki war was more than a year old, and Mason aligned himself at once with the party in power, headed by Stafford, and dedicated to the energetic prosecution of the war.

At Howick, alarm was greater than in Auckland for the villagers and settlers felt themselves exposed to war parties travelling up the coast from the Thames. The Military Pensioners of 1847, who had already served twenty years before taking up their allotments, were no longer much protection. Early in April, Lush noted in his diary that 'the talk everywhere and with everyone has been about stockades and redoubts and guns and rifles and cavalry and militia. Our life seems quite changed; we are living with things packed up for a moment's start, and with our plate already buried for the sake of concealment.'

In Parliament, Mason's only major speech had to do with these hostilities. Speaking against a Want of Confidence motion on the conduct of the war, he tackled William Fox who a week later (12 July) succeeded Stafford as leader of the Government: 'The honourable gentleman has expressed an opinion that if the military had not been employed to protect the survey of the Waitara block at Taranaki there would have been no war; that it has been brought on by haste and mismanagement of the Governor and the Colonial Government. I cannot agree with him. The cause of this war I trace to a very different source, far removed; and I venture to state had the Imperial Government pursued a different policy towards the natives of New Zealand when they took possession of this country for the

[4]Thomas H. Ely, a customs officer and stalwart of the Choral Society, was commissioned in the Auckland Volunteer Rifle Company at the formation of which, in 1858, he took the chair. See Minutes A Battery N.Z.F.A., A.I.M.

[5]Warrington was a physician living at Onehunga. He and his wife had been shipboard companions of the Lushes on the voyage from England.

[6]John Alexander Smith, a merchant who had been mate of the Government brig, *Victoria*, was the founder of the Auckland Museum with a collection he had gathered for the London Exhibition of 1850. The collection was subsequently housed in the old Government Farm House near the Symonds Street corner of Grafton Road. See *New-Zealander*, 27 October 1852; *Southern Cross*, 25 October 1850.

[7]Lush diary, 27 February 1860.

[8]David Burn diary, 25 June 1850. Microfilm, A.I.M. Burn had been naval officer, Shakespearian actor and playwright but, at this time, he was a journalist with the *New-Zealander* and editor of the *Maori Messenger*.

purpose of colonisation we should not now have been at war with them.

'A system of secular education in addition to teaching the natives the English language would have led to the fusion of the two races. A scheme of this kind was proposed to Captain FitzRoy in 1845 and would in all probability have been carried out but for the arrival of Sir George Grey. Had this course been adopted at that period, instead of our now being at war with the Natives, William King, or perhaps some other influential men amongst them, would now be sitting in this House, assisting to make laws to guide their fellow men.

'Great stress has been laid on the cost of this war, and elaborate calculations made to show it; but this is looking at only one side of the question; and if the war goes on sufficient land must and will be taken from the insurgents not only to repay the Imperial Government and the expenses of the militia force employed in the Colony, but amply to compensate the settlers for their pecuniary losses. Therefore I look upon the monetary cost as a secondary consideration.

'I have been many years in this country – I came with Captain Hobson – and have seen a great deal of the Natives, and think I understand something of their character. We have heard from the opposite side of this House cries of "God forbid this war. Take time to negotiate. Let it be avoided if possible." This I believe to be impossible, but I assure this House if any terms less imposing than the ultimatum of the Governor were proposed, the Natives would expect further change and negotiations would become interminable. Instead of two or three months being required for this purpose, two or three years – perhaps ten – would be insufficient. As I do not agree with the honourable member for Rangitikei I must vote against his motion for want of confidence and support the Government.'

That same day Mason complained to the House, in seconding a motion of James O'Neill for provision of proper accommodation for meetings of the General Assembly, that he was suffering from acute rheumatism from a draught from an open window the previous evening, in what O'Neill had termed 'this ill-ventilated barn'.[9]

On 27 August and 3 September he moved for the encouragement of rifle shooting by competitions and prizes. It was a field in which Mason himself excelled for he won the first prize offered by the Government for rifle shooting and was second for the Colonial Belt in the first annual competition organized by the New Zealand Rifle Association.

Also serving his first term in Parliament, and concerned with much bigger, self-rewarding affairs, was thirty-two-year-old plausible Tom Russell, a lawyer of modest antecedents who had recently formed a partnership with Frederick Whitaker. Russell, who became Minister of Defence in Domett's government a year later, and continued as such under Whitaker, had already secured to himself sufficient legal business to give him control of very large sums of money, which he habitually over-employed, to the extent that he had recently found himself in an awkward position with his bankers, the Oriental Bank Corporation, who were in process of withdrawing from the New Zealand market and handing their business over to the Bank of New South Wales. The Bank of New South Wales showed some unwillingness to accept an account requiring such accommodation as Mr Russell's. Russell saw the opportunity to found a new bank, the Bank of New Zealand, and within a very few weeks issued a prospectus which, published sixteen days after the opening of

[9]This building had been hastily put up in 1854 to a design by Reader Wood.

13. William Mason, 1861.

Parliament, included in its list of Trustees six members of the House –
Brandon, Rhodes, Stafford, Weld, Cracroft Wilson and McGlashan. No
more respected names could have been secured in the country. Six weeks
later an Act of Incorporation was passed by Parliament.

All this was to have a profound influence on Mason's later life for the
Bank's directors learnt almost at once of the gold discoveries in Otago
and soon sent their manager Falconer Larkworthy[10] down to Dunedin to
take what advantage he could of the situation. He opened a branch there
in October and shortly had such a large staff at work that a new building
became an urgent necessity. Mason was commissioned to design these
premises and also premises at Wellington.

Parliament had finished sitting in early September and it seems very
likely that Mason accompanied the members returning to Dunedin to see
for himself the effect of the gold discoveries. He was plainly anxious to
return to practice and Dunedin promised more favourable circumstances
than Auckland.

He had allowed his name to go forward for the Pensioner Settlements
for the Provincial Council elections held in October. At the election by
show of hands, on 16 October 1861, he and McGhee and Wynn were given
the show but the two unsuccessful candidates, Foley and Griffin, called
for a poll, the results of which were published on 6 November. Quite
clearly, between the show of hands and the poll, Mason had made known
his intention to go south. Twenty-four devoted supporters still gave him
their votes but the newspaper publishing the results published also, in the
same issue, an advertisement of an auction sale of his effects at Howick.

All Sarah's furniture went under the hammer – mahogany and kauri
tables, a first class cottage piano, couches and sofas, mahogany and cane-
seated chairs, carpets, rugs, bedsteads and hangings, washstands, fenders,
fire irons, lamps, candlesticks, a dinner and dessert service, glass and
china; and Mason's own six-barrelled revolver, one single Manton gun and
one regulation rifle.

Vicesimus Lush in a valedictory paragraph in his diary noted that East
Head had been sold to a captain in the 70th but evidently he, like the
Braithwaites, was unable to proceed with the purchase and in early
December a transfer was finally executed between William Mason, late of
Auckland but now of Dunedin, Gentleman, and Alfred Buckland, Auction-
eer. The terms were £2,500 payable immediately and an annuity of £150
payable to 'William Mason and his wife Sarah Mason during their lives
and that of the survivor.'

So ended the central phase of Mason's life. The honours and successes
he would accumulate in Dunedin would be as differently flavoured as
Dunedin was from Auckland. Little of his known architecture in Auckland
much longer survived intact. St Paul's was soon to be altered, the Courthouse replaced. Government House was at last accepted. His own house
at East Head and Paton's at Eden Hill would serve for many years. Of
his other work, in point of style, it is possible only to surmise – the single-
storeyed villas for his fellow officials in Official Bay? Hulme Court?
Bleazard's house in Sylvan Avenue? The Gordon cottage in Waterloo
Quadrant, since John Gordon was his shipmate in the *Westminster*? Every
McLean's Bleak House at Howick? Selwyn's first buildings at Purewa?
The documentary evidence is unfortunately lacking. More than likely the
Queen's Ferry Hotel for James Robertson, one of his original mechanics,

[10]Larkworthy's autobiography *Ninety-one Years* (London, 1924) gives an all too
little known account of
these events and an illumi-
nating though biased anal-
ysis of the character of
Thomas Russell.

and other buildings on the block he once owned in Queen Street and Vulcan Lane were to his design. And perhaps he was the architect for the elegant little house which once stood at 9 Mount Street, which was built with slabs of kauri in exactly the same way as Government House.

XI GOLDEN PROVINCE

Gold in the hills, gold in the rocks,
Gold in the river gravel,
Gold as yellow as Chinamen
In the bottom of the shovel.
            – Denis Glover: 'Arrowtown'.
            The Wind and the Sand. Christchurch, 1945.

At the beginning of 1862 the whole of New Zealand stood on the brink of conspicuous economic and material development. Dunedin, as a result of Gabriel Read's astonishing gold discoveries six months before, was in a specially privileged position. It was a phenomenon with precedent. Many old hands who had gone off to the goldfields of California or Victoria now streamed back, bringing with them thousands more, anxious to try their luck. Dunedin, which had been little more than a village, suddenly expanded, with that marvellous promptitude then witnessed only in gold countries, into a township of 20,000 and the population of the whole province rose to 61,000.

Three years later, when the full-pocketed city fathers opened an Exhibition on a scale which would have seemed incredible before, they set up, in the entrance, a gold obelisk representing 103 cubic feet of solid gold, being the quantity exported from New Zealand in the intervening period, or 1,814,026 ounces valued at £6,250,000. The annual produce of the Otago goldfields was more than half a million ounces.[1]

To this swarming community largely accommodated in calico tents or, more exactly, to the established business houses where they spent their money and to the official and governing bodies who ministered to them, Mason now offered his services. But his name does not appear in the Dunedin newspapers until 26 September 1862 when notice of partnership is advertised and then on 13 October when Messrs Mason and Ross call for tenders for building premises for the Bank of New Zealand in Wellington (Plate 49). Earlier in September builders had been notified that plans and specifications might be seen at the office of David Ross, Architect, of Manse Street, for the new Bank of New Zealand building in Dunedin. Mason must partly have occupied the intervening period between the sale of his household goods at Howick and his appearance in practice in Dunedin by silent attendance at the session of Parliament from July to September in Wellington. Before that he had evidently visited Dunedin

[1] *Illustrated London News*, 13 May 1865.

and decided to settle there and had almost certainly met David Ross and come to some agreement with him. Ross seems to have set up in practice on his own account about the middle of the year – by no means without competition for more than a dozen other architects and so-called architects had recently called tenders[2] – in the offices in Victoria Chambers where Mason now joined him. He already had some reputation, having gained prizes in Melbourne in architectural competitions for Government House, Chalmers Church and St Mary's Catholic Church, Geelong.[3] Subsequently he designed the Otago Museum building, the Bank of Otago, the Imperial Hotel, the Congregational Church, Johnny Jones's Fernhill and Dalgety Rattray's warehouse, all in Dunedin, and the Harbour Board offices in Auckland; but his association with Mason did not last long.

On 5 February 1863, Mason notified readers of the *Otago Daily Times* of the dissolution of the partnership and his removal to Belgrave House in Princes Street. On the following day Ross inserted a much larger advertisement stating that '. . . the following works, undertaken by the Firm, are to be finished by it as arranged, viz:–

> Bank of N.Z., Wellington
> Fittings do.   Dunedin
> Alterations Bank of N S Wales, Wellington
> Office Building, T. B. Gillies Esq
> Villa & Cottages, Captain Inverarity
> Do.   Henry Clapcott Esq.
> Houses Mr John Riordan
> Mr Osgood's Empire Hotel
> New Club House
> Villa Mr Justice Richmond etc., etc.,
> I still carry on business as before.'

Nearly all, if not all, of these works were in fact Mason's while the alterations for the Bank of New South Wales were almost certainly not for Wellington but for the building in Dunedin which served the Bank until the construction of Mason's fine new premises in 1866. Other jobs had been completed during the partnership. Mason had been called to the rescue when the almost finished Wesleyan Church in Dowling Street, designed by Edward Greenfield, had practically collapsed in a storm, and had solved the problem by shoring it up with transepts.[4] He had been called in also, to examine and measure the new St Paul's Church of England which had just been built to the designs of Charles Abbott, a builder turned architect.

The several houses for Thomas Cargill, Charles Black, William Hall and Robert Gillies, for Captain Iverarity in Brown Street, for John Riordan in Hope Street, for Henry Clapcott at Caversham and another in Elm Row for the Rev. Isaac Harding, that robust intellectual preacher of Methodism, were rated as cottages. There were numerous other small buildings in Princes Street or Rattray Street which, main streets as they might be, were still muddy tracks lined with predominantly single-storeyed wooden buildings on narrow frontages. Architects in general practice, even today, are constantly required to design small buildings so subject to restrictions of use, site or finance, that they offer little scope for imaginative solution. These buildings seldom make any impact on the eye though they may serve their simple purposes very well. They are the bread and butter work of many practices, filling in the spaces between

[2]W. H. Monson, George Mallinson, George and Edward Greenfield, Ben Smith, Chas. Smith, – Lambeth, E. Mills, W. C. Vahlaud, R. C. Luscombe, Augustus Poeppel, C. J. Toxward, Sanders and Anderson, R. A. Lawson.
[3]*New Zealand Herald*, 9 August 1883.
[4]William Morley, *The History of Methodism in New Zealand*. Wellington, 1900, p. 475.

the bigger prestigious commissions and providing the architect with a regular though modest flow of fees. Mason's many little buildings round Dunedin – shops, warehouses, or stables – were of this kind and few of them have survived. Those few have generally been altered beyond recognition.

His Bank of New Zealand building, (Plate 51) in contrast to these others, made some pretence of elegance and was stonebuilt and lavishly furnished. Some idea of its impact is conveyed by a reporter for the *Daily Telegraph*: 'The new Bank of New Zealand, designed by Wm. Mason, Esq., architect, internally will not belie its exterior. The fittings are chaste and classic. On entering, the eye is met with cedar pillars of an order approaching the Corinthian. The acanthus leaf twines everywhere, trained as it were upon the cable mouldings. About the prosaic counter, where the sleek clerk asks, "how will you have it, Sir," is there also a wreathing of poetry. Between each distributant of filthy lucre, there is a partition still of the cedar of Lebanon, carved in the forms of the luscious vine, clustering with graceful leaves and festoons of the ripened grape. The ceiling is divided into panels, each panel being wrought inwards, in the egg and dart style. The whole of the ceiling, however, maintains its conformity with the general Grecian style of the building. As the Bank will be opened in a few days for the dispensation of £. s. d. we shall reserve a more detailed notice for a future occasion.'[5]

Little more advantage was taken of the future occasion than to state that the fittings 'are of polished cedar, beautifully carved[6] in multiform, fantastic shapes, and designed as is the building generally, by Mr Mason, architect.' The octagonal public desk is now preserved in the Otago Pioneer Settlers Museum (Plate 52). The whole building cost £9,192. It bore some resemblance in the use of a segmental pediment, broken front and tripartite windows to Mason's Government House at Auckland. Or it might modestly be compared with Robert Adam's Edinburgh College. There was here, in the complex projections and recessions, a hint of Adam's theory of movement in architecture just as there was in Government House and in the Wellington offices of the Bank, a hint of the 'brawny simplicity'[7] of Adam's later Scottish houses. Adam was a Scot and it may be that the characteristic Scottish austerity of these buildings satisfied Mason in the depression which had settled on him with the death of his son, the oppositions of public life, and no doubt certain difficulties of private life as his wife retired into the preoccupations of old age, even as it must have appealed to the Scottish settlers of Dunedin, homesick for Edinburgh or Kilmarnock or Aberdeen. As success came to him again and the Victorian love of ornament became a demand, he abandoned this simplicity but returned to it in the final years of his practice. In 1883 it became necessary to enlarge the bank and W. B. Armson designed a new building for the same site. It is Armson's building which is in use today.

The Wellington offices of the Bank (Plate 49) which Mason no doubt supervised while attending Parliament in Wellington during the year, were also replaced on the same site (a difficult sharply triangular one bearing some resemblance to the Tivoli corner of the Bank of England) and no traces of the original building remain. If anything was retained it was so overlaid with additions that Mason's work is unrecognizable. He carried out other work for the Bank at Tokomairiro and Queenstown and even

[5]*Daily Telegraph*, 12 March 1863.
[6]by J. L. Godfrey.
[7]John Fleming, 'Robert Adam's Castle Style', *Country Life*, 30 May 1968.

designed a portable bank for the goldfields.

T. B. Gillies, who had recently gone into legal partnership with his and Mason's fellow parliamentarian, C. W. Richmond, called on him to design first an office building in Princes Street next to the Bank of New Zealand and then a gardener's cottage. Their associate James Prendergast soon wanted a house and so did Richmond. All three of these men became Judges of the Supreme Court, Prendergast holding office as Chief Justice for 24 years. Richmond's house, Highlawn, (Plates 55, 56) on a site fronting Queen Street and Heriot Row, was described by the *Telegraph* as an 'Italian villa . . . of a most elegant and recherche style.'[8] It was built in wood in a style to which Mason was, of course, always sympathetic, allowing him once more to use Venetian windows of a modified kind and loggias; but it is probable that Richmond himself played a greater than usual part in the design. The low-pitched roof with wide eaves introduced a new element. The same kind of roof covers Fernhill, the house David Ross built four years later for Mr Johnny Jones. Fernhill has survived while Highlawn was demolished in 1901-2 but, on the evidence of photographs, Highlawn, in spite of its timber structure, would seem to have been a more successful design. Ross's buildings are essentially Victorian, Mason's display earlier influences and, to that extent, please us more today.

Gillies's narrow-fronted, three-floored office building (Plate 51) was also strongly Italian, the facade having paired arcaded windows on the upper floors and three arched openings on the street level. A busy cornice, sculpted heads over the columns and an exotic tenant on the ground floor, Mr Nathan Salomon, watchmaker and jeweller, all contributed to the effect, but it must be assumed that Messrs Richmond and Gillies had been more impressed than Mason by their reading of Ruskin for he did not again make use of these Venetian motifs until he came to design the Stafford Street premises of Ross and Glendining and the offices of the Standard Insurance Company (Clarion Buildings) in the following decade.

Other clients flocked in. In a matter of nine months and in addition to the work already noted, Mason designed stores or factories for Monson Lane and Co. at Molyneux, for a Mr Gray in Maclaggan Street and for Cargill and Co., F. Luhning and William Dalrymple all in Princes Street, post offices at Port Chalmers, Tokomairiro and Waikouaiti, and major buildings for the Bank of Australasia, Captain Peter Williams, and Alfred Cleve. He also fulfilled minor commissions for such well-known Dunedin personalities as Edward McGlashan, James Fulton and Henry Howarth. It was not done alone. He had in his employ an engineer-draughtsman, William George Jackson,[9] and a clerk of works, N. Y. A. Wales,[10] both of whom remained with him a long time, Wales eventually becoming the firm's principal. Mason's office rent in those days at Belgrave House was £120 per annum while Jackson and Wales were each paid £5 a week. Fees on commissions were usually charged at five percent on the full service of designs, working drawings, specifications and superintendence of construction, so that it may be assumed from the volume of work that Mason had a net income approaching £1,500 a year, a not inconsiderable sum at that time.

The Bank of Australasia's building in High Street (the site is now occupied by No 152 and remnants of the bank building can still be found) earned him further prestige as a man to design banks. He treated

[8]*Daily Telegraph*, 16 June 1863.
[9]From 2 February 1863. William Mason, Accounts Book. Office of Mason and Wales.
[10]From 30 March 1863. ibid.

14. *Dunedin, 1863.*

it very differently from the Bank of New Zealand. Where the first building seemed to recall the architecture of the Regency, the later one (Plate 53) was more obviously Victorian. The vertical proportions were more exaggerated and this, coupled with the symmetry of the facade, gave it a rather prim appearance. It is interesting to notice that cast iron work was imported to ornament it,[11] a feature of Dunedin buildings in the next few years which may in its popularity be attributed to the many immigrants and architects who came from Victoria in the wake of the gold discoveries. In the forthcoming Exhibition of 1865, Wilson Brothers and the New Zealand Iron Works, both of Dunedin, were able to show castings and ornamental railings and later the name Shacklock was to be associated with ornamental ironwork in Dunedin.

The Bank has virtually disappeared and so have the premises built for Captain Peter Williams in Maclaggan Street. Williams[12] was an old whaler who had first come to New Zealand in 1829 to the whaling station at Cuttle Cove, Preservation Inlet. He had been a purchaser at the first Auckland land sale in 1841 at which Mason was the auctioneer. His future association with Mason was not always to be a happy one but at this time he seems to have provided the members of the Otago Club (of whom Mason himself was one) with a solution to their problem of finding a clubhouse. The Club, later to be known as the Dunedin Club and to be domiciled at Fernhill, had occupied a building on the north side of Maclaggan Street which was taken over in March 1863 by three men named Waters, Morton and Robertson who in turn employed three cooks named Ude, Careme and Francatelli to attend to the wants of the 'Aristocracy, Gentry and mercantile community of Otago and the neighbouring provinces.'[13] This, however, did not satisfy the Club members and in casting round for new premises they found Captain Williams ready to put up a large building which would provide both clubrooms and residential accommodation. This building, called Abbeyleix House, cost £6,900 and was on the south side of Maclaggan Street on a rise behind the present New Club Hotel. It appears to have been a rather uninteresting building (Plate 14) with large double-hung windows and an awkwardly handled, low-pitched roof. The Club stayed there only two years and its rooms were then taken over for the use of the City. When Mason became Mayor and Chief Magistrate in 1865 he held his court there.[14] Later again, it was known as the Universal Hotel. Mason's remaining large building built in 1863 was a warehouse for Alfred Cleve in High Street between the Arcade and Graham Street. It is important only as the forerunner to Edinburgh House, now the offices of the State Advances Corporation, often known as the Universal Bond, or Neill's Bond, but originally built in 1865 for Messrs Cleve and Lazarus.

As if Mason's architectural practice were not enough, a request came from the Government for him to open a recruiting office for volunteers for military settlements in the Waikato. 'Write Mr Mason M H R now in Otago and inform him of the desire of the Govt to raise recruits to the number of 500 in that province under the regulations for the formation of military settlements in Waikato . . . . Mr Mason's knowledge of the province of Auckland and the interest it may be presumed he takes in its welfare are an additional reason why this duty should be entrusted to him. Proper remuneration would of course be given for his services.'[15] This memorandum, apparently from Alfred Domett, that aggressive poet whose attitude to the Maoris was, as Thomas Arnold said, more Roman than

[11]William Mason, Accounts Book.
[12]Williams was the father-in-law of W. H. S. Roberts, the first historian of North Otago.
[13]*Otago Daily Times*, 31 March 1863.
[14]The rather obscure history of this building may be traced through various newspaper reports: *Otago Daily Times*, 1 October 1862; *Daily Telegraph*, 5 January, 13 February, 9 March 1863. Clues to its use are also given in a manuscript letter from W. D. Murison in Dunedin Public Library.
[15]National Archives, A.D.1, 65/3399.

Christian, was dated 6 August 1863. In fifteen days time Mason advised that fourteen men had been despatched by the *Ladybird*. He pointed out that 400 men had already been drafted from Dunedin for Wellington and Taranaki and asked for recruiting posters.

In the following month he promised eighty to one hundred men and proposed raising a Highland company under Mr Cameron and offering any two gentlemen who could raise one hundred men commissions as Captain and Lieutenant. In October he sent per *Airedale* 123 men in charge of Lieutenant Frederick Nelson George of the Mounted Police, twenty-three more per *Stormbird*, then chartered the small craft *Corio* in agreement with Captain A. Orbell, Master, to transport thirty or forty men to Auckland at £8 per head. He gives as his reason for this charter trip the reports made to Mr Commissioner Branigan of finds of from two to ten pounds weight per man per day on the Taieri goldfield. He was afraid the men would bolt if they heard the news. This recruitment went on until December when Thomas Russell, now Minister of Defence, wrote thanking him for his very great services and advised him to close the office.

By now Mason's position in Dunedin, after two years residence, was completely assured. Regrets he must have had for Auckland were over-come by the greater opportunities Dunedin offered. Into the bargain both he and Sarah, who suffered from asthma, found the climate more congenial. He decided to buy the property in London Street which Richmond now vacated to move into Highlawn. Richmond had lived in a house called Winchester Cottage which belonged to W. C. Winchester, a builder who later described himself as an architect. Mason paid him £600 and built his own house on the site, a tall two-storeyed house (Plates 57-60) now 104 London Street, whose present occupant, Mr Patric Carey, has added a small theatre to the building. As always when Mason bought land, the site is magnificent; and the house, if the timber-into-stone detailing is ignored, is easy and dignified, elegant without being pretentious, spacious though of modest proportions. It is notable for some good plaster work in ceilings and cornices. The drawing room and the main bedroom over it had superb views of the harbour and the city, looking down to the city's centre where, in a very short time, his too grand Post Office and his Provincial Council Chambers would start to rise.

XII HEAVY COMMITMENTS

Unless a modern architect is allowed to borrow his pillars, his cornices, his details, wholesale from some other building, he never could get on. James Fergusson, *History of the Modern Styles of Architecture*. London, 1862.

Mason now received two commissions of greater magnitude than anything proposed in the Colony before. One was a building to house the great Exhibition planned for 1865 and the other a new Post Office, a building which somehow got rather out of hand in the comparative magnificence of its design – a circumstance which may have had something to do with the recent appointment of Mason's old friend George Eliott to the office of Secretary to the General Post Office but which was taken by the men of Otago to be an earnest of government and a warning against the follies of provincialism. Whatever the circumstances, Mason obviously had more work than he could handle and so he looked round for a partner.

In May 1863 an advertisement had appeared in the Otago papers setting out the qualifications of Mr W. H. Clayton, Architect, Land Surveyor and Civil Engineer, who had recently arrived from Australia. 'Mr Clayton is a member of the Victorian Institute of Architects, has had 15 years colonial experience and erected about 300 buildings, including 5 churches, 3 banks, 1 mechanics' institute, 1 theatre, 3 steam and water mills, breweries, mansions, villas, 5 bridges etc and for several years held a Government appointment as land surveyor and road engineer.' Clayton was twelve years younger than Mason having been born in 1822 in Tasmania where his father, one of the last free settlers to leave Norfolk Island, had taken up land in 1813. The father, Henry Clayton, had been an energetic and enterprising settler and had accumulated considerable property. William Henry, who had trained at Brussels and worked in London under Sir John Rennie, had built him a fine house (no doubt one of the 'mansions' of his advertisement) on his estate, Wickford, at Longford. Whether the father or the son first became interested in New Zealand is not clear. But in August 1863 Henry Clayton chartered the brig *Creole*, 131 tons, of Launceston, took 35 head of cattle, 12 horses and 200 sheep on board and with passengers including women and children, a total complement of 31 persons with crew, sailed for New Zealand on what was purely a trading venture.[1] The ship was evidently overloaded and her wreckage was soon found on Waterhouse Island and along the coast.

[1] E. Graeme Robertson and Edith N. Craig, *Early Houses of Northern Tasmania*. Melbourne, 1964. Vol. 1, p. 140. Harry O'May, *Wrecks in Tasmanian Waters*, 1797-1950. Hobart, n.d., p. 66.

No one was saved. News of this disaster must have adversely affected Clayton's first few months of practice in Dunedin. He did, however, put up several minor buildings and when he entered into partnership with Mason, in February 1864, he brought with him a commission to build a synagogue for the Jewish community who were now investing their profits from the goldfields in the commercial prosperity of Dunedin.[2] Clayton was a well-liked man. George Augustus Preece, who won the New Zealand Cross for bravery at Ngatapa and who later married Clayton's very much younger sister, wrote of him ten years later: 'I called at Claytons in the evening they were just going out so I promised to call another evening – I met Mr Clayton he seems such a pleasant person such a nice face . . . .'[3] Whether or not he had a nice face, his association with Mason seems to have been a fairly fortunate one.

On 18 February 1864 a holiday was declared and all Dunedin turned out for the laying of the foundation stone of the ambitious Exhibition building which was to be, when completed, the largest masonry building in the Colony. A procession of tradesmen on foot was followed by the Executive Councillors, Provincial Councillors and Royal Commissioners (of whom Mason was one) all on horseback. Clayton having played no part in the design of the building his name was not coupled with Mason's as architect, but he took part in the Masonic ceremony of laying the stone. The Exhibition had first been promoted a year previously when the Provincial Council had indicated its readiness to construct 'some one of its public buildings in such a manner as would afford the necessary accommodation for such an exhibition.'[4] In August they had placed £9,500 on the estimates for a market, to be granted temporarily to the Committee of the Industrial Exhibition, for the purposes of the Exhibition, and £20,000 for a post office.[5] The Exhibition prospectus, issued in November,[6] pinned its colours to a typically high-flown nineteenth-century statement by Sir Robert Peel: 'It is a noble thing to test by actual experiment to what extent the ingenuity and skill of the nations of the earth have corresponded to the intentions of their Creator, and to improve the advantages which each country can offer the other, in supplying the wants and adding to the happiness of mankind.'

Mason as one of the fourteen commissioners[7] produced a sketch at one of their meetings – like Paxton sketching the Crystal Palace on a sheet of blotting paper – on precisely the same plan as he had before used for a market house and in consequence the question of design was left entirely to him. This led to an unfortunate misunderstanding. The first crude sketch had been produced gratuitously but the Superintendent, John Hyde Harris, later chose to believe that Mason's complete architectural services were gratuitous also. The absurdity of his attitude was suitably recognized by an independent committee of enquiry which awarded Mason £800 in fees. The whole job was fraught with difficulty. The tender price had been £10,250 but the Superintendent ordered a change from the middle of the site between Cumberland Street and Great King Street to an area nearer Great King Street. The change made it necessary to build a basement where it had previously been intended to leave the ground unfloored and, as if this interference were not enough, the Town Board then raised the level of the road and shed water on to the site which had to be extensively drained. Mason, after examining the ground with an iron rod, had thought that the extra cost of foundations would be between

[2] Clayton's links with the Jewish community are interesting. His elder daughter married Sir Julius Vogel and a niece married N. Alfred Nathan of Auckland, long acknowledged as the leader of New Zealand Jewry.
[3] G. A. Preece, 'Diary'. Manuscript, A.P.L., 20 March 1874.
[4] National Archives, O.P.4, Minutes, 28 January 1863.
[5] ibid. 6 August 1863.
[6] *Otago Daily Times*, 19 November 1863.
[7] James Hector, MD; Thomas Dick, MPC; T. B. Gillies, MHR; James Paterson, MHR, MPC; William Mason, MHR; E. B. Cargill, MHR, MPC; John Cargill, MPC; R. B. Martin, Chairman of the Chamber of Commerce; James Rattray; Alfred Eccles, FRCS; Henry Clapcott, MPC; R. S. Cantrell; W. H. Reynolds, MHR, MPC; and Julius Vogel, MHR, MPC.

£2,500 and £2,700. In fact, extra foundations and basement cost £6,319, the ground floor cost £637 and the drains £800, bringing the total almost to £18,000 or nearly double the amount granted by the Provincial Council. The whole argument was thoroughly ventilated in an enquiry in October 1864 at which Mason at first made use of his legal immunity as a member of the House of Representatives and refused to give evidence until his fees were paid. When this was done he opened his case with the statement that 'We court the present enquiry.' He was completely vindicated. [8]

The Exhibition was duly opened in January by the Superintendent of the Province, the Governor, Sir George Grey, having failed to arrive. 'The interior of the building' we are told, 'looked light and exceedingly pleasant, despite the absence of chromatic colouring on the walls and ceiling, which one is apt to consider as the necessary and only appropriate decoration of the interior of an Exhibition building.' [9] It was (Plates 61,62) a great four-square Italianate pile of stuccoed brick, planned round a covered courtyard, the main entrance being from Great King Street under the clock tower. Without doubt it would have looked better without the hastily inserted basement. Charles Fowler, the architect of Covent Garden, Hungerford and Lower Exeter markets, had established this style thirty years before when he found that the corner towers were very useful for the water tanks necessary for a market and the appearance of Italian arcades accorded well with the open courtyard plan. It is, however, interesting to note that Fowler had proposed a very similar use of arcades and corner towers in an unexecuted house design for Mamhead, Devonshire, in 1822, thus predating Charles Barry's use of the Italian palazzo style by six years. [10] Hungerford Market, more highly developed than Covent Garden, was opened in 1833 and would certainly have been familiar to William Mason. But these square, loggia-topped towers had recently come to be much used in England – the Queen herself had accepted them at Osborne – and they continued in use in New Zealand, with W. H. Clayton one of their chief exponents. For the Exhibition building they were 26 feet square and 120 feet high.

Mason and Clayton as architects now took the opportunity to show a number of their drawings in the Fine Arts Section of the Exhibition. (Mason also lent for exhibition a painting of a sleeping girl.) The Exhibition building itself, the Post Office, All Saints' Church, the Bank of New Zealand, [11] and drawings for a villa were included. Some if not all of these were perspective drawings by the topographical painter and draughtsman, George O'Brien, [12] who did so much to record the Dunedin scene. Mason was accustomed at this stage to make fairly small perspective drawings of his proposed buildings and then to hand them over to O'Brien for enlargement if they so warranted. The careful oil sketches he had made in England were now beyond the scope of a busy man. The firm did, however, exhibit two other drawings which were not identified in the catalogue and someone, most likely Edward Rumsey who had recently won this section of the competitions for public buildings in Auckland, exhibited a design for Government House, Auckland. Out of this list, only O'Brien's drawing for the Post Office seems to have survived. Other architects' names appear also: Rumsey [13] was awarded a medal for his drawings for the Supreme Court at Auckland and R. A. Lawson, now established in Dunedin, and Robert Speechley of Christchurch also showed some of their work. Speechley was Sir Gilbert Scott's supervising

[8] Otago Provincial Council, *Reports of Select Committees.* Session XIX, 1864; *Otago Witness*, 3 October 1895.

[9] *Otago Daily Times*, 13 January 1865.

[10] Christopher Hussey, *English Country Houses, Late Georgian*. London, 1958, p. 194.

[11] The catalogue prints 'Bank of New Zealand, Auckland' which may be an error or may indicate that Mason and Clayton prepared a scheme for the building carried out by Leonard Terry of Melbourne in 1866. An abortive competition was held in November 1865 after local architects protested at the employment of an Australian. The premium of £75 was awarded to Mr G. Stafford but the directors were unshaken in their determination to employ Terry. *Weekly News*, 25 November, 16 December 1865.

[12] George O'Brien, born 1821 at Dromoland, co. Clare, was the fifth son of Admiral Robert O'Brien and a first cousin of the 13th Baron Inchiquin and his more famous brother, William Smith O'Brien, who spent six years as a political prisoner in Tasmania. O'Brien was a member of the Victorian Institute of Architects.

[13] Edward Rumsey, who later practised in Sydney, had won a gold medal at the Royal Academy in 1847 with his drawings for a cathedral. These also were exhibited in Dunedin.

architect for Christchurch Cathedral, a position later assumed by Mount-fort.

When the Exhibition closed, it was expected of course that the building would be put to its intended use. The Provincial Council, however, decided that this would be a wanton waste[14] and that for the expenditure of £2,000 on the building and £2,230 on the grounds it could be converted to a hospital. This was done but not by William Mason. The work was entrusted to John Turnbull Thomson, the Provincial Engineer, an austerely intel-lectual man who was one of the most versatile and able of Otago's early colonists. Thomson had come to New Zealand from Singapore in 1856. In Singapore he had been the Government Surveyor but he had also tried his hand at architecture and engineering and had made quite a good showing at both, being responsible for the Horsburgh lighthouse on Pedra Branca, the tower to old St Andrew's Cathedral and two hospitals.[15] It was no doubt this experience with hospitals in Singapore which brought him the task of converting the Exhibition building. In later years the building came back into the care of Messrs Mason and Wales and satis-factorily fulfilled its role as a hospital for another seventy years.

Concurrently with the work on the Exhibition building Mason and Clayton were engaged on three major buildings all within a stone's throw of each other. The post office was clearly Mason's design, the other two – the bond store for Messrs Cleve and Lazarus and the Provincial Council Chambers for which they had won a competition – show evidence of Clayton's hand.

Cleve and Lazarus's bond store, later known as Neill's Universal Bond or Edinburgh House, still stands much as it was built, a very satisfactory and harmonious building occupying the whole block of reclaimed land between Crawford, Water, Bond, and Liverpool Streets. Completed in March 1865, it is 135 feet long by 81 feet wide and has three storeys including a basement. The building was planned with private offices at each end and a cartway through the middle from Bond Street to Crawford Street. Walls were of imported bricks built off a bluestone basement and plinth, which was broken forward to receive the brick pedestals. Window and door heads were semicircular with cement archivolt dressings, and a Doric rusticated ordonnance took its rise from the impost band (i.e. the level of the springing of ground floor window arches) instead of the more usual rise from the platband above the keystones. (Plate 66.) 'This feature', wrote the *Times* reporter, 'gives the composition a charm of originality and harmony, which we do not recollect having previously witnessed.'[16] At the eaves the building was finished with what was called 'a block entablature of Vignola in cement.' The slated, hipped roof was built on kingpost trusses in three spans, carried off *miro* posts. The bluestone bases to these posts bore on concrete pads, 2 feet 6 inches square by 12 inches deep, while the concrete foundations to the exterior walls were 3 feet 6 inches wide by 2 feet thick. It is interesting to find concrete being so used at that time.

An important discovery in the use of materials was made with the building of the post office. (This building, at a later stage the premises of the Colonial Bank and then of the Stock Exchange, tends to be known as the Exchange Building but it is intended here to refer to it as the post office which was its original designation.) Stone for building had until this time been imported from Hobart Town but Mason saw no reason why

[14]*Reports of Select Commit-tees*. Session XX, 1865, Re-port 1.
[15]Thomson's architectural skill was probably derived from long association with George Drumgoole Coleman (1795-1844) an Irish archi-tect whose feeling for tropi-cal architecture was develo-ped in Calcutta and Batavia and perfected in Singapore. Lithographs of Thomson's paintings of early Singapore are much sought after in that city, but his architect-ure, unlike Coleman's, was more correct than suitable. See T. H. H. Hancock, 'Coleman of Singapore', *Architectural Review*, Vol. CXVII, pp. 168-79.
[16]27 February 1865.

a satisfactory stone should not be found locally and, on his recent visit
to Auckland to attend Parliament, he had taken with him a sample of
limestone from Pleasant River near Waikouaiti for testing by Dr Knight[17],
the Government auditor who was much respected for his scientific knowledge. He had it tested also by Dr Hector in Dunedin and was assured
that it was superior to the Bath stone which was at that time being
imported at Auckland. A dyke of the stone opened up on Mr Hepburn's
property six miles from Waikouaiti was practically without flaw and in
the same area Mason obtained a sample of Dove marble.[18] These discoveries of building stone were made through the insertion of a notice at Mason's
suggestion in the *Provincial Gazette*, 12 August 1863.[19] In fact the Pleasant
River stone was ultimately considered inferior in weathering to Oamaru
stone from the Kakanui Range and the latter was used for the post office
instead. The degree of interest in building stone was made apparent by
the extent of the section devoted to it at the Exhibition.[20]

The post office building must be regarded as Mason's finest achievement
and it is ironic that its overpowering success contributed chiefly to its
regrettable subsequent history. As built its nobility evidently shocked the
post office officials and the Provincial Council alike and long before its
completion in 1868 it was agreed that it was altogether beyond the
requirements of the Department.[21] The Government agreed to hand it
over to the Province and after being used for a bazaar, a ball and a flower
show it was opened as the Museum in October 1868. In 1871 it was handed
to the University, for whose purposes it was no more suitable, and then
sold for £27,000 in 1877 to the Colonial Bank. The original tender price
had been £22,960 submitted by Dalrymple and Company of Melbourne.
Occupation by the Bank was probably its most happy phase but the
Bank was liquidated and the Stock Exchange took over in 1900. It is the
Dunedin Stock Exchange which must be held responsible for the disgrace-
ful manner in which the building was converted into a rabbit warren of
tenancies, building another floor over the single storeyed portion and
filling the arcade with shops. Nothing could have been more ludicrous than
the way in which offices were built on either side of a passage down the
middle of the central hall.

As originally designed the building was in a style which the architects
described as Palladian with Italian and Grecian features. The lower storey
consisted of rusticated pilasters between dwarf Doric columns supporting
moulded arches with enriched spandrels. A richly carved frieze and cornice
was crowned with low balustrading. The upper storey was Corinthian
with full paired columns supporting the entablature and relieved windows
between the pairs of columns. The central clock tower, Mason's sketches
for which survive in the office of Mason and Wales, rose 120 feet from the
ground to the weather vane and the whole building was 150 feet long by
130 feet deep. The arcaded lower storey was 22 feet high. Through the
arcade was a central hall 60 feet by 40 feet and 50 feet high with a highly
decorated coved and painted roof and painted frieze. It has become
virtually impossible to judge the degree of success Mason achieved with
this central hall, intended as a place where the townspeople might gather
for the arrival of mail from the 'Old Country', but it seems probable that
Rumsey's hall to the Auckland Supreme Court, under construction at the
same time, at least solved the problem of lighting more satisfactorily.
Rumsey used a twenty-five by ten feet lantern; Mason's skylights in the

[17]Charles Knight, FRCS,
came to New Zealand from
South Australia with Sir
George Grey who placed
great reliance on his financial knowledge. His brother
was Auditor General in
Western Australia.
[18]*Otago Daily Times*, 21 and
25 March 1865.
[19]National Archives, O.P.4.
Mason to Provincial Secretary, 5 August 1863.
[20]New Zealand Exhibition,
1865. *Reports and Awards of
the Jurors*. Dunedin, 1866.
[21]*Reports of Select Committees*. Session XXI, Report
III, 1865.

plane of the roof preserved an intact skyline, without conflict with the dominating tower, but lacked subtlety when viewed from within. On either side of the hall was an arcaded wall screen over which the balustraded first floor corridors were placed. A great stone staircase was to rise from the centre of an area 30 feet square. Not much of these interior arrangements survived the alterations made by the Stock Exchange. Over the false ceilings of the shabby little offices the old painted decoration, very William Morris in this rather un-English building, reminded the curious of the care with which the architect planned his details. J. L. Godfrey's carved swags and lion masks still made a brave show on the outside. The tower was structurally suspect through neglect. Eventually in 1969, it became expedient to demolish the building altogether.

Early in 1865 the partnership began two churches, one Anglican, All Saints' North Dunedin, and the other, St Paul's Oamaru, Presbyterian. Each was planned in two stages with the nave comprising the first stage. This worked out splendidly in All Saints' (Plates 74,75) where the work was completed by Mason ten years later, but the Oamaru congregation found their part-built church (Plate 73) merely curious and, unable to visualize its completion, pulled it down and built a new undistinguished structure on its foundations, thus destroying the concept of what might have been one of the more interesting of the Province's early churches. The nave as built had a ridge line 45 feet from the ground but walls only 10 feet high. It was the extremity of these proportions which disturbed the congregation. They could not see that transepts[22] and chancel and a square tower and spire, rising to the 126 feet planned, would have thrown the first stage into proportion. All Saints', on the other hand, built in the so-called Early English style but with High Victorian details, was accepted at once. Built of red pressed brick, it was considered rather advanced in having no wall buttresses and in relying on bands of black and white glazed bricks to give relief to the plain wall surfaces, and bands of differently shaped slates to decorate the roof. There is a refreshing plainness inside also. It was originally intended to paint the ceiling of the roof blue and gold but this was not done, nor was the intended campanile built. There is a feeling of true partnership in the building – neither Mason nor Clayton did anything quite like it again – and there is the evidence also of their willingness, though neither was now young, to experiment with new ideas and to prove their awareness of the changing architectural climate abroad. All Saints' was gentle Butterfield and it was the identically named All Saints', Margaret Street, completed several years before in London, with which William Butterfield had signalled the beginning of the High Victorian phase of English architecture. In the next decade Mason's church work returned again to the more historically correct forms of Early English or Early Decorated. It is interesting to compare these two churches with the rather utilitarian St Peter's, Caversham, (Plate 71) which had been consecrated in February 1864. In this building Mason had obviously been very restricted and the result excited nobody – 'an unpretending building in wood but well finished,' said the *Times* 'and in every respect neat, comfortable and appropriate.' But the interesting feature is of course the square campanile with its pyramidal roof, a structure much more High Victorian in its reliance on French or Italian models than the main body of the church behind it. Such towers (the campanile in the Piazza San Marco in Venice is for most people the

[22]The walls of the transepts were to have been 17 feet high to give room for galleries. A similar scheme was followed at All Saints'.

supreme example) were commonly used by the High Victorian architects in England but they are curiously rare in New Zealand. At Caversham the result was rudimentary in the extreme, particularly as it was built in wood, and in the next few years (it was removed to Mornington in 1883) it must have offended the eyes of many Dunedin citizens enchanted with the soaring pinnacles of Lawson's First Church in Moray Place. The point is made, however, that a tower such as this was probably intended for All Saints', Dunedin, and in these more congruous circumstances and with further interior enrichment of the church itself, it would probably have made the kind of High Victorian statement which is otherwise scarcely to be found, ecclesiastically, outside some of Mountfort's work in Christ-church.

Mason and Clayton now had a new building for the Bank of New South Wales on the boards and, more important still, a residence for the Governor at Wellington; and there were, of course, other buildings designed at this period – the Colonial Museum commissioned by Dr Hector[23] in 1865 (Plate 70) is an example of a building partly fabricated in Dunedin for erection in Wellington – but while Mason's account books are available for the first period of his Dunedin practice and again during his later partnership with N. Y. A. Wales, nothing can be discovered of records for the partnership with Clayton. It is, for instance, not known what houses they did together, though something like the Driver house, Driver's Road (Plate 77), may be fairly certainly attributed to them. The synagogue built in Moray Place (not, of course, Louis Boldini's later structure but a building afterwards used by the Freemasons) is assumed to have been entirely Clayton's work.

Back in October 1863, the Provincial Engineer, C. R. Swyer, who had designed Dunedin's affectionately regarded Cargill Monument,[24] prepared plans for new Provincial buildings which the *Times* described as 'exceedingly pretty' but lacking in 'stately grandeur'.[25] Their extent may be judged from his estimate that the cost would be £70,000, but their imaginative nature is made clear when we are told that no site had been determined on. Swyer's scheme was not proceeded with. It was anyway too costly.[26] But a number of architects submitted designs by general invitation and the Council narrowed this number to two, the cost, which was not to exceed £16,000, being the deciding factor. Mason and Clayton were given the job in August 1865.[27]

A month before this, however, Mason had received a requisition signed by 140 citizens, including many leading merchants, seeking his consent to nomination for the office of Mayor of Dunedin. Dunedin was about to become a city, the first City Corporation in New Zealand, and Mason, not even one of the 'old identities' and an Episcopalian at that, was to be its first Mayor. He was invited also to stand for the higher office of Provincial Superintendent but considered his serious objections to the Provincial Council's land policy sufficient reason for declining.

[23]James Hector, later knighted, had been persuaded to transfer himself and the staff of his geological survey to Wellington on completion of his three year contract with the Otago Provincial Government. Like Mason he had been one of the fourteen Exhibition Commissioners. Correspondence is preserved in the archives of the Dominion Museum with reference to the building of the Colonial Museum.
[24]*Daily Telegraph*, 18 June 1863.
[25]21 October 1863. A perspective drawing was engraved for the *Otago Witness*, 19 March 1864.
[26]C. R. Swyer was the first treasurer of the Victorian Institute of Architects on its foundation in 1856. Before coming to Dunedin he practised in Melbourne with Albert Purchas, an elder brother of Dr A. G. Purchas, Bishop Selwyn's associate in Auckland. Swyer appears to have left Dunedin in 1866.
[27]National Archives, O.P. 11/10. Public Works Office to Mason and Clayton, 24 August 1865.

XIII   FIRST CITIZEN

. . . how many pages of doubtful record might we not often spare for a few stones left one upon the other – John Ruskin, 'The Lamp of Memory', *The Seven Lamps of Architecture*, 1849.

Since his arrival in Dunedin, Mason had taken very little part in public life. His attendance on Parliament was perfunctory and his constituents at the other end of the country can have seen him seldom. In November 1864 he travelled to Auckland with nine others[1] in the specially chartered steamer *Phoebe* for the three weeks sitting until 13 December, but took no part in the proceedings of the House. John Bathgate, who in this party of ten was the only non-member but travelled with them as chairman of the recently formed Dunedin Waterworks Company, wrote an account of their journey which was later published under the title *Bathgate Expeditions*.[2] The voyage to Onehunga which took six days with calls at Lyttelton, Wellington, Picton, Nelson, and New Plymouth to pick up other 'senators', was uneventful except for the overturning of a coach when the party was on shore between Christchurch and Lyttelton; but Bathgate tells of their enjoyment of the coastal scenery, whether for the grandness of Egmont and the snowy Kaikouras or for the evidence of good farming land in North Otago and Taranaki; and their enjoyment of a different kind in the impromptu concert given one fine calm evening out of Nelson: 'As we steamed out of Tasman Bay the night was beautiful, Sirius gleaming brilliantly with a bright reflection in the calm waters. As we sped on our way . . . towards the Northern Island the passengers assembled on deck. At every port we had an accession of senators, and at Nelson the Speaker of the House of Representatives, Dr Monro, came on board. It was quite a picture to see the legislative cluster seated and standing round the companion door, many of them with tumblers of grog in their hands, trolling out their best songs, and in the intervals bandying about joke and repartee. The Speaker sang *The Barring O' Our Door* in excellent style, and the chorus was stunning.'

Bathgate was pleasantly surprised at the standard of debate in the Lower House: 'The debates . . . were characterised with considerable ability, and the tone of the whole proceedings was far removed from the democratic rowdyism which ocasionally disgraces the legislatures of the sister colonies. The members are chiefly men of education and social

[1] Dr Buchanan, Mr W. H. Reynolds, Mr Paterson, Major J. L. C. Richardson, Mr Julius Vogel, Mr T. B. Gillies, Mr Brodie, Mr Wayne and Mr John Bathgate.
[2] Edited by A. H. Reed. Wellington, 1952.

position, many of them of good English families, and all this tells on the general bearing of the House.' Whatever Mason's position in this scheme of things he took no part in debate and it must be assumed that his time was occupied at Howick in seeing his constituents and perhaps referring their wants to the various Parliamentary Committees. Before he left Auckland, however, he was verbally instructed to examine with Dr Featherston various sites at Wellington and to give his opinion of their suitability for a residence for the Governor who would soon be required to remove with Parliament to the new capital on Cook's Strait. This he did and chose the site in Bowen Street which was ultimately used.[3]

Back in Dunedin, Mason at once prepared plans for a house estimated to cost £18,000. These he took to Wellington, had them approved and then, two and a half months after receiving his first instructions, called tenders throughout the Colony. No drawings for the house are now available, and its form is discoverable only from a sketch photographed at the time. (Plate 79.) The sketch shows a spiky, many gabled house with steep roofs, towers, and romantically irregular elevations. It was the kind of house Gore Browne had wanted at Auckland ten years before. But the climate had already changed and building was deferred on the grounds that the site was not immediately available. This may or may not have been the full reason but, in August, Clayton, on a visit to Wellington, saw designs prepared by another architect 'by direction of Mr Weld' and wrote to the Postmaster General to enquire whether Mason and Clayton's services had been dispensed with. He was reassured and himself had the satisfaction more than three years later of redesigning the house and carrying out the commission.

If Mason was not to build the new Government House in Wellington he was shortly to be elevated to the position of first citizen and chief magistrate for Dunedin. He was approached for his consent on 15 July 1865, and a few days later was nominated by R. B. Martin, the chairman of the Chamber of Commerce, and James Smith, a solicitor. This was the major step in what seemed to be a reawakening of his interest in public affairs, a reawakening which was no doubt made possible by the certainty of his partner's attention to their architectural practice. At the end of the previous year he had been gazetted a trustee of the Dunedin Savings Bank and soon afterwards, as one of the sixteen lay members, he attended the very important third General Synod of the Anglican Church held in Christchurch, where he presented a Bill for the appointment of a Board of Trusts in the Rural Deanery of Otago and Southland. The Synod, incidentally, was a body of considerable distinction, its sixteen laymen including such notable names as Sir William Martin, J. E. FitzGerald, John Hall, H. J. Tancred, Robert Stokes and John Grigg. It was this Synod, presided over by Bishop Selwyn, whose members accepted and signed the reworded and expanded constitution of the Branch of the United Church of England and Ireland in New Zealand. Mason, with Bishop Abraham, the Rev. Francis Tripp and J. E. FitzGerald, was appointed to the Standing Orders Committee. His bill for the appointment of a Board of Trusts was more apposite than might at first appear as on it depended the acceptance into the constitution of one of the demands of the Diocese of Christchurch – the right of an individual diocese to set up its own trusts for ecclesiastical purposes, which was one of the points at issue in diminishing Selwyn's personal authority.[4]

[3]National Archives. I.A. 135/1.

[4]It is of interest here that Bishop Selwyn's ledger in the Diocesan Office at Auckland lists the following subscriptions to the Dunedin bishopric in pencil and then notes that they were unpaid: Judge Chapman and the Bishop of Christchurch £100 each, Messrs Gorst, Strode, R. B. Martin, Fraser, Mason, and Capt Boyd £50 each.

From the rarefied yet rebellious atmosphere of Synod in April and May, he was pitchforked two months later into the hurly-burly of the mayoral election.[5] He was opposed by James Paterson, a Scottish Presbyterian member of Parliament shortly to be a member of Stafford's executive but not, evidently, the man by whom even his fellow-countrymen wished to be represented as Mayor, by two lawyers, Macgregor and Wilson, and by the Sheriff of the Province, R. H. Forman, soon to be the subject of a major scandal. Since he belonged to neither it was probably hoped that Mason would be impartial to the two main factions, the Scotch settlers or 'old identities' and the Victorian immigrants or 'new iniquities'. After nomination he made his first statement while suffering from a heavy cold. 'I am almost a stranger among you,' he said. 'I have been here two or three years, but I have, during that time, been living a quiet, secluded life; I have been attending to my own private business . . . . We have had a fever and we are now feeling the effects of that fever; and we must remain quiet for a short time, until we gather strength, and then go to work as men with strong arms and sound heads.' He stated his intention of resigning from Parliament should he be elected, 'though I believe the forthcoming session will be the most important we have ever had in New Zealand. Therefore I should regret not being able to be in my place in the House of Representatives.'

It had been originally intended to place the choice of a Mayor in the hands of the City Council, but the attempt was frustrated and the election was made popular. Mason's committee hired two or three of Cobb's four-horse coaches, together with several cabs, and these, covered with placards, were constantly drawn to and fro, conveying voters to the various booths. Other candidates' committees followed similar methods without having the advantages of Cobb's coaches. The placards advised candidates to vote for Mason 'if you want your streets properly made, if you want your money judiciously expended, if you want drainage through the city.' Handbills were plentiful and imitated a voting paper with a cross against Mason's name. The excitement was considerable, yet, from a roll of four thousand, only one thousand electors cast their votes. Mason polled 495 votes with Paterson, his only serious rival, polling 398. Forman polled 10. David Ross, Mason's former partner, was elected a Councillor at a separate poll some days later.

Mason's term as Mayor was not remarkable for any great advances but he pushed forward with the levelling of streets as funds permitted and strongly backed the inauguration of the City water supply. He was later remembered for introducing a by-law forbidding the ringing of auctioneers' bells and for being temporarily frustrated by Mr Shadrach Jones who introduced the greater nuisance of blowing horns in their stead. Much of his time was taken up with presiding over the Mayor's Court which sat at ten o'clock each morning. As Chief Magistrate he had very soon to sit in judgement on one of his opponents for the Mayoralty, the Sheriff, R. H. Forman, who was arrested at the Heads when fleeing a charge of embezzlement. The charge related to his appropriation of the effects of a suicide. He was certainly guilty but Mason felt bound to discharge him on the technicality that no one had required him to hand over the effects. Before the error in the indictment could be rectified Forman left the colony. This provoked a public uproar which had not died down when the following year's election took place and Mason appeared on one

[5]He made one other public appearance in April when he presented the Otago Rifle Association with a Challenge Cup for competition and it would appear that he had also taken some part in the formation of the Waterworks Company and had given much gratuitous advice to that body. *Otago Witness*, 3 October 1895.

15. *Punch cartoon: Mason with wings spread.*

occasion waving in his hands, as justification of his action, the Government Gazette containing notice of renewal of his appointment as a Magistrate.

The City was extremely unfortunate, during this initial period, in the quality of its paid staff. As well as the Sheriff, the City Clerk, the Engineer and the Collector were dismissed. The first had been guilty of a financial irregularity which was not indictable – he connived at the rate collector's paying in a cheque after an enquiry was begun – the second, John Millar,[6] had already had a not undistinguished career in Melbourne and survived his dismissal to become a member of the Provincial Council, but he unfortunately found it difficult to get contractors to tender for work under his supervision. The third man, the City Collector, was arrested for rioting and was then found to be out in his accounts. Mason's problems with these men, particularly his dismissal of Millar, lost him some supporters and gained others.

The shortage of funds was desperate and casting round for some means of raising money the Council decided during Mason's second term to lease portions of the Town Belt. The leases, for fourteen years, prevented any building and the public were to have right of way at any time, but there was a tremendous outcry against this alienation of public land and those people – the Superintendent, Hyde Harris, was one – who had taken up leases with the intention of running a cow or securing grazing for their horses, had soon to give them up. Again Mason bore much of the animadversion.

At his re-election in 1866 he polled 612 votes against J. G. S. Grant with 231 and David Ross with 16. This time he was proposed by E. B. Cargill and seconded by Job Wain, some of his earlier supporters having ostentatiously withheld themselves as a protest over the Millar affair. Grant, a disgruntled Scotch schoolmaster, whom the *Witness* described as a lasting disgrace to the city and whom others called 'this clever clown', proved a lively opponent. He complained that the business of the Corporation had been conducted in an arbitrary and tyrannical fashion savouring of King 'Bomba' of Naples. What had been done, in dismissing the Town Clerk, had been more like a bit of Muscovite government or the act of a scion of the House of Hapsburg than British fair dealing. He taunted Mason with his dismissal of the charge against Forman and with his absenting himself for two months of the year to attend Parliament. Mason, waving a copy of the current Gazette, replied that he was responsible to His Excellency as a Resident Magistrate and not to the electors and, as for his attendance to parliamentary duties, he had not immediately resigned his seat as a member of the House of Representatives because Council had thought his voice in Wellington would be helpful in passing the Empowering Act[7] and perhaps in getting possession of the Maori Reserve.

The feelings of the citizens towards their members of Parliament were not always the happiest. In October 1866 Mason was requisitioned to call a public meeting to demand an explanation of their conduct from the local members. His attempts to keep good feeling prevalent, in an overcrowded meeting in the theatre, were of no avail. In the following May a similar meeting was called to consider the relationship between the provincial and general governments. Though out of sympathy with them, Mason had to forward its resolutions to Wellington. This was the period when Vogel was busily advocating the separation of the North and South Islands to relieve the latter of any responsibility for the costly

[6]John Millar, FSA, trained under Thomas Hopper, architect to King George IV during his regency. He was a Gold Medallist at the Royal Academy and claimed some association with Nash, Smirke, Pugin, Haydon, Turner, Roberts, Baines, Etty, Carew, Westmacott, etc. *Otago Punch*, 12 January 1867, p. 153.
[7]Presumably the Otago Municipal Corporations Empowering Act 1865.

Maori Wars.

The squabble over the Town Belt erupted at the end of 1866. In February 1867 Sir George Grey's long-awaited visit eventuated. He landed at Port Chalmers and was met by the Mayor and Corporation of Dunedin at the boundary of the city. It was, said the *Times*, a simple formality properly performed, and the effect of the long line of the procession was capital. For Mason it was a meeting with an old friend.

The public welcome on the following day astonished everyone with its fervour. At its conclusion Mason called for three cheers for the Governor, adding, 'And now, let the voice of Otago be heard!' At the subsequent *déjeuner*, in the not yet completed central hall of the Provincial Government buildings, the Mayor presided, while Mrs Mason, making one of her rare public appearances, sat between the Superintendent and Judge Richmond. Mason proposed the health of the Governor. In returning the compliment, Grey said ' . . . it is with great pleasure that I recognise in the position of Mayor of this town, an old friend, whom I have known in other parts of New Zealand.[8] It has been with great satisfaction, also, that I have seen with how many specimens of his skill as an architect, the town of Dunedin has been adorned; and I feel certain that those abilities which he has exhibited in the respects I have mentioned, will be equally devoted to the service of the inhabitants of the town, in all those local improvements upon which the future of the city so much depends.'

Naturally enough the Governor, whose suite comprised the Hon. Major Richardson, his cousin and military secretary, Major Grey, the Rev. Frederick Thatcher and Captain Hope, was taken on a tour of public works. Starting at the new Post Office he was accompanied by Thatcher, now filling his role as secretary but curious, no doubt, in his other capacity of architect, to see what was going on.

'His Excellency accompanied by the Rev. Mr Thatcher and conducted by the Mayor (William Mason, Esq.) visited the works about one o'clock yesterday. The architects of the building were Messrs Mason and Clayton, up to the time when Mr Mason retired from the profession; so that the Mayor was fully qualified to conduct the Governor over the works and the building.

' . . . the cutters for a simple architrave moulding were in place; and steam having been got up – nearly all the men were holiday keeping – His Excellency was enabled to see how easily the stone can be worked. He stood by while ashlar was cut from blocks, by means of a steam-driven circular saw, and while men with a hand saw made deep cuts into a block which was being worked into a capital; he was shown the speed with which balusters can be turned – 36 can be finished in a day of eight hours, by one man, so that the labor for each costs less than 4d; and he watched the first chippings by which a block was roughly moulded, in its progress towards an elaborately finished capital. His Excellency examined with great interest two beautiful cabinet specimens by Mr J. L. Godfrey – samples of real art, as well as proofs of the delicate working of which the Oamaru stone is capable; and he also saw how easily the stone yielded to the chisel of Mr Godfrey and of other of the workers.'

On the following day, 16 February, Grey visited the Provincial Government buildings. 'Here His Excellency was received by his Honor the Superintendent; the Mayor (William Mason, Esq.) – the architects of the pile were Messrs Mason and Clayton; Mr J. T. Thomson, Engineer of

[8]Mason had been one of the two 'croupiers' at the farewell dinner tendered to Grey on his departure from Auckland in 1853. At that dinner Mason had proposed the toast to 'The Author of Auckland and its Neighbourhood' who was, of course, the Attorney-General, William Swainson.

Roads and Works; and Mr S. Cornwell, contractor for the Buildings. The plans were laid on a table in the Central Hall; and the Mayor explained the peculiarity of the design. The Hall will have arranged round it, a series of counters, which will be assigned to the different departments; behind which there will be a room or rooms for the chiefs. . . . He [Grey] was then conducted to the rooms at the south west corner of the pile which are temporarily occupied by the Roads and Works Department; and there Mr Thomson submitted the plans for bridges in the course of construction – such as those over the Clutha and the Mataura.'

The party then proceeded to the Fire Brigade's building, the Gaol, and the former Exhibition building, already converted by Thomson to its use as a Hospital. ' . . . the Governor was first conducted into the central hall. There the obelisk representing the bulk of the gold got in Otago up to the end of 1864 still stands. During the period between the closing of the Exhibition and the opening of the Hospital, curious visitors stripped off pieces of the gold-leaf-covered calico forming the sides of the obelisk; but the whole has been renovated, and looks now smarter than at first.'

As a strange finale to the day's activities, the Governor and his suite accompanied by Mason and Judge Chapman attended the Lunatic Asylum Ball, given to the patients, where Grey assured the Master and Matron of his deep interest in their work.

Grey's visit took place in February 1867. Mason was now much taken up with an estate at Maheno which he had leased from Captain Williams with the right to purchase. The Mayoralty was established and he decided not to stand again for election. Before J. Hyde Harris took over in the following July, Mason was able to tell the last meeting of his Council that the by-laws and standing orders of the Corporation had been gazetted. A few days later, after an election without excitement, he announced the name of his successor to a crowd of 400 citizens in Maclaggan Street.

During his term as Mayor he had virtually retired from the practice of architecture but he had seen the completion of several buildings for which he had been responsible. The Post Office, the Exhibition building and the Provincial Chambers were the most notable of these but the premises for the Bank of New South Wales, opened in May 1866, (Plates 16,72) provide one of the most attractive nineteenth-century facades in New Zealand. It appears to have been designed by Mason rather than Clayton and some contemporary references mention his name exclusively in connection with the building. 'The new building for the Bank of New South Wales, in Princes Street, is now completed', wrote the *Times* reporter. 'It is specially adapted to the business requirements of the Bank with a residence and domestic offices for the Manager; and it is about the most handsome building in the city.' The instruction had been to design a building not exceeding £6,000 in cost and the tendered price was £5,937. The main design problem was to achieve an impression of importance on a site which was only 48 feet wide and was further reduced by the necessary provision of vehicle access to the rear.

'In consequence of the limited frontage, it became necessary to treat the elevation so as to add to the apparent width of the building. The Architects have succeeded in this by recessing the front and adding return wing-walls, by which arrangement also a great security against fire is obtained, and the lighting of the basement storey is facilitated. This basement is Port Chalmers bluestone (a conglomerate), quarry-faced, with

16. *Punch cartoon: Mason carries an earth closet.*

chiselled margins, terminating in a moulded plinth on the level of the ground floor, and returning round the area to that next the street, thus forming a retaining wall on which, above the footpath, is placed a dressed kerb and ornamental iron railing. There are also neat gas-lamp pillars and folding iron gates. The front is Oamaru stone. The ground storey comprises three arched recesses, rusticated with vermiculated piers and arch stones. The centre recess is the business entrance and has two Ionic columns the shafts of polished Port Chalmers stone forming a strong contrast with the cream-coloured Oamaru stone. These columns carry a moulded and denticulated entablature, the space above the springing being filled with plate glass. There is a window in each of the two side recesses, each having two detached Doric columns with polished Port Chalmers stone shafts, and pilasters of Oamaru stone, on pedestals, carrying an entablature ranging with the impost on the piers, but terminating and returning on each side of the windows. From this entablature springs a moulded archivolt, extending to the soffits of the voussoirs. The arches are designed with extending arch stones, from the springing upwards, and terminate with sculptured keystones. There is also a moulded and denticulated entablature, returning on the wing walls, with moulded corbels over each arch, supporting a projection of the cornice and forming a balcony to each window on the first floor. Here there are coupled engaged Corinthian pilasters supporting an entablature proportioned to the height of the building, and broken over the pilasters, but also returning on the wing walls; this entablature being enriched with dentils and modillions, as is usual in the order. Each window has architraves and panelled jamb-pilasters, carrying enriched consoles, with dentilled cornice and segmental pediment. The attic storey has piers with moulded sunk panels ranging with the pilasters below, and terminates with a denticulated entablature, triplicate blocking courses, with square balustrade and pedestals over. The basement contains messengers' rooms, vaults for vouchers, strong room, three rooms for the smelting of gold, lumber room, stationery room and clerks' lavatory. The ground storey consists of the public banking hall, 35ft 6in. square in the clear, and 25ft high. The hall has a deeply coffered and enriched ceiling. The lighting is by a lantern in the roof, with ground plate glass panels immediately under in the ceiling. The hall is chastely handsome throughout. It is approached from Princes Street by a lobby and vestibule, separated by elegant folding swing cedar doors, with ground plate glass panels. The floor of the lobby vestibule and the space in the hall set apart for the public, is flagged with black and white polished marble in diamond pattern. The fittings of the hall are of cedar, French polished. On the right of the vestibule is the manager's office with strong-rooms, while on the left of the vestibule is the inspector's office. Next to this office and corresponding with the strongrooms on the manager's side, is the staircase, leading to the manager's apartment, which is approached by a private door to the right-of-way from Princes Street. The first floor comprises a drawing-room, dining room, kitchen, scullery and pantry. From the kitchen, a shute is provided, whereby cinders, ashes &c, can be shot to the basement. The attic floor consists of four bedrooms, and conveniences. In the yard there are chaise-house, stable &c. The whole of the work has been excellently done by Mr Cornwell.'[9]

[9]*Otago Daily Times*, 18 May 1866.

This hypnotic newspaper account is given at length as an example of what the educated reader was expected to appreciate at that time and of the knowledge it was assumed he had, of the grammar of architectural ornament.

Less exacting was Anthony Trollope's description of the Provincial Council Chamber when he visited it a few years later. 'The members sit, like Siamese twins, in great arm-chairs, which are joined together, two and two, like semi-detached villas. I was specially struck by what I cannot but call the hyper-excellence of the room. There has been, in most of the New Zealand provinces, a determination that the Provincial Assembly shall be a real parliament, with a Speaker and Speaker's chair, reporters' galleries, strangers' galleries, a bar of the house, cross benches, library, smoking-room and a "Bellamy," – as the parliament refreshment-rooms are all called, in remembrance of the old days of the House of Commons at home. The architecture, furniture and general apparel of these Houses – such of them as I saw, – struck me as being almost grander than was necessary. The gentlemen as they sit are very much more comfortable than are the members in our own House at home, and are much better lodged than are the legislators in the States of the American Union. The Congress of Massachusetts sits in a building which has indeed an imposing exterior, but the chamber itself inspires less awe than does that of Otago.'[10]

This 'awesome' hall, 80 feet by 34 feet by 24 feet high, became the Supreme Court Chamber on the abolition of the Provincial Councils, but from the beginning the building also housed the Post Office and two magistrates' courts. Trollope found the interior 'hyper-excellent'. Externally the building was very satisfactory (Plates 68,69) except on the Princes Street front which housed the Post Office. Perhaps the architects were trying to belittle the expression of this department after their over-grand gesture in the still incomplete building originally intended for it, but certainly the treatment of the Princes Street front is insignificant, with nothing more than an awkwardly handled pediment to give it character. The hand appears to be Clayton's. His handling of the contract, during Mason's mayoralty, led once more to argument – with the Secretary for Public Works and with that inflexible man, J. T. Thomson, who, as Engineer of Roads and Works, was given the responsibility of signing certificates for payment on the contract – a responsibility which Clayton evidently chose to ignore. Mason and Clayton's claim for fees was again submitted to arbitration and the Council, having refused to pay a balance of £68 16s 11d in January 1867, was compelled to pay them rather more than double that amount in July.[11]

That all was not well with the acoustics of the Council Chamber before it was furnished may be supposed from a mock advertisement in *Otago Punch:*   'Lecture
MESSRS MASON AND CLAYTON
will, on Monday next, deliver
a lecture in the new Council
Chamber. Subject –
ACOUSTICS
with practical illustrations,
demonstrating the historical
truth of the record of the confusion
of tongues, which occurred at the
TOWER OF BABEL.'[12]

[10]Anthony Trollope, *Australia and New Zealand.* London, 1873. Vol. II, p. 344.
[11]National Archives, O.P.4, Council Minutes 1866-8, 22 January, 4 July 1867.
[12]*Otago Punch*, 24 November 1866, p. 99.

XIV   THE PUNCHBOWL

'Brother,' said Richard, 'do I hear aright?
Does the land truly give so much delight?'
  — George Crabbe, *Tales of the Hall.*
  Book IV, Adventures of Richard.

Mason's connection with North Otago went back at least to 1863 when he had designed a store for Traill[1] and Roxby[2], the pioneer storekeepers of Oamaru, described by Elwell as 'two very nice gentlemanly men who seemed to prefer that life to sheep farming.'[3] But he would also have heard something of the area from his old Auckland friends, the Rich family, for in 1861 F. D. Rich had established himself at Bushey Park, near Palmerston, to become the leading sheep breeder in the colony and a generous host to the Dunedin sportsmen who came north to hunt his game birds and red deer. Mason, as we know, was a famous shot.

Land in the hundred of Otepopo had become available for freehold purchase in 1864 and a large area was then awarded to the old whaler, Captain Peter Williams, in settlement of his claims at Preservation Inlet. Mason, who had recently designed the building known as Abbeyleix House for him and established his Mayor's Court there, leased a part of this land, it would seem, either immediately after its allocation or at the time of his election as Mayor of Dunedin and his virtual retirement from practice. The lease was for 2,647 acres of land south of the Island Stream and included a purchasing clause. Mason called the property the Punchbowl, a name which is retained to the present day. In addition to this he owned the freehold of some 340 acres, half of it nearer to Herbert, and a small block in Hampden township. This last was held jointly with his associates R. B. Martin and E. E. C. Quick and may have been in trust for the Church. A single reference in Elwell could indicate Clayton's interest in the Punchbowl, also, but it is nowhere else borne out and may be explained by the fact that Elwell's 'boy colonists' had been working on the property of F. T. Walker, whose father, Thomas Walker of Rhodes, was a neighbour of the Clayton family in Tasmania, and that Clayton's association with Mason would therefore have been uppermost in their minds. In fact the homestead at Rhodes, a not unoriginal building, may well have been designed by Clayton. Walker was associated with the Otago lands of Sir Henry Young, a former Governor of Tasmania.

[1] Charles Traill, born in Orkney, was an amateur naturalist who discovered oyster beds during a visit to Stewart Island and later settled there on the island he called Ulva.
[2] Eustace Wriottesley Roxby, afterwards Town Clerk for Oamaru, 1870-87.
[3] E. S. Elwell, *The Boy Colonists or Eight Years of Colonial Life in Otago.* London, 1878. p. 213.

Mason lived on his property between the years 1867-71 but he retained the house in London Street where his wife, now in her seventies, probably remained. He, too, though fifteen years younger, must have begun to feel the weight of his years but he set about farming with characteristic energy. In 1869 the lists of runholders show that he had 1,960 sheep on the property, a small enough flock in the company of such men as Robert Campbell of Otekaike who had 27,000 there and another 51,500 jointly with Low at Benmore, or Young with 46,795, Teschemaker and Co. with 37,000 or Borton and McMaster with 50,000. But these were vast runs different in character from the down-like arable country of the Punchbowl.

Elwell's reference to an overnight stop at Mason's farm, when driving sheep from Longslip near the Lindis Pass to Palmerston, occurs in May 1865. In December of that year Mason wrote from Belgrave Chambers to the Secretary of Public Works: 'I have expended a large sum of money in fencing two thousand acres of land in Block 5 Otepopo district, the whole of which expenditure is rendered almost useless to me from my being obliged to leave portions of the fence down to accommodate the present traffic.' Four months later he wrote again: 'I think the decision as to the road being as suitable to traffic as that now in use should not be an open question. I would suggest this question might be decided by Cobb & Co (their coaches travelling over the road every day are interested in having this arrangement properly carried out . . .)'. He had undertaken to form an alternative route by-passing his property and this offer had been accepted. It was the main north road and required a cut nine feet deep. This cut was the section to be tested by Cobb's coaches.

Roads in country districts were always a matter of contention. The Punchbowl came under the Sydney Road Board[4] for rating purposes. In January 1868 the General Road Board received a petition from twenty-three landholders, of whom Mason was by far the largest, protesting against the levying of a rate of one shilling per acre by the Sydney Local Road Board. Soon afterwards the Local Board informed the General Board that the petition had been got up by Mr William Mason; and soon after that, no doubt with the spirit of protest still strong within him, Mason was elected to the Board by his fellow ratepayers. He served two years as Chairman. On 10 December 1869 the Sydney Road Board enquired from the General Road Board whether it was essential to employ an engineer on all works. 'Our Chairman, Mr Mason, is willing to prepare specifications for any work not involving too much labour. Would the General Road Board object to this counsel?'

His other activities were various. On 15 September 1868 the *North Otago Times* learnt that 'Mr Mason, Otepopo, brought up from Dunedin by yesterday's coach, from the Acclimatisation Society, seven brace of Californian partridges and three brace of Californian teal. The partridges are to be let loose on the east side of the Otepopo bush on Mr Mason's property, where there is plenty of waste grain. . . . The teal are to be set at liberty on the Otepopo side of the Kakanui.'

Oamaru, where the *North Otago Times* was published, was already a thriving town centred on Tyne Street and Itchen Street. In the next decade the centre shifted to Thames Street and Oamaru then qualified for its description as the best-built and most-mortgaged town in Australasia. No doubt the availability of local stone spurred its citizens to build beyond their needs, but perhaps the character of the surrounding run-

[4]North Otago was divided between nineteen Road Boards increased to twenty when Windsor was added in 1867. Each board had six members with jurisdiction over a minimum territory of fifteen square miles. (Sydney, despite the different spelling, was apparently named after Sidney Herbert, who became Secretary of State for the Colonies in 1855. His mother was the sister of Edward Blore's old client, Prince Michael Voronzoff.) The Otepopo hundred comprised six of these road districts. The records of the Sydney Road Board are preserved with the Waitaki County Council.

holders, many of whom were men of education and good family, contributed also to the quality of the buildings. Tyne Street and Itchen Street, deserted by the banks and public offices, form today an architectural setting which is unlikely at least in this country where Florentine reminders are rare – and one which has been curiously overlooked by cameramen. Already in 1866 W. B. Armson had begun to practise there as an architect. By 1869 he had gone but Grenfell, Glass, Clarke, and Moore had taken his place. Mason, however, pricked by the local dislike of his half-built St Paul's Church, took no part. His interest seems, rather, to have been directed south to Moeraki.

In March 1868, at one with the settlers' agitation formulated some months before with a meeting at the Kakanui Hotel, for a railway between Moeraki and Waitaki, Mason wrote personally to the Superintendent of the Province to urge its immediate construction. Moeraki, as a port, offered more shelter than the exposed roadstead at Oamaru and, loading costs being cheaper there, settlers were accustomed to ship their wool and quarry-masters their stone and lime from the port. By May the Provincial Council had agreed to give its support and two years later John Millar, the engineer whom Mason had once dismissed, was instructed to make a survey of the route. The first contracts were let in 1873, but by that time the scheme had been taken over by the General Government.

As with his term as Mayor of Dunedin, Mason once more had staff trouble in the Sydney Road Board. On 1 June 1869 the Board resolved that it would no longer place confidence in its clerk, W. R. Speid. On 7 June Mason reported that steps had been taken to arrest Speid in Dunedin. This was done and a charge against him, for the misappropriation of funds, was adjourned to Oamaru and there dismissed. On 6 May 1870 the Board resolved 'That the money paid by the Chairman to Mr Speid to prevent any action being taken for defamation of character should be paid out of the rates.' Speid had won and Mason did not again offer himself for election to the Board.

Sections in the township of Maheno, just outside the north-eastern extremity of his land, had been offered for sale in April 1869. Mason's lease was the last big holding in the immediate area and he now cut this up in sub-leases. The Sydney Road Board wrote plaintively to the General Board on 11 October 1870: 'Mr Wm Mason had 2,647 acres 39 poles on the Punchbowl estate for which he was rated last year: he has now however leased the greater part of it to 10 different parties. Some of the lessees pay the highway rate while others, according to their agreement, are not entitled to do so. Mr Mason has appointed an agent in Oamaru to manage his affairs.' They complained of the difficulty of getting an accurate list of lessees and suggested levying Mason with the whole rate and letting him collect. Whatever the outcome or, indeed Mason's right to sub-lease, Captain Williams, the true owner of the land, was evidently inadequately consulted, for seven years later he brought an action against Mason which was settled by the latter's paying him a sum of £500. This it would seem was due, at least in part, to the agent who had been appointed in Oamaru.[5]

The freehold block of 162 acres near Herbert was sold in April 1870 to F. D. Rich for £1,000 and by Rich to W. H. S. Roberts for £800. But Mason didn't immediately get his money and some years later, when Rich was in temporary financial difficulties, he was asked to accept collateral security over 1,000 acres of Rich's land in the North Island.[6] Rich's Otago

[5]N. Y. A. Wales to Mason, 2 December 1879. Personal Letterbook, Office of Mason and Wales.

[6]Probably a part of the Patetere block for which Lichfield, near Putaruru, was proposed as a cathedral city. N. Y. A. Wales to Mrs Mason, 23 October 1885. Letterbook, office of Mason and Wales.

estate, Bushey Park, was eventually handed over to the Bank of New Zealand's Assets Realisation Board.

Though Mason seems to have returned to Dunedin in 1870 he maintained an interest in the North Otago area through his shareholding in Rowley, Wilson and Company who worked the Shag Point coal mines from 1871. From 1875 to 1877 he appears as joint owner with John Cotton Rowley and Charles James Wilson of the two vessels, *Jane* and *Shag*, the little colliers which plied to Dunedin and Oamaru. The s.s. *Shag*, 42 tons gross, built for the company by Kincaid, McQueen and Company, made a trial trip on Otago Harbour in January 1875 and ran on to a sandbank where she remained stuck for three hours. She was able, however, to negotiate the port facilities at Shag Point, a stone jetty built in a narrow fissure in the rocks not more than thirty feet wide, and was eventually broken up in Wellington in 1900. Rowley, Wilson and Company were absorbed in the Shag Point Coal Company formed by F. D. Rich in 1878.

17. *Maryhill, Otepopo.*

XV   RETURN TO PRACTICE

It can well be imagined with what boredom a Greek architect would have thumbed through illustrations of the newly erected Parthenon if he had been subscribing to the 'Athenian Builder's Weekly' since 490 B.C. – Peter Collins, *Concrete, The Vision of a New Architecture*. London, 1959.

When Mason retired from architectural practice in 1865 to give his time to mayoral duties, his partner Clayton carried on with the assistance of W. G. Jackson, the engineer who had been some time in their employment. The demand for building fell away and many architects who had attended the feast provided by the gold-rush returned to Australia or moved to other towns.

Clayton inherited the task of building Government House at Wellington. In 1865 the partnership billed the Government for something over £500 for the work they had done on designs, preparing documents and advertising tenders. The basic charge was 2½ percent on £18,000, being the estimated cost of the unbuilt house. Stafford, Prendergast and Gisborne were unwilling to pay this much, Gisborne noting that at this rate it would pay an architect much better not to erect buildings than to build them, but Charles Knight, the Auditor-General, gave his opinion that the charge was very reasonable and must be paid. They deducted, however, a sum of £59 2s which it was claimed Mason owed the Government as the balance of his expenses account in recruiting for the Militia in 1862.

Clayton acquired some influence with the Government as his son-in-law, Julius Vogel, drew the reins of power into his hands. In October 1868 he forwarded a photograph of the design for Government House, selected by Mr Weld, and offered, as the fee had already been half paid, to supervise the job for the remaining 2½ percent. He signed himself as late of Mason and Clayton. On 26 November he was appointed by Minute to carry out the work and nearly three months later he claimed £300 from Felix Wakefield, Secretary to the Government House Commission, for professional services.

He was no doubt glad of the work for in July 1868 he had been reduced to offering his services to the Superintendent in making good the damage to roads and bridges caused by recent floods. 'I was appointed by Sir William Denison (a Civil Engineer of eminence) Engineer of Roads and Bridges in the Northern districts of Tasmania which appointment I held for five years when the colony was divided into road districts and the office abolished.'[1] Such worries were now overcome by his appointment in April 1869 to the newly created post of Colonial Architect at a somewhat miserly salary of £200 a year but with a commission on certain works and permission to practise privately.[2] Mason may well have smiled wryly in recollection of Hobson's refusal to allow him this designation, twenty-nine years before.

With Clayton's removal to Wellington the loose ends of the old practice in Dunedin appear to have been tied up to some extent by N. Y. A. Wales[3] who had been originally employed by Mason as clerk of works on the Bank of New Zealand building. He had acted in the same capacity for the difficult Post Office job and then moved to Port Chalmers to supervise the construction of the graving dock, an important and arduous task lasting two years. The dock was completed on 6 April 1871 with general praise for the part Wales had played.

In the same month that Wales ended his work with the graving dock, April 1871, he and Mason opened an office under the style of Mason and Wales. Wales, of course, had had no strict architectural training but nor had many men describing themselves as architects at that time. His matter-of-fact approach to the profession, untroubled by fine points of aesthetics, seems to have appealed to Mason. What he had was an outstanding knowledge of the practical side of building and a sound head which soon after this took him into Parliament and subsequently made him Mayor of Dunedin. He had also an outstanding military career in which he rose from the ranks to be a lieutenant-colonel of militia and honorary colonel of volunteers. While at Port Chalmers he had apparently been commissioned to design the new Presbyterian church there. He called for tenders in February 1871. What would have been more natural than to ask the advice of his old employer, Mason, with whom he had been and always would be on the best of terms?

Mason, it would seem, had been living quietly in London Street since giving up his interests in North Otago. He appeared occasionally in the news – as one of those presented to the new Governor, Sir George Bowen, at a levee on 31 March, or as a candidate for the Provincial Council three weeks earlier. Seven councillors were elected from a field of twenty in which Mason polled ninth. In his one reported election address he spoke on immigration and the Public Works Act, averring that the country must borrow to carry out public works and that more people and more capital were needed for building railways. He advocated making a large proportion of the land in the hands of squatters available to immigrant farmers with families and some capital. He did not approve the use of prison labour but preferred the more humanitarian American system of teaching prisoners a trade and insisted that released prisoners should not be turned adrift with nothing in their pockets. He stated that no class of public works would give such an immediate return as the supply of water to the goldfields.

Church affairs occupied him also. At the Diocesan Synod in March he represented Otepopo, Hampden and Moeraki and was appointed to the Board of Nominators. He became a vestryman at St Paul's and with Henry Howarth led the procession into church at the consecration of Bishop Nevill in the following June. Dunedin was settling down. From the brash settlement of the previous decade the provincial capital was

[1] National Archives, O.P.4.
[2] *Otago Witness*, 17 April 1869.
[3] Nathaniel Young Armstrong Wales (1832-1903) was born in Northumberland, educated at Jedburgh, Scotland, and went to Dunedin from Victoria in 1861. On termination of the Post Office contract he received from Mason and Clayton a testimonial which said 'In parting we have to express our great satisfaction at the able and honourable manner in which you have discharged your duties as Clerk of Works over a period of nearly four years, notwithstanding the difficult and unpleasant nature those duties often assumed.'

emerging. In the same month as Nevill's consecration the University opened its doors in, of all places, the Post Office building.

The new partnership of Mason and Wales set up its offices in a building owned by the New Zealand Insurance Company in High Street. Where Mason's practice in the preceding decade had been largely concerned with putting up offices for the Provincial Government or impressive buildings for banking houses, this new phase was less spectacular. In the next three years before he again retired, they built many houses, shops and offices but few public buildings other than churches. Probably the two most outstanding buildings were St Matthew's Church and Bishopscourt, the latter now forming part of Columba College.

Houses form an interesting group for they ranged from the stone magnificence of Bishopscourt, a house which was in no way inferior to the better country houses built in England at that time, to such a place as Keith Hall at East Taieri, a smallish wooden house remarkable for a floor plan which bears strong resemblances to the accepted planning of many houses built in New Zealand since the Second World War. (Plate 98.)

Bishop Nevill, a man with full sympathy for the fine arts, visited New Zealand in 1870 at the instigation of Bishop Selwyn who was by this time installed at Lichfield. The unfortunate episode of Henry Lascelles Jenner's[4] rejection by the new See of Dunedin, after his consecration by the Archbishop of Canterbury, an affair in which Mason's associates, R. B. Martin and E. C. Quick, had taken a leading part, had been dealt with by the General Synod of February 1871 which Nevill had attended at the invitation of the Primate, the Bishop of Christchurch. The Dunedin Diocesan Synod, meeting in March, then sent an invitation to Nevill, who was waiting in Queenstown, to accept nomination as their Bishop. Following his consecration in June he left soon afterwards for England to wind up his affairs and raise funds for the diocese, but instructed Mason in the building of Bishopscourt before he went. The diocese, being without funds, pledged itself to find a sum of £2,500 for the building of a 'See House' on which Nevill was to spend what he thought fit, with the condition that the £2,500 be paid him with interest within ten years. Expenditure in excess of £2,500 was to be paid from Nevill's own resources. Nevill at once purchased twenty-five acres at Roslyn and accepted Mason and Wales's design for the house, which altogether cost him more than double the amount the Diocese had undertaken to provide. He gave as his reason for building such a large house, his plan to receive students for the ministry to live with him. The arrangement produced a house (Plates 89,90) which was probably unequalled by any other in the country at that time, though other houses of some magnificence were to be built in Auckland or Canterbury, or in Dunedin itself, within the next few years. Nevill moved into it, still unfinished, on his return from England in November 1872.

Not unexpectedly the style of the house was a freely detailed Gothic somewhere between Perpendicular and Elizabethan. It was built by David Hunter in grey Caversham stone with facings and quoins of Oamaru stone. Inside, much of the woodwork is walnut, ceilings are plastered or moulded papiermache and floors in the hallways are Minton-tiled. With its tall mullioned and transomed windows, square dripstones, distinctive terminals to the gable verges and high elaborate chimneys it recalls the school Mason designed for Bishop Selwyn in 1845. It is disconcerting on closer examination to realise that the sashes in the gables and in the bay windows

[4]Jenner was at one time secretary of the architecturally-minded Camden Society.

are double hung, but by and large the amalgam is successful and the whole building masses up convincingly. Its 'all roundness' is in interesting contrast to the 'facade' architecture of Government House at Auckland. Rooms within the house are handsome, the only major criticism being of a meanness of dimension in the entrance hall and stairway. Additions have been made in the same style.

While Bishopscourt was building, Mason completed a large single-storeyed house, Grendon, for James Macassey (Plates 92-96). This place, in timber, differed completely from Bishopscourt and may have been largely Wales's design though the commission was certainly Mason's. It spreads widely as a colonial house on an open site might be expected to do, with rooms disposed on either side of a long transverse corridor and a subsidiary corridor forming an 'L' on the north-eastern end. There is a remarkable curving window occupying the whole north-western end of the drawing room but otherwise the house is chiefly notable for the freedom of its planning and its divorce from any accepted style. This kind of house continued to be built up to the time of the First World War. At Grendon the verandah is paved with Minton tiles and coloured figured glass makes its appearance in sidelights to the exterior door. There is an excellent iron gate and gateposts.

Even more modern in feeling is the much smaller house called Keith Hall (Plates 97,98) which was built for William Shand on the Taieri plain in 1873. Once again it is built round a transverse corridor but the extreme simplicity of approach and the reduced scale of the house, both in height and area, recall many houses built seventy and eighty years later. It forestalls the return to eighteenth century proportion which marked the early years of the next century. The Shand family, leading farmers at the Taieri, were good clients. For Mrs Barbara Shand, Mason built a 3,000-square-feet house, now demolished, at Green Island, and for James Shand in 1872 a bakehouse at Outram and substantial farm buildings at Abbotsford nearby. Another major house was built for Professor James Gow Black on the site of the old Vauxhall pleasure gardens beyond Anderson's Bay. It is not to be confused with a small house in the same area retained by Dr Black after he went to live in the University precincts. Black's house cost £1,300, Mrs Shand's £1,000, James Macassey's £1,484 and Bishop Nevill's £3,620. Keith Hall, however, cost only £500 and a whole host of small houses done by the firm at this time ranged from £140 for a concrete cottage to £619 for the rather unattractive two-storeyed North Dunedin Manse for Dr Copland (Plate 78) or £940 for a 'town residence' for Mr Frederick Muir. There were several pairs of houses – for Messrs Isaac and Marks in Hope Street and for Mr M. Fleming in Melville Street – and a row of seven in George Street, for A. T. Dunning, which were apparently never built.

The character of all these houses was considerably changed from those designed in the previous decade. No longer would they have taken their place unnoticed in an English setting. Though it is true that houses like them were being built on the outskirts of London or Birmingham or Liverpool, they seemed to take their inspiration as much from America as from England or, for that matter, Australia. Such books as Samuel Sloan's *Homestead Architecture*, first published in Philadelphia in 1866, provided models of Italian villas, Gothic cottages or Bracketed farmhouses which seemed eminently suited to the greater freedom in ways of living which New Zealand now shared with the United States, and the informality of planning and the irregularity which had been elevated into a virtue, found favour in Dunedin as elsewhere. The mixing of styles was less blatant and the houses were less tall, if only because there was no large class of servants for whom to provide attics; but the informality of the planning allowed additions and improvements, as in the States, in a fluid society where the owner might wish by these means to indicate his increasing importance or affluence. Not all American styles were immediately adopted however. Because Dunedin builders built ideally in masonry, it was left to timber-orientated Auckland to provide, twenty years later, the few good New Zealand examples of the so-called American Stick style,[5] a style which bore remarkable similarities to Frederick Thatcher's manner of building in timber, developed in Auckland either before or about the same time as the American style. There are, however, interesting examples of 'stick-work' in the South: it will be seen under the verandah canopy at Keith Hall in a form which recalls a similar use in the house called Maryhill at Otepopo in which Mason may well have had a hand though no documentation is available (Plate 17). The other major style typifying the 1870s in England and the United States, Norman Shaw's Manorial, is similarly lacking in Dunedin, perhaps because of the bulk implied, but it had a late flowering in Hawkes Bay and the Wairarapa district where F. de J. Clere of Wellington and C. Tilleard Natusch of Napier designed timber variants, sometimes crossed with the Stick style, for numbers of station homesteads around the turn of the century.

Commercial buildings – shops, warehouses, hotels and offices – were the mainstay of Mason and Wales's practice. For his old friend R. B. Martin, Mason designed both offices and a warehouse in High Street and included in them an office for Robert Campbell from Oamaru, thus forming an architectural association which culminated in Otekaike House built by Wales for Campbell in 1876.[6] His association with Job Wain likewise bore fruit for Wales rather than himself. In this period the firm altered Wain's Hotel in Manse Street and formed a billiards saloon for him in the old Masonic hall in Moray Place but, in 1878, soon after Mason's final retirement, Wales had the pleasure of designing the splendid new hotel in Princes Street which has since been one of Dunedin's most interesting and frequented buildings. Buildings which seem to typify the period are the premises (Plate 83) for the *Otago Daily Times*, 1873, and those for A. T. Dunning and Thomson Strang and Company built as neighbours to each other in the same year, to replace earlier buildings destroyed by fire. (Plate 84.) All three buildings are plastered brick with flat-arched window openings as wide or wider than the wall space between them. The *Times* building has decorative hoods over the entrances and the other two buildings have similar hoods over the windows of the intermediate floors. Floor levels are marked by moulded bands in character with the very modest cornices and low parapets. Over the ground floor fronts of the Thomson Strang and the Dunning buildings, the use of iron girders permitted wide spans for shop display fronts. The careful handling of these very simple elements shows a more practised hand than, let us say, the shops in George Street for Mr Chiaroni, the picture framer and print dealer, though these were built at much the same time. There, vases on the parapet and other superfluous ornament destroy the very kind of distinction which, presumably, they were intended to give.

[5]Henry-Russell Hitchcock, *Architecture, Nineteenth and Twentieth Centuries*. London, 1958. p. 263-64.
[6]Otekaike is interesting among New Zealand houses as being perhaps the first to have a lofty, pillared and galleried hall, the full height of the house. It claimed unmistakably to be a mansion. John Burnside, sometimes described as the first New Zealand-born architect, worked on the drawings for Otekaike while training in Mason and Wales's office.

In the following year, 1874, Mason designed Dunedin's (and, it was claimed, Australasia's) most luxurious dining rooms for his old acquaintances, the Watson brothers, in whose long-room at the Exchange Hotel in Shortland Crescent he had presided over meetings of the Auckland Farmers' Club, twenty years before. The facade of this three-storeyed building in High Street, immediately next to the Grand Hotel, laid emphasis on the intermediate floor, a kind of *piano nobile*, not only through its greater height but also through the denticulation of the wall surface between and over the semi-circular heads of the three great twelve-feet-high windows. (Plate 87.) This floor was carried at street level on freestanding columns spanned by an iron girder. The effect was not particularly beautiful but at least it had character, that most sought-after Victorian architectural virtue. The building cost £5,580.

For a site round the corner from Dunning's buildings, in Moray Place, the firm now prepared drawings for a new hall intended to be called the City Hall but more often known as the Choral Hall or, for a brief period until 1886, as the Temperance Hall. This was commissioned by a Mr R. G. West who was conductor of the Choral Society until 1873 in which year, on a hot night, he was so lacking in proper feeling as to rehearse the ladies of the choir in shirt sleeves and was accordingly required by the gentlemen to resign. Whether this loss of position affected the proposals or whether they ran into financial trouble is not, at present, clear, but the finished product (Plate 88) was much less interesting than the description given by the *Otago Witness* of 30 August 1873. It would seem that the narrow corner frontage to Princes Street, left after the construction of Dunning's building, had been intended to be brought in for entrances and for a double staircase branching right and left to the main galleried hall, 100 feet long by 35 feet high, with a width of 35 feet at the orchestra and 45 feet at the back. Particular attention was to be paid to acoustics. The Moray Place frontage was to have had a pilastered ground floor and second and third floors with three-quarter, fluted Corinthian columns all surmounted by a pediment. 'Undoubtedly', said the *Witness* reporter, 'a harmonious whole different from any building yet erected in Dunedin.' The drawings were exhibited at the Club Hotel which seems to indicate that West was looking for financial backing, but his lack of success may be estimated by the modest nature of the building finally erected to occupy only the Moray Place frontage – no Corinthian columns, no ornamental vases and no pediment.

Churches, of course, had their share of the partnership's attention. All Saints', the nave of which, with a temporary sanctuary, had been built by Mason and Clayton in 1865, was now completed by Mason and Wales with transepts, chancel and sanctuary in the same style. The foundation stone of St Matthew's, at the corner of Stafford Street and Hope Street, was laid with Masonic ceremony on 11 July 1873. This grey stone church with once white quoins and door and window dressings, built by James Gore, contractor, at a cost of £4,854, is probably the most successful of all Mason's ecclesiastical commissions and accords remarkably closely with accepted practice in England and the United States at that time. It is in the English style following the reaction against French and Italian models begun by Street, Pearson, and Bodley about this time and promulgated by magazines like the *Building News* (to which Mason subscribed) in drawings reproduced by the new photo-lithographic process. St Matthew's (which was first to have been called St Thomas's) is cruciform in plan with side aisles, and has a well-proportioned broach tower at the south-west end of the nave over the main entrance porch. Internally it has octagonal piers to the nave, a clerestorey lit by quatrefoil windows in circular openings and a timber roof with simply decorated braces under the collars and principals. The aisles are lit by single lancets and three lancets, the middle one taller than its neighbours, light each of the transepts and the west end. (Plates 80, 81). The chancel is apsidal and is unequal to the rest of the building. The experiments made with tiles, pattern, and colour at All Saints' are here nowhere evident.

The Scotch settlers, intensely proud of their First Church on Bell Hill, had before this set the stage for a comic opera affair in building Knox Church in George Street. They apparently invited architects to submit designs, for Mason and Wales employed George O'Brien to draw a perspective of their proposals in May 1872 and then received a premium of £25 from the trustees in that same month. But this was not the beginning. Five months earlier R. A. Lawson, the architect for First Church and a natural choice on the present occasion, had called for tenders on plans he had drawn and had been unable to obtain a satisfactory price. Now, having awarded Mason and Wales a premium, the trustees delayed action until July when they decided to adopt a design submitted by David Hunter, no architect but the builder of First Church. This evidently profited them nothing for in October Mason's former partner, David Ross, advertised for tenders and got as far as having the foundation stone laid on 26 November. But he too ran into trouble and before the job had progressed at all Lawson was brought back. Mason and Wales, well out of this architectural *mêlée*, were employed in September 1873, to examine correspondence and report on the rights and wrongs of the case.

David Hunter was not the only builder to mix in an architecural situation. The rather grand woolstores designed by the firm for Driver Stewart and Company, near the wharves at the foot of Rattray Street, were expanded by the builder, Walter Bell, from one storey to two and were then claimed by him for credit. Whether the bold detailing of parts of this building is attributable to architect or builder it is therefore impossible to say. Warehouses were, however, completed for numbers of other clients notably Cargill McLean and Company (£3,168), John Edmond and Company (£1,784) and Ross and Glendining (£2,250). Of these, the work for Ross and Glendining (Plate 86) took the form of additions to an existing building in Stafford Street next to the Provincial Hotel and included the highly decorated street front with paired Venetian windows and free-standing columns with sculpted capitals. As with Watsons' the size of the windows is remarkable.[7] The style in much modified form was also used for the offices of the Standard Insurance Company in Princes Street (Plate 85) undertaken shortly before Mason's final retirement.

Mason's retirement came at the end of September 1874 when a number of commissions including additions to the Otepopo Presbyterian Church and alterations for the Dunedin Savings Bank had been recently received. Almost certainly he planned the Otepopo Church alterations (Plate 99) for they take a leaf from Colonel Mould's book in his additions to St Paul's, Auckland, and make use of transepts to provide extra accommodation. The tower and spire, placed rather oddly at forty-five degrees in an angle of the crossing, echo St Paul's and, even more closely, St James's, Bright-

[7]A few years later Wales extended glazing to its limits, for that time, with his design for the Auckland warehouse of Sargood, Son and Ewen in Victoria Street.

lingsea, designed by Mason thirty-six years before. But for some time he had been giving less time to the practice. The reason is not hard to find. On 22 September 1873, his wife Sarah had died after years of ill-health. He did not grieve long but on 20 December 1873 in St Paul's Church, Dunedin, married a widow, thirty years younger than himself, Catherine Fenn.

Catherine, or Kate as she was always known, was the daughter of Joseph Allison of Bilby, a good property north of Retford in Nottinghamshire. Her mother, born Elizabeth Hodgkinson, belonged to another well-known north Nottinghamshire family and was a first cousin of Samuel Hodgkinson, a surgeon settler in Canterbury in the eighteen fifties, who had returned to England for a visit in 1857. The close friendship as well as the marriage ties existing between the Allison and Hodgkinson families would have ensured that Kate, seventeen years old at the time of cousin Samuel's visit, heard much in praise of New Zealand. When she married John Fenn, ten years later, the young couple emigrated. Her husband came of a family notable in the history of the Church of England in the nineteenth century, his father, Joseph Fenn, Minister of Blackheath Park Chapel in Kent, having been a London barrister who gave up brilliant prospects to become a missionary in the Malabar Syrian Church, whose members lived mainly in the Indian states of Travancore and Cochin, the Christians of St Thomas, originally a Nestorian church but reorganized by the Portuguese and then the Dutch who had brought a Syrian Metropolitan from Antioch to preside over them. Joseph Fenn had many sons of whom eight (but not the sixth, John) were at Cambridge: Christopher Cyprian Fenn became general secretary of the Church Missionary Society, Joseph Finch Fenn (whose son also came to New Zealand) was a Canon of Gloucester, Thomas Foster Fenn was headmaster at Trent College, David was Canon of St Paul's Covent Garden and Nathaniel was Vicar of Loughton in Sussex. Another, curiously named William Mason, probably in honour of a missionary of that name once stationed in Canada, was conduct master at Eton and was said to have refused the bishopric of Brisbane.

From May 1860 to June 1861 the Samuel Hodgkinsons[8] lived in Dunedin in a cottage at Caversham Rise and then moved south to Riverton until their house was built at Mount Fairfax, a property they had bought under the Longwood Range. Their young relatives, the Fenns, settled in Dunedin in York Place (their name appears in the first pew book of St Paul's Church) but were soon overtaken by disaster. John Fenn sickened and died on 3 July 1868 when only thirty-three years old. Instead of turning tail, home to England, Kate stayed on. Fenn seems to have left no estate of value but his widow evidently had some resources, perhaps from the estate of her father who had died in 1860. Their extent may be gauged from the fact that Mason made a will in 1875 leaving £2,000 to her sister, no doubt to offset the circumstance that, before the Married Women's Property Act, a woman's property became her husband's possession. Later, in 1877, Kate's uncle William Allison, a physician at Retford, died leaving £12,000 to be shared between his sister, five nieces including Kate, and one nephew.

Where Mason met her is not known. They were both parishioners of St Paul's Church and it is not impossible that Kate had become a member of the Mason household to care for poor sick Sarah. Kate made him a good wife. His first gift to her was a piano, an amenity Sarah had evidently done

[8]Hodgkinson declined nomination for the superintendency of Southland but became a member of the Executive and sat in Parliament from 1876 to 1890 as member for Riverton. His manuscript 'Autobiographical Sketch' written in 1903, is in the Hocken Library.

without since the sale of her cottage piano at Howick twelve years before. The newly-married pair had both suffered sadness in their lives and no doubt needed the kind of help and companionship each could give the other.

The partnership of Mason and Wales was dissolved on 30 September 1874, and two years later the Masons removed themselves to Queenstown. For those two years nothing is known of their activities but it is not unlikely that they visited England. If Mason still hoped for a son, his hope was not to be fulfilled; and, had Sarah's son, William, still been alive, he would have been more than forty years old.

18. William and Kate Mason, c. 1885.

XVI   QUEENSTOWN AND PARADISE

Every man, he observed, at last wishes for retreat; he sees his expectations frustrated in the world, and begins to wean himself from it, and to prepare for everlasting separation. – James Boswell, *The Life of Samuel Johnson, LL.D.*

Queenstown in 1877 was a straggling settlement of fewer than 1,000 people beside an alpine lake of such beauty that it already drew tourists from all parts of the world. Anthony Trollope visiting it five years previously had been struck by the town's unexpectedly English appearance: 'It is built close down upon the water, and is surrounded by mountains. . . . There are many towns so placed in Switzerland, and on the Italian lakes, – which in position this New Zealand mining borough much more closely resembles than anything at home; but the houses, and something in the fashion of the streets, the outside uses and bearings of the place declare it to be unmistakably English.'[1]

The Masons' stay in Queenstown was probably at first in the nature of an experiment, for the London Street house was not finally sold until 1879 – for £1,790 – but their affection for the town and its superb setting quickly grew. They rented a house which had been the home of Richmond Beetham, son-in-law of William Swainson, the naturalist, and for the previous twelve years goldfields warden and resident magistrate for Wakatipu. From its windows and elevated garden they looked obliquely down the long wall of the Remarkables, and across Queenstown Bay to Walter Peak.

The town itself, founded in 1862 after the discovery of great quantities of gold in the nearby gorges, gullies and rivers, had grown quickly and at this time supported two architects, F. W. Burwell and John Turner. Years before, Mason had designed temporary premises for the Bank of New Zealand there, but these had been replaced in 1873. His account books for 1871, preserved in the Dunedin office of Mason and Wales, show periodic payments from May to July of a total of £27 to a Mr Burrell; in August 1872 they show a payment of £2 10s. for George O'Brien's perspective drawing of the Queenstown church and in March 1875 N. Y. A. Wales's account shows a credit of £21 for an undetailed payment by Wesley Turton. The proposed building for the Queenstown church evidently came to nothing. The other two items are noticed because of their probable connection with the single-storeyed stone villa called

[1]Anthony Trollope, *Australia and New Zealand*. London, 1873. Volume II, p. 331.

Hawkshead (Plate 19) which seems to have been built in the early seventies and which is sometimes connected with Mason's name. Its owner, Wesley Turton, was a Queenstown lawyer who had prospered greatly from the litigation of gold-happy miners.

It is said[2] that the house was built entirely out of the fees paid by a miner named Grace in defending a claim for £12,000 damages brought against him by the owner of a neighbouring claim. Whatever the truth of the matter, Hawkshead was a remarkable house to find in Queenstown at that date. Marble fireplaces graced all the main rooms, hot and cold water emerged from porcelain lion masks over elaborate wash basins in the bedrooms, while the bathroom, the size of many living rooms, was equipped with an intricate wrought-iron shower screen and a turkish bath cabinet in addition to all the usual fittings. The architecture of the house is compatible with much of Mason's work and it may be that the payments to 'Mr Burrell' were made to Mr Burwell for local supervision. On the other hand Turton employed John Turner on other minor work in 1874. Burwell was the architect for many of Queenstown's well-known buildings, the Courthouse (1875) and Council Chambers among them, and he later carried out such commissions as the Bank of New Zealand in Invercargill. Turner evidently had some experience of naval architecture and designed the lake steamer *Antrim*.

Mason's diary,[3] written at Queenstown, records that he was planning a house in May 1877 for John Butement of the 54,000 acre North Station, at the head of the lake, but no further involvement with architecture is known. Instead the diary is concerned with the *minutiae* of day to day living: 'Played croquet in the afternoon . . . Piano and pictures arrived . . . Mr Jones [the parson] assisted us to unpack . . . joined us in a game of croquet . . . Kate, Lucy and self went out in the morning to pay bills . . . High wind all night. Lake particularly high . . . letter stating Buller's book was lost . . . Mowing machine arrived . . . Sat on Bench for three hours . . . putting ferns in books all day . . . Posted reply to Mr Wilson enclosing Bill for £1000 . . . Went to church in the evening . . . Mr Kirk [?Thomas Kirk, the botanist] called and looked at the ferns . . . Kate and Lucy went to purchase tobacco for I had discovered aphis on the vines. Smoked them with tobacco . . . went to head of lake . . . went up tramway collected a new fern . . . returned by steamer. Mr and Mrs Selwin called [John Richardson Selwyn, about to be consecrated Bishop of Melanesia] . . . packed fern books for Annie and my mother . . . Eichardt [Captain Albert Eichardt of the Queen's Arms Hotel] here in the evening. Judge Harvey came . . . broached new cask of beer . . . Mr Turton, Mr Adair, Miss Purchas, Mr Jones and Smith [his old Auckland friend John Alexander Smith, then of Napier] dined with us in commemoration of my birthday . . . Smythies came to breakfast . . . Saddle arrived . . . Mr & Mrs Finn came to dinner [H. J. Finn, see below] . . . building bathroom with Mr Jones . . . Sir John Richardson [Speaker of the Legislative Council] came up and stayed with us . . . Kate and I went out rabbit shooting. Got one. Went up one side and down the other of Queenstown hill . . . Received a letter from Cook & Son announcing Peter Williams intention of entering an action in equity against me . . . wrote to Fulton re settlement of Kate's money on her self . . . Hodgkins [W. M. Hodgkins, the water-colourist] called in the afternoon.'

In September they returned from a visit to Dunedin, even then an

[2]F. W. G. Miller, *Golden Days of Lake County.* Dunedin, 1949. p. 141-43.
[3]Office of Mason and Wales, Dunedin. The firm founded by Mason has remained one of the most important architectural offices in the country, carried on by N. Y. A. Wales's son, grandson and great-grandson.

19. Hawkshead, Queenstown.

19a. Hawkshead, detail of veranda.

arduous journey, but less so than Trollope's snow-impeded traverse of the road in the opposite direction when the journey had taken six days and 'the inns at which we stopped were not delightful.'[4] They brought with them a servant girl and all slept the night at Eichardt's before opening the house next morning. Mason set down the costs of the journey:

'Cab fare to station		5.	6
Railway fare for 3 – 15s.	2.	5.	0
Van Luggage		2.	0
Dinner at Lawrence		5.	6
Coach fare from Lawrence to Queenstown	10.	10.	0
Dinner or supper, beds and coffee in morning, Teviot		18.	0
Breakfast at Stoney creek		7.	6
Dinner at Cromwell		8.	0
	15.	1.	6
Eichardts Tea breakfast & beds	2.	12.	6'

As well as the servant girl they brought back cuttings and shrubs from the garden at London Street. Their residence in Queenstown now seemed to be confirmed. He resumed his diary but only for a few weeks before he gave it up. 'Saw Mr McArdell [partner with J. A. Hodge in the Mt Nicholas run] about proposed Steamer on the Lake. Saw Women who wanted me to attend a railway meeting at 7, had it postponed until Tuesday. Telegraphed Kincaid & McQueen re steamer. Had a long conversation with Mr Johnstone re quarrel with Mr Finn . . . Received telegram from Kincaid & McQueen re Steamer £7000 . . . Mr Finn came in . . . Called with Mr McArdell on Robertson & Co re steamer. Propose that should we obtain Govt subsidy it should be offered to their Co if they would undertake to put steamer on the Lake . . . Stove for greenhouse came . . . three cucumbers up . . . wrote to Beetham offering £750 0s. 0d. to buy.'

So, with many callers and many calls, time passed. Peter Williams won his action which depended on the purchasing clause in the agreement for lease of the Otepopo land and Mason had to pay £500. Kate became a major shareholder in the Wakatipu Steam Navigation Company and Mr Finn became chief villain in the piece.

Mason, by 1879, was not only sitting on the Bench but was a member of the Hospital Board and the Library Committee and became Chairman of the Licensing Committee. In the Parliamentary elections of 1879 he and his erstwhile friend, Finn, were both candidates for the Wakatipu seat in opposition to the sitting member Henry Manders, who had earlier been a mining agent and then editor of the *Lake Wakatip Mail*, and had two years before suffered a sordid and ridiculous persecution by his housekeeper which was published throughout the country.[5] Hugh Joseph Finn (1847-1927) was an Irish-born lawyer who had been educated at the Jesuit College at Amiens, served for a short time with the Papal Zouaves and came to New Zealand by way of Melbourne in 1874. Though no longer a very good Catholic, he made no scruple about securing the Catholic vote with promises of educational preference, and further promised a railway to Martin's Bay and the benefits of a 'million dollar' loan. He not unnaturally beat Mason to the post with 266 votes to Mason's 232 and Manders's 143. Both Mason and Manders spoke after the election, Mason bitterly and Manders, who had campaigned without a committee, with more reserve. 'He could not but thank Mr Manders', said Mason, 'for the handsome manner in which he had conducted the election; he had acted as a gentleman throughout, and the speaker should always treat him as such; but the less he said about the other candidate the better.'[6] A rumour went about that the legality of Finn's election would be contested and three weeks later the *Lake Wakatip Mail*[7] reported from Wellington that 'There has been considerable amusement in the lobbies today, owing to Mr Mason having written to Mr Sheehan (ex-Minister) asking for his assistance in unseating Mr Finn; and saying he would support Sir George Grey. At the same time Mr McLean[8] received a telegram from Mr Mason asking for his assistance and offering to support Mr Hall if successful. Mr Turton has wired Mr Pyke[9] on the subject, but all the members decline to interfere. Mr Finn is prepared for a petition.'

Mason's rancour stayed with him a long time. Nothing, of course, came of the proposed petition though the *Southland News* lost no time in accusing Finn of charlatanism. Altogether it developed into a disagreeable year, for Mason had to move house through failure to strike a bargain with Beetham, Wales was finding conditions difficult for architecture in Dunedin and there was a general tightening up of financial arrangements as the long slump of the late seventies and early eighties made itself felt. The new house was less satisfactory and neither Mason nor Kate was very well. Wales wrote philosophically from Dunedin toying with the idea of a week's fishing at the head of the lake. 'But as Stevenson is away there is no one I can leave in charge and I am living in hope that I may be wanted one morning.'[10] Investments had one bright spot in that the Shag Point coal mine was apparently thriving, and Marianne North, the English botanist, apparently saw nothing to dismay her when, in 1880, she visited 'Mr and Mrs M. . . . those nice people', and found them acclimatizing Engl sh song-birds for release.[11]

The head of the lake had always been for Queenstown people a fabulous place, feared by the hotelkeepers lest its beauty take tourists and travellers from their own doors. There the glacier-fed Rees and Dart rivers enter the lake and the great shoulders of Earnslaw, topping 9,000 feet, seem to fill the sky. W. G. Rees, the man who had given W. G. Grace his first cricket bat, had established a sheep station there in 1862 and sold it to John Butement in 1864. Another well-known Dunedin family was represented in the Rees valley by H. W. Valpy. Twelve miles from the Glenorchy landing where Butement had his headquarters, beyond a fine birch forest, the dark waters of Diamond Lake reflect Mount Alfred and here on the northern shore a legendary character, Joseph Cyprian Fenn, nephew of Kate Mason's first husband and son of Joseph Finch Fenn, Canon of Gloucester, had taken up a considerable holding obtained partly by grant and partly by purchase from James Whitbourne whose name is commemorated in the Whitbourne glacier. He had a grant also of 516 acres on the south-west side of Mount Alfred, fronting the Dart river, but this he leased to G. S. Fulton in 1892.

Beyond Fenn's Diamond Lake block was the area known as Paradise Flat – from the congregation there of the paradise duck – a grassy stretch of land at the 1700 feet level. This now engaged Mason's interest and he selected an area of 317 acres (sections 29, 30, 31, 32, 33, 39, 42, Block II) which gave him frontages of half a mile to the Dart river, which is three quarters of a mile wide in this part, and a few chains to Diamond Lake. The place is so well named that it has sometimes been argued whether the

[6] *Lake Wakatip Mail*, 20 September 1879.
[7] 10 October 1879.
[8] Sir George McLean, not at that time knighted, was a member of the Vogel and Atkinson administrations and was well-known to Mason as a partner in Cargill McLean and Company, and a former Dunedin manager of the Bank of New Zealand.
[9] Vincent Pyke, M.H.R., closely associated with the goldfields, had been the editor of *Dunedin Punch*.
[10] Wales to Mason, 9 December 1879. Thomas Stevenson, briefly in partnership with Wales, died at Russell, Bay of Islands, 8 December 1881, at the age of twenty-nine. It is probable that he had been responsible for the design of Iona Church at Port Chalmers, superbly sited and one of the finest examples of Gothic Revival work in New Zealand.
[11] Mrs John Addington Symonds (ed.). *Recollections of a Happy Life being the Autobiography of Marianne North*. London, 1892. Volume II, p. 182.

20. *The Dart Valley from Paradise.*

duck was named from it or it from the duck. But quite clearly the name was used before the Masons went there to live and the duck, which is really a goose, was called paradise, said improbably to be a corruption from the Maori name *putangitangi*, at least as early as 1843 when Ernst Dieffenbach published his *Travels in New Zealand*. The Maori name refers to the bird's mournful cry, remarked on by Samuel Butler: 'The paradise duck is a beautiful bird. The male appears black, with white on the wing, when flying: when on the ground, however, it shows some dark greys and glossy greens and russets, which make him very handsome. . . . He says "whiz" through his throat, and dwells a long time on the "z". He is about the size of a farm-yard duck. The plumage of the female is really gorgeous. Her head is pure white, and her body beautifully coloured with greens and russets and white. She screams, and does not say "whiz". . . . The old birds are very bad eating. I rather believe they are aware of this, for they are very bold, and come very close to us. . . . Being geese, and not ducks, they eat grass.'[12]

Here at Paradise Flat, slightly elevated above both river and lake, Mason built a small house in 1883 and called it Eden Grove in allusion to its site, but also in recollection of the house of that name which he had once owned in Auckland. The house faces the lake with a distant view of the Rees Valley and the Richardson mountains. Beech forest grows close behind it with Mount Alfred giving shelter on the south. Immediately north the turrets of Earnslaw seem to rise straight out of the fields. From the banks of the Dart the sight of peak after peak – Momus, Somnus, Nox, Chaos, Cosmos and Poseidon – engraves itself on the memory.

Here the Auckland artist, Charles Blomfield, exploring these regions in the early summer of 1884, was caught in a thunderstorm and 'made for shelter to a house in the distance. On receiving a kind invitation to enter I saw at once that this was something more than a shepherd's hut or runholder's shanty. The house was well built, and furnished with grace and comfort; handsome pictures hung on the walls, and a well-stocked library filled up one side of the room. Feeling surprised at such signs of refinement in a place so far away from civilisation, and no doubt showing my surprise in my face, I soon learned that the owner of the house was Mr Mason, a retired architect, who has chosen this spot for his summer home. When he heard I was from Auckland he told me he was one of the earliest pioneers of Auckland; and that he was architect for Government House, St Paul's Church, and other public buildings in Auckland; and that after a successful career there, at Dunedin, and other places, he had settled down at Queenstown, but making a visit to the head of the lake last summer, he was so enamoured of the charming situation of his present home that he made up his mind to build there. He and his wife have now been living there for two months. They are both fond of grand scenery, and also of the study of botany, and find plenty of occupation in their favourite pursuits. He told me they had already found several new varieties of Alpine flowers. After partaking of Mrs Mason's kind hospitality, and the weather having cleared, Mr Mason took me to some of the best views round his place, and certainly for wild magnificence, combined with picturesque beauty, the scenery is equal to anything to be seen anywhere. . . . Just behind the residence, which is sheltered by magnificent beech forests, a grand view is obtained of the Valley of the Dart, and the wild precipitous mountains of the Humboldt and Forbes Ranges, seamed

[12]Samuel Butler, *A First Year in Canterbury Settlement*. Oxford, 1964. p. 107.

21. *Glenorchy*

with icy glaciers, peak beyond peak – a glorious vista vanishing into the clouds, and culminating in the snowy crown of Mount Cosmos, 8,000 feet high. "There," said Mr Mason, "tell my old Auckland friends how you found me here, amongst some of the grandest scenery in the world. People say I am mad, but that does not matter. I like it." '

The *New Zealand Herald* (7 February 1884), quoting Blomfield's letter, added that 'Mr Mason asked after a number of old Auckland residents, and took a great interest in Auckland matters, particularly the Art Gallery and Free Public Library. . . . Mr Mason showed Mr Blomfield a fine painting in his collection, by one of the old Dutch masters, valued at £150. It is quite on the cards that Mr Mason may yet present it to our Art Gallery, as a souvenir of the pleasant days he spent here, and in token of his interest in Auckland, her citizens and her future.'

Scenery, however, even on such a grand scale, does not in itself provide an occupation and here there were at first, and then only in summer, few of the callers the Masons had received in Queenstown. So Mason began, with the aid of a married couple, quite seriously to farm. In the beginning it was a matter of cultivation of oats and barley, with the aid of two single men, but in 1885 when, in a hand grown shaky, Mason once more began a diary, David Aitken and his wife moved into the staff cottage and farming operations began in earnest. English grasses were sown, Southdown sheep and stud cattle were brought up on the steamer *Antrim* and driven from the heads (as Glenorchy was usually called) to Paradise. A Brahma cock was obtained from England to improve the poultry. Turkeys were established. Pigs came from Christchurch. Aitken's trips to the heads were seldom fewer than twice a week, if not to collect stores and stock, then to take letters down or to bring back the mail bag. Wales, writing to Mrs Mason in October 1885, noted the stir of activity at Glenorchy as other settlers came in. He had seen them both in Dunedin the previous August when Mason had talks with Kincaid, McQueen and Company about the lake steamer and then went on to Invercargill.

J. C. Fenn, their neighbour, through whose land the Paradise road passed, might have been expected to provide them with some society but did not. Their relationship seems to have remained quite formal if not, at times, strained. This strange recluse, who had been a famous oarsman, rowed for Cambridge in 1877 and won the title of Champion of the Cam, seems to have been stirred from his solitariness only once, when in later years he proposed unwelcome marriage to the Aitkens' daughter. From Glenorchy the hotel proprietor, J. K. Birley, often made the journey to Paradise, sometimes driving the Masons in his trap when Mason himself, plagued by rheumatism, was unable to do so. Visitors in summer were taken climbing to Invincible in the Richardson range or up the slopes of Earnslaw: 'Mrs Mason, Alice Worthington, Mr Walker with Willie Prior ascended Mount Earnslaw for mountain lilies, brought down a quantity. Started at 9 a.m. and returned 7.30 p.m.' So reads Mason's diary.

Farming received a setback with the departure of the Aitkens to land of their own and Mason then conceived the idea of adding fifteen bedrooms to his house to provide accommodation for the tourists who were now finding their way to Paradise. So Eden Grove became a guest house with a Mr and Mrs Mark Harris to run it. The Harrises stayed for nearly two years and then David Aitken, always greatly favoured by Mrs Mason, took a six-year lease of the property from October 1890 and finally bought it three years later. The Aitken family remained there until 1932. The Masons moved down to Queenstown, to live for a while at Eichardt's Hotel, but left when objections were raised to Mrs Mason's spaniel, Dart.

As infirmity grew on the old man his mind had turned back to past days when the young men of Hobson's party set out to civilize a scarcely explored land. Dr Hocken, in Dunedin, had already begun his researches into that period and embodied them in a series of lectures which were later published under the title *Early History of New Zealand*. Reports of the fourth lecture had prompted a long letter from Eden Grove (Appendix II) about the forestalling of the French at Akaroa, early tensions between Auckland and Wellington, the inhabitants of Official Bay, the first Auckland land sale, and the mounted police under Captain Smart. Dr Hocken, who was not above recording that 'Daniel Wakefield . . . was a great rascal and ill treated his wife' or that 'Polack married the widow of Hart who escaped from his Sydney creditors by coming to Auckland in a piano case', was delighted to find this first-hand evidence from the sole survivor among Hobson's officials and prompted Dr Martin Chalmers, Mason's physician, to question him. Hocken's notebooks accordingly contain the following:

'Mason spoke highly of Lieut Shortland as an . . . intelligent man of strong opposition which often placed him in antagonism with the new-comers who had no good word for him. He [Mason] recognised my photograph of him in a moment, also those of de Thierry and Busby which he said were excellent. . . . de T. gave much trouble to the infant Govt with his letters – some a quire in length – re his fanciful pretentions to N.Z. These were all burnt in the fire of 1841. He was a clever man says Mason but apparently not quite "right". . . . Hobson had sailed much in the West Indies – his wife was a native of Bermuda & had a strain of native blood in her.'

Of the *New Zealand Herald and Auckland Gazette* Mason told Dr Chalmers: 'The plant and five men were brought from Hobart town. Amongst them were John Williamson afterwards editor of the *New Zealander* and Superintendent, Wilson of the *N.Z. Herald* and J. C. Moore afterwards Govt Printer. The original proprietors Major Richmond, Dr Johnson, W. Mason and Montefiore (Montefiore wrote more than anyone else) knew nothing of newspapers nor that they depend indeed on advertisements. They lost their money and were glad to sell the plant and paper to the Govt who constituted it as the *Auckland Standard*. The policy of the paper was against the Govt though three of the number (Richmond, Johnson and Mason) were connected with the Govt. This was owing to Cap. Hobson's officialism and often overbearing manner, also of Shortland and Coates. Hobson though honourable was often overbearing and passionate and had much of the quarter deck manner. Mr Wm Mason bought one of the first sections opposite Govt House, the street being a chain wide. One day some Maoris were employed erecting a fence in the middle of the street by Hobson's instructions. Mason complained; the Govr said "In a hot sunny climate like this what do you want with so wide a street, narrow ones are more suitable, more cool and shady, let the work go on." However, Mason insisted and gained his point. On his section was a spring. Hobson, learning this, said he would have a water tank built over it. Mason objected on the ground that the section with its spring was his. "No such thing," said the Govr "you may have bought the land but you

22. *William Mason, c. 1895.*

have no title to the water." Of course Mason won. Coates – the private
secretary – was troublesome. Petty tyranny like these begat enemies who
worried Hobson into his grave.'

Mason himself was nearing his grave. In 1894 he moved to Dunedin and
for three more years lived there quietly but more confidently with doctors
close to hand. It seemed natural enough to call in Dr Hocken. He himself
was not forgotten. The *Otago Witness* gave him pride of place in a series
of historical portraits and up to a fortnight before his death he maintained
his interest in the day by day happenings of the city whose physical shape
had been so largely his own creation.

In 1897 he was living at the Grand Hotel on the corner of High Street
and Princes Street which was then under the management of his old
clients, the Watson brothers. Built in 1883 to the designs of Louis Boldini,
the Grand Hotel was more lavish than any other New Zealand hotel. Its
galleried public spaces with great mosaic-tiled floor and glass roof dome,
and its handsome dining room, were matters of civic pride. But for Mason
its chief advantage must have been the not-long-invented electric lift,
perhaps the fruit of Sir Julius Vogel's curious visit to New Zealand in 1882
as the representative of the Electric Lighting Company.

Eighteen-ninety-seven marked the sixtieth anniversary of Queen
Victoria's accession to the throne, and Dunedin, not to be outdone by
lesser populations, determined to express the Empire's pride and glory
with all the revelry a good Scottish town might decently countenance.
The culmination of the festivities was timed for 23 June. Visitors flocked
in from the province to swell the population by more than a quarter.
Everywhere through the town, buildings were festooned with lights.
Shops set up prism lights and transparent portraits of the Queen. Candles
were placed in windows, gaslight was put to uses never attempted before
and that still remarkable illuminant, electricity, spelled out names and
loyal mottoes. Bonfires were built on the Peninsula heights and coloured
fires on the tops of buildings. From the windows of the Grand Hotel,
Mason might have looked across to the Colonial Bank whose design, as
the Post Office, had occupied him so long, or to the Provincial Council
Chambers in which he had partnered Clayton. Looking obliquely down
High Street to the waterfront, though his eyes were now dim, he might
have seen his *Times* newspaper building or the Garrison Hall and the
New Zealand Insurance building done by his later partner Wales.

He might have seen these preparations but death claimed the old man
on 22 June, the day before their culmination.

The festivities had their columns of praise in the newspapers. After it
was all over the obituaries for Mason appeared, informed and respectful,
but faintly astonished that anyone so linked with history should have
survived. The world's thoughts were already on the new century.

Kate Mason had him buried beside his first wife in the Northern
Cemetery in Dunedin and then travelled north to Auckland where she had
a tablet to his memory set up in St Paul's Church. But it was not the
St Paul's he had built. That had given way to street improvements in
1885. Auckland, the city of which he had been a founder, had grown far
bigger and grander than his native Ipswich.

Kate seems to have visited the Pacific Islands, stayed some time in
Wellington, and then gone back to Queenstown to live with her companion,
a daughter of James Macandrew, second Superintendent of Otago. She

was a considerable benefactor of the Queenstown Anglican Church and enjoyed the particular friendship of Dr Douglas, a bachelor of her own age, and of the Salmond family who were her neighbours in Sydney Street. Dr J. D. Salmond has recounted in his *Hearts of Gold*[13] how she arranged for the continuing support of a needy acquaintance during an absence in England, while Miss Mary Salmond recalls her own mother's insistence on her immediately visiting Mrs Mason each time she returned from University in Dunedin; and Miss Salmond would chide her mother with her wish 'to keep up with the aristocracy'. In 1914, in Dunedin, Kate too died.

St Mary's Church, Mornington, contains a memorial tablet to Catherine and William Mason and the brass lectern commemorates the architect. A few relics of the Masons are preserved at Arcadia House, Diamond Lake, books in the tiny Glenorchy library record their tastes and birthdays. But William Mason's memorial is his legacy to New Zealand architecture and the buildings for which he was responsible. Some of these have already been demolished, others are in imminent danger as their sites become too valuable to escape development. Their modern neighbours overshadow them and they seem to have shrunk in size, but their human scale still finds a response in those who appreciate that buildings, like people, were once individuals, before the race of giants stepped out of fable into the twentieth century.

[13]J. D. Salmond, *Hearts of Gold*. Dunedin, 1962. pp. 32-33.

XVII RETROSPECT

What is wanted in architecture, as in so many things, is a man. Shall we find a refuge in a Committee of Taste? We only multiply our feebleness and aggravate our deficiencies. But one suggestion might be made. No profession in England has done its duty until it has furnished its victim. . . . Even our boasted navy never achieved a great victory until it shot an admiral. Suppose an architect were hanged? Terror has its inspiration as well as competition.

                         – Benjamin Disraeli, *Tancred.* 1847.

How good were Mason's buildings and how did they compare with the work of other architects both in New Zealand and abroad?

First it is necessary to remember that he practised on his own account for nearly forty years during a period of fluctuating tastes and frequent revivals of styles, when architects everywhere were conscious of the need for a new kind of architecture but were so bemused by archaeology or historicism, and the insistence by such men as John Ruskin on the paramount importance of ornament, that they were quite unable to conceive anything better than the grudgingly approved Eclecticism which was elevated into a Style towards the end of the period – the practice of combining in one building the desirable features of several styles as opposed to the practice of designing different buildings in different styles according to whim, theories or realities of suitability, or preferences of clients. It is the latter practice which Professor Peter Collins[1] describes as Indifferentism and it seems fair, in these terms, to describe Mason as an Indifferentist for he seems to have been the only one among early New Zealand architects to have worked with reasonable success in each of the current nineteenth-century styles or revivals. But few men forget the principles in which they were trained and Mason clearly showed his preferences. He had his architectural beginnings in an age which valued proportion and had not yet fully accepted the proposition that visual pleasure in architecture may be derived instead from associations of images – a proposition which occupied architects throughout the Victorian period.

None of this is to claim for Mason any position as a theorist. His views remained fairly limited and it would be absurd to judge his work by recent standards. In his youth, the architect as such had only recently attained true professional status, divorced from earlier connections with the trade of building, but the scholarship he was now assumed to possess was still

[1]Peter Collins, *Changing Ideals in Modern Architecture.* London, 1965. pp. 117, 177.

concerned with the grammar of architecture and had not spread, except in a rather naive way, to philosophical and sociological argument as it was to do during the next century. Even such a familiar concept as space in architecture was not formally recognized in England until the latter half of the nineteenth century though it had always been implicit in any major work. Mason was more sensitive to landscape than to urban patterns and apparently saw his buildings standing alone without any particular relationship to their neighbours. This is hardly surprising since planning in the wider sense was a contradiction of Victorian individualism. But his original delight in the panoramas of land and sea, of forest, lake and mountain, remained undiminished.

The first New Zealand architects were necessarily men who had received their training in other places, nearly always Britain. Mason's fellow practitioners in Auckland, in the first years, were in two cases at least – Kempthorne and Thatcher – men of some distinction but were so far from being Indifferentists that neither found himself able to practise his profession in the full sense.

Sampson Kempthorne (1809-1873) arrived in the country in 1842 having already carried out a number of commissions in England; but the talents with which he was credited seem to have been little evidenced in these antipodes. It may be that he simply had good friends in England: he had joined with S. S. Teulon in submitting competition drawings for the new town hall and market place in Penzance in 1835[2] and was able to call on the young Gilbert Scott for assistance when engaged by the Poor Law Commissioners to design workhouses. He was described then as a good, kindly fellow[3] and perhaps he simply could not face up to the realities of the profession. But, with his considerable experience in church building and his intimate connection with the Church Missionary Society, he was employed by Bishop Selwyn, as a matter of course, for the building of St Stephen's Chapel at Parnell, St Thomas's Church at West Tamaki, and the Stone House at St John's College. Of these, only St Stephen's Chapel showed much merit and it very soon collapsed and was replaced by a wooden chapel designed by Frederick Thatcher. The other two buildings lasted a few years longer.

Kempthorne may be assumed to have been in full sympathy with the views of that extremely influential body, the Camden Society or Ecclesiologists, as they came to be called, men whom one suspects William Mason would have regarded as well-intentioned busybodies while respecting their less extreme views. Frederick Thatcher (1814-1890), like Kempthorne a member of the Institute of British Architects, landed at New Plymouth, became Superintendent of Works at Auckland in 1845 and shortly afterwards private secretary to the Governor, Sir George Grey. During his secretaryship, which lasted until October 1848 when he entered St John's College as resident architect and a candidate for holy orders, he superintended Selwyn's building programme at the College and also carried out some civil commissions such as stables for the Governor (1848) and a hospital (1847) for Auckland. He, too, subscribed to Ecclesiological doctrines. His competence seems to have made it unnecessary for any watching brief for which the bishop may have thought it necessary still to retain Mason's services, but from May 1846 until he became resident at St John's he had the help of Reader Wood who was described as Civic Bursar.[4] It will be remembered that Mason had designed a school for Selwyn

[2]H. M. Colvin, *A Biographical Dictionary of English Architects, 1660-1840.* London, 1954. p. 338.
[3]Basil Clarke, *Church Builders of the Nineteenth Century.* London, 1938. p. 162.
[4]'Senior Bursar's Abstract Book', Diocesan Office, Auckland.

(Plate 43) and examination of this drawing will show how different his approach was from Thatcher's. The plan is symmetrical about a centre line, the elevational treatment echoes his attachment to eighteenth century notions of proportion, only the steep-pitched roofs and the detail are Gothic and those in a fashion which Thatcher, now under Selwyn's influence, would probably have regarded as debased, the kind of thing which was well enough for Lambeth Palace, where Mason had first made its acquaintance, but unsatisfactory for this new diocese in the Southern Hemisphere.

Thatcher's one known building in England, the parsonage at Halton near Hastings[5] was itself in the same debased style but it must not be thought that he thenceforward became nothing more than the interpreter of Selwyn's architectural ideas. The hospital he designed for Auckland in 1847, before finally entering St John's, showed all the peculiarities later to be characterized as Selwyn-inspired. Selwyn's chaplain, W. C. Cotton, writing in his diary on 20 April 1848, referred to a suggestion he himself had made for the College hospital and noted that 'This improvement in his Peculiar style of building Mr Thatcher gladly introduced . . . '. This same improvement, the projection of the gables beyond the walls beneath 'in the manner of a Swiss building . . . securing the most vulnerable point viz the junction of the boards above and below the wallplate', was also incoporated in the town hospital as was the exposed framing which was another feature of Thatcher's 'Peculiar' style.

It is worthy of note that Cotton, so close in all ways to his bishop, had his own architectural connections of a most influential kind, for his brother-in-law, Sir Henry Acland, was the intimate friend of John Ruskin who had already published a widely noticed series of articles called 'The Poetry of Architecture' in the *Architectural Magazine*. Not many years later, in 1854, Acland was to embark on that most controversial of Gothic Revival buildings, the Oxford Museum, with Deane and Woodward as architects and Ruskin always at his elbow. 'Entirely satisfactory very few issues are or can be', wrote Ruskin; and ' . . . precedent has shown sufficiently, that very uncomfortable and useless rooms may be provided in all other styles as well as in Gothic.'[6]

Thatcher continued to supply designs for buildings for the diocese after his ordination as priest in 1853 and Bishop Selwyn's ledger book, preserved in the Auckland diocesan office, indicates that he was paid for these architectural services in addition to his work as a cleric. Thus he was responsible for old Bishopscourt at Parnell, 1863, (now known as Selwyn Court), for the nearby Deanery and Dr Kinder's house, both belonging to 1856 or 1857, and for several churches in the diocese up to his visit to England in the latter year. His best known work is undoubtedly St Paul's Church, Wellington, built after his return.

Besides Mason, Kempthorne, and Thatcher (and Edward Ashworth who had no practice), three other architects were in Auckland in those early years but, of the three, Reader Wood and James Baber were at first much engaged in land survey work and re-entered the architectural field in the following decade, making little impact design-wise, though no doubt carrying out a large number of commissions. Wood was responsible for the additions to the Northern Club premises in 1883, when he was President, but they were carried out in the manner of the original neo-Renaissance building designed by James Wrigley in 1867. Earlier than

[5]Alan Savidge, *The Parsonage in England*. London, 1964. pp. 129, 136; Margaret Alington, *Frederick Thatcher and St. Paul's*. Wellington, 1965. Plate 3.

[6]Acland and Ruskin, *The Oxford Museum*. London, 1859.

this, in 1854, he was commissioned as architect for the regrettable Parliament buildings about which it was sometimes said that he forgot the staircase and had to put it on the outside. Much more successful were the Melanesian Mission buildings at Mission Bay (1859), built in stone with steep shingled roofs, lattice windows and a broach-stop chimney in typical 'Selwyn' style. His partner James Baber took over the practice when Wood became Colonial Treasurer, a position in which the latter may be thought to have shown greater talent than as an architect,[7] but specialized in houses of which a number survive in the Remuera district. Together they had been responsible for additions to the old Queen Street wharf in 1862, and it would appear from a tenders advertisement of 1846 that Wood was the designer of the stone building in Fort Street, long familiar as Grahame's Bond.

This left Walter Robertson who arrived in Auckland from Sydney in 1847 and died suddenly in May 1851. Robertson, however, seven years Mason's senior, was probably nearest to him in the degree of professionalism in his approach to architecture and though none of his buildings is of great distinction they were nicely judged for the period and for the resources of his clients. He worked mainly in modified Georgian terms, or what might be called English vernacular, but frequently built in the local bluestone which gave his buildings a kind of Gothic gloom. It was a gloominess which failed to achieve the sublimity sometimes associated with that description. In fact it must be admitted that it sometimes had the appearance of an architecture for peasants. In the four years of his Auckland practice he was responsible for St Andrew's Church (without the portico or tower though a portico was included in his design), the multi-purpose original St Patrick's Cathedral, schools for the Wesleyans at Three Kings and for the Roman Catholics at Shoal Bay, the Methodist Chapel in High Street, the steam mill in Official Bay and the smelting house for the copper mine at Kawau Island. He also designed a number of houses, among them those for Dr Moffit in Princes Street, and Dr Ford near St John's, and extensions to the old Felton Mathew house then owned by Colonel Wynyard, and most notably, perhaps, the stone house called St Keven's, built for David Nathan but leased to Sir George Grey, who considerably altered it, after the burning of the first Government House.

Military building was of limited significance in the early years although Fort Britomart and the Albert Barracks were major features of the town. Britomart was built under the supervision and to the plans of George Graham, Clerk of Works in the Board of Ordnance (Royal Engineers) who was also chiefly responsible for laying out the Barracks. At the Barracks he had the assistance of E. I. Matthews who later described himself as an architect. More interesting from an architectural standpoint was Colonel Thomas R. Mould, C.B., Royal Engineers, who entered into the Government House controversy in 1856 (see Chapter 9) and while himself submitting a design to the Government, also reported on the proposals of Benjamin Mountfort. Mould extended St Paul's Church shortly after Mason's departure for Dunedin and about the same time designed a defensive police station and courthouse for Kohekohe in the Waikato, the plans of which, and the very pleasant Georgian elevations, are preserved in the Appendices to the Journals of the House of Representatives for 1865. It is not generally appreciated that the Royal Engineers maintained

[7] Wood's own house at 26-28 Brighton Road has considerable charm and character. No account is given here of G. E. Vaile who arrived in 1842 and carried out one or two minor architectural commissions as an architect-builder before taking up a commercial life.

a school in which the principles of architecture were taught and that men like Mould could therefore claim a sound training.

Mason's Government House (1856) was in a sense the second big architectural gesture in Auckland. Its Georgian facade (unlike Sir John Soane he seems to have been lacking in the feeling that a building, like a piece of sculpture, should be equally satisfactory from all aspects) was in contrast to the Early English style of the first gesture, his St Paul's Church. Architects did not again make much impact until the middle and late 1860s when the general expansion throughout the Colony produced in Auckland Rumsey's Supreme Court, Wrigley's Lunatic Asylum, Terry's Bank of New Zealand and Union Bank, Philip Herapath's Pitt Street Methodist Church, T. B. Cameron's Star Hotel and other buildings of similar pretension. Edward Rumsey (1824-1909) and Leonard Terry were Melbourne architects but the Italian Gothic Supreme Court was supervised by Rumsey himself who stayed some time in Auckland and Dunedin to do other work, while Terry was represented by Richard Keals (1817-1885) who founded an architectural practice running through two generations. Two familiar buildings by Keals are the present offices of the National Mutual Life Association (1882) at 41-43 Shortland Street and the malthouse and stores for the Great Northern Brewery (1863). Leonard Terry's best known building is the Melbourne Club in Collins Street, Melbourne, but the very beautiful Auckland house built in 1867 on the side of Mt St John for David Murdoch, manager of the Bank of New Zealand, may also be attributed to him. Rumsey died in Sydney after spending his last working years in the office of the Colonial Architect there.

The main architectural episode of this decade in Auckland was the setting up of the Public Buildings Commission at the beginning of 1864 with Sampson Kempthorne as secretary. The members were W. C. Daldy, Alfred Domett, J. A. Gilfillan, William Gisborne, Robert Graham, Charles Knight, Albin Martin, Joseph Newman, William Swainson and Frederick Whitaker.[8] Kempthorne drew up an extremely ambitious programme for a kind of Whitehall in the area between Princes Street and Symonds Street and forestalled the criticism that its comprehensiveness must inevitably have bred, by invoking the precedents of Inigo Jones's and Sir Christopher Wren's far-sighted plans for London.[9] Included in his 'idea of a plan on paper' were the Supreme Court, a rebuilt St Paul's Church and other places of worship, a Music Hall, General Assembly buildings and Government offices, Provincial Government offices, and a Town Hall and Exchange with an internal quadrangle and a piazza or colonnade for promenade and military bands. There were to be two large hotels each capable of furnishing 150 beds, a Colonists' Union Club, a Public Library and Museum and a Hall for philosophical lectures, a Grammar School, Law Courts and Library, a Mechanics' Institute, a Medical College, and a Society of Fine Arts with schools for Drawing, Engineering and Architecture. It was suggested that some of the more imposing buildings might surround a grand square or arena on the crest of the hill, with a monumental column or campanile in the Italian or Byzantine manner in the centre, as a memorial to men who had died in the local wars. At the top of this column an electric light would guide mariners to harbour.

It was a brave but impossible conception. The Commission in the meantime offered prizes for a new Government House, a Supreme Court House and a combined Post Office and Customhouse. First prizes in each case

[8]*Auckland Weekly News*, 5 March 1864.
[9]ibid, 3 September 1864.

were valued at £200 and second prizes at £100. For the Government House Mr Rumsey of Dunedin was placed first with Mr Baston of Hobart Town second; for the Court House, Mr Honey of Sydney and Mr Clark of Melbourne and, for the Post Office, Mr Baston of Hobart Town and Mr Matthew Henderson of Auckland were the winners.[10] Government House was not built but both the other buildings were given to Rumsey.

The grander work of this period in Auckland paralleled but slightly post-dated the flush of Mason's practice in the South. Architecture in New Zealand had no Capital. The removal of Government to Wellington did nothing architecturally for that city for at least a decade but, instead, the initiative rested first with Auckland and then, on the discovery of gold in Otago, with Dunedin. Only Thatcher and Mason had made much contribution during the first twenty years in Auckland and neither had given his full time to practice, while Thatcher's work was confined to churches and houses for what was virtually a single client. In Christchurch, Mountfort and Maxwell Bury had a corner in Gothic until the arrival of W. B. Armson in 1871 to prove that it was possible to build in the Renaissance style in that dedicated city.

The Dunedin scene, if little different from Auckland when Mason went south – indeed the town itself was even less formed – quickly changed. Australian architects began to take an interest in Auckland about 1865. They appeared in Dunedin some four years earlier.[11] Mostly they were young men from Melbourne, ten to twenty years Mason's junior, who had been brought up on the rich display of Renaissance Revival work with sufficient smattering of other things to design a commercial block in Venetian Gothic or a church in the Decorated style as required. The Greek Revival which had imparted a certain severity to Mason's natural manner, evinced in some of his houses and small buildings, had affected these later men not at all. It might be thought that they would have influenced him but this seems not to have been so until he had perforce to admit the suggestions of his partner W. H. Clayton (1822-1877). Quite clearly Mason was the architectural superior of his first partner, David Ross, a man of excellent Melbourne references, nor could Swyer or Armson at that time match him. This is remarkable when it is considered that he had been more than twenty years away from England and for at least half that time engaged in farming rather than building. Architectural magazines and published collections of drawings were of course available as they are today and we must assume that he had kept in touch by means such as these.

R. A. Lawson (1833-1902) surpassed him in a single building, First Church, a superb example of Decorated Gothic viewed from without, but disappointing within, for the forms of the Presbyterian Church give little occasion for the spatial complexities suggested by the exterior. Seacliff Lunatic Asylum (1877), the vast baronial edifice north of Dunedin, also by Lawson, is inconceivable from Mason's hand until, shorn in imagination of all its turrets, it looks suddenly like one of his workhouses of forty years before. F. W. Petre[12] (1847-1918), who from Dunedin designed the domed Roman Catholic Cathedral in Christchurch, considered by that arch-critic George Bernard Shaw to be the finest Renaissance cathedral outside Italy, followed Mason in practice so that his work has no chronological comparison.

It was, of course, a matter of age but also of youthful training and eager

[10]ibid, 10 September 1864.
[11]The influx of Melbourne architects to Dunedin certainly followed the Otago gold discoveries and the decline of building in Melbourne, but the architects were served like other men by shipping schedules which demanded that sailings from Melbourne went first to the Bluff, then to Port Chalmers, Lyttelton, Wellington, Nelson and Hokitika before returning to Melbourne – or took the trip in reverse. Port Chalmers, the port for Dunedin, was a natural place to disembark. By the same token Hokitika briefly played host to several architects who would otherwise have been unlikely to penetrate there.
[12]F. W. Petre, son of the Hon. H. W. Petre, first Postmaster-General, and grandson of the 11th Baron Petre, a director of the New Zealand Company. He is said to have designed more than seventy New Zealand churches.

inclination which made Mason what he was and turned his hand to each of the nineteenth-century styles and revivals as it came uppermost: Norman St Botolph's, Early English St Paul's, the so-called Palladian Government House, the Greek-influenced Bank of New Zealand buildings in Wellington and Dunedin, the Italianate Exhibition building and Renaissance Post Office, the plainer almost 'Queen Anne' Provincial Council Chambers and the Universal Bond and the even plainer buildings of the 1870s which came close to the Eclecticism which many believed was the proper solution to the great architectural problem. To this last period, also, belong the several single-storeyed houses which have such a modern look today, which might be regarded as developing, for the first time, characteristics which were specifically New Zealand in their adaptation to climate and ways of living, were it not for the conviction that the lost houses of Official Bay, built soon after 1840, themselves foreshadowed the future and then were unfortunately forgotten in the long heyday of Victorian diversity and ostentation.

A final word needs to be said on materials. Mason had learnt in Australia that low-pitched roofs, favoured anyway in the first years of the century, were suitable for the climate and were more economical unless the roof spaces were to be used for attics, and he had learnt that verandahs were not merely charming Regency gestures but a matter of near necessity to give protection against the sun. He had not learnt, however, to accept timber as a desirable building material and his sudden arrival in a country where timber grew in such profusion must have been disconcerting. His early attempts (Courthouse and Government House, Auckland) to imitate stone forms in a material which has its own proportions and peculiarities deserve excuse. Similar imitations were common in New England and, not long since, timber palaces were being built in Russia. That he began at once to prefabricate cottages at the Bay of Islands for transhipment to the Waitemata, an experiment incidentally which gave some trade to Auckland builders and merchants a few years later, Thomas Flower Russell and James Macky among them, in shipping prefabricated houses to the Californian goldfields, showed his understanding of the nature of timber and indeed he could not have long remained ignorant with Hobson's prefabricated Government House already on its way from London. But public buildings in his view deserved stone and so he did his best to copy it. If, instead of being a classicist at heart, he had been more sympathetic to Gothic forms, he might, as Thatcher did, have evolved at once a timber style suited to the occasion.

In building St Paul's in 1841 he had first to manufacture bricks and for the Post Office in Dunedin, or the Exchange as it came to be called, he had first to find a stone which would not only weather satisfactorily as ashlar but would also yield to the sculptor's chisel and lathe. This led to the development of the great quarries of Oamaru stone. Concrete came to be tentatively used by a few architects in the early 1870s – Clayton experimented with it in Wellington and James Wrigley in Auckland was encouraged in its use by the magnate miller J. C. Firth[13] – but its true pioneer in monolithic form in New Zealand was the remarkable F. W. Petre, once known among engineers as 'Lord Concrete'. Apart from two small concrete cottages designed with Wales for John Burnside senior in 1874, Mason seems to have thought of it only in terms of foundations, floors, or cast ornament like that 'block entablature of Vignola in cement'

[13]Firth's interest in concrete may well have been derived from his friend Sir John Logan Campbell. Campbell records in his manuscript autobiography, 'A Short Sketch of a Long Life', (Auckland Institute and Museum), that in 1870, before returning to New Zealand, he made plans in England for an addition to his house, Logan Bank, 'to be built in concrete according to a new invention just patented.' He then made arrangements for the necessary apparatus to be sent ahead of him. The quality of the concrete may be observed in the ruins of the house still standing on the north side of Anzac Avenue in Auckland.

which was placed on the Universal Bond. This is perhaps strange in light of the knowledge that his brother's family became proprietors of a considerable Portland Cement manufactory at Ipswich and that Ipswich, his home town, also has a place in the development of reinforced concrete construction in that it was the scene in 1844 of Frederick Ransome's experiments to reconstitute the crushed metal otherwise wasted in the dressing of mill-stones. The smallness of the nineteenth-century world is emphasized if we consider that Ransome's son E. L. Ransome, working in San Francisco, is credited with the development of reinforced concrete construction in America, while the architect first described as applying Californian building methods to New Zealand conditions, the Scotsman Thomas Turnbull, who spent nine years in Melbourne before going in 1861 to San Francisco where he designed Trinity Church (1867) among other buildings, paid Dunedin a long visit on his arrival in New Zealand in 1871 and formed a lasting friendship with Mason and Wales before going north to Wellington to work briefly with Mason's old partner, the Colonial Architect, Clayton, and then to set up one of the most extensive practices in the country. The later application of Californian aseismic design to New Zealand structural codes is well known.

In spite of his early training under that late-Georgian giant, the engineer Thomas Telford, Mason seems not to have had any ambitions to excel in or to explore new structural methods. Cast iron columns were used to support the roofs of the exhibition halls of the Colonial Museum but even this was probably at Clayton's suggestion, for Clayton had worked more recently under Sir John Rennie, engineer to the Admiralty. Admittedly iron had to be imported and was costly and therefore limited in use. Two drawings of bridges are among the Mason material held by Mr Lloyd Veint of Diamond Lake but they are undated and unidentified. The bridges are on a fairly modest scale showing stone piers and abutments spanned by girders of uncertain material (one at least has the appearance of ironwork) and they probably belong to that period in Auckland when, from 1855 to 1857, Mason was Provincial Architect and President of the Board of Works.

What does this all add up to? Obviously there was no architect in New Zealand in its first years of settlement to compare with Greenway at a similar stage in Australia. But, of the handful of men working in each of the main centres, several were considerable in their talents and in the volume of work they produced and, among these, Mason, the first of them all, always held his place honourably. No great masterpieces or innovations came from his drawing board, no outstanding political triumphs from his public life, few startling episodes from his private life, but, because of this, perhaps, his life sums up the lives of many other young men who came to New Zealand, eager to build their Britain in the South, who accepted responsibilities and undertook tasks for which they lacked training and, at the same time, worked in their proper professions when they were able, and so became old men, but old men secure in the knowledge that in most cases their lives had been far richer than they ever could have been had they remained in their homelands.

APPENDIX I
GOVERNMENT HOUSE, AUCKLAND

Costs as stated by the Superintendent, Auckland Province, to the Colonial Secretary, 26 May 1859.

'On grounds and approach	258	16	0
Iron gates	24	0	0
On Excavation, Foundation & Drains	1208	5	3
Well	19	0	0
Building Government House pd William Hay	11765	16	10
Water closets, cistern & plumber work	344	2	0
Bells	36	17	6
Mason work at cooking stove & cellar	37	5	0
Cooking stove, steam chest etc	89	18	4
Repairing & fixing Royal Arms	10	0	0
Venetian blinds	89	12	9
Furniture & fittings per William Hay	263	19	0
Hooks etc	1	1	4
Table, sofa & carpets	79	18	3
Insurance	150	0	0
Architect's allowance	203	4	6
	14581	16	9

Repaid by the Colonial Government for furniture £250
,,   ,,   on account of
                       labour on approach   11 10   261 10 0

                                     14320   6 9

Interest on the above amount from first of
          January 1856 @ 10 pCent   4892 15 7

                                     19213   2 4

                   (signed) R. B. Lusk
                       Provl. accountant.'

'Provincial Council Papers,
APL.

APPENDIX II

William Mason to Dr Thomas Morland Hocken. Some punctuation has been added to this letter but mis-spellings have, with minor exceptions, been retained. The original is in the Hocken Library, Dunedin.

Eden Grove
Paradise
Glenorchy 12th Octo 1888

Dear Doctor Hocken

I have been very much interested in reading the report of your fourth lecture lately delivered at a meeting of the Otago Institute. It is particularly interesting to me because it is a lesson showing how differently matters that transpired between forty and fifty years back are viewed at the present moment to the impressions made on the minds of actors on the scene at the time they were enacted; for instance the New Zealand company are now looked on as a body of British gentlemen who in face of every opposition &c; at the time that company was looked on as a trading community pursuing the same course that Gibbon Wakefield had pursued a short time before in South Australia and really led by that gentleman's experience in forming that New Zealand land company. No doubt the formation of this company forced the British Govt against their will to colonise New Zealand.

Believe me I am not finding fault with the correctness of your facts but many of them lack the surrounding incidents that gave zest to them at the time of their occurrence. I will relate the way in which the French Govt were outgeneraled by Captn Hobson in their attempt to take possession of the South Island of New Zealand. In August the corvette L'Aube arrived at the Bay of Islands. I am not certain but believe she came from Sydney and brought dispatches from Sir George Gipps informing Captn Hobson she was going on to Akaroa. The Britomart was lying in the Bay at this time but as she was known to be a very slow sailing vessel it was impossible she could reach the South Island before the corvette if she tried unless by stratagem and Captn Hobson whose mind had been trained to meet such cases during his long experience on the Malabar coast, watching and chasing pirates, at once determined on a plan in which Captn Stanly fully concured.

Orders were given for dismanteling the Britomart prior to a thorough overhaul. This was done under the very nose of the Frenchmen and the gear as taken down sent up to the Govt Store at Russell (as it was then called) a distance of four or five miles from the ship. This act entirely lulled all suspicion of any idea of Capt Hobson's attempting to superceed the French in taking possession of the South Island or watching the French at Akaroa, indeed they were then in no hurry and said they intended calling in at Port Nicholson on their way. I forget the date but the French vessel sailed early in the morning but as soon as she was out of sight every available boat and man that could be procured in the Bay was set to work re-conveying the gear &c back to the Britomart, Captn Hobson himself assisting in sending the various articles away in such order as they would be required by Captn Stanly for replacing on board the ship as they arrived; it was the smartest thing I ever saw done, as before night just at dusk every thing was replaced and the ship underway with orders to sail North about and through the straits to avoid the L'Aube and if possible to raise the flag on the peninsular before she arrived. This was all done and only a few hours before. But for this act of Captn Hobson the South Island would have been a French colony.

Your information in relation to what you have called crimping and the surrounding sentences must be from Wellington and quite *untrue* the circumstances were these: our difficulty of communication with home at that time was very great; our letters were carried all round the Islands in the Govt brig (you have truly related what she was) on their way to Sydney and it would be sometimes two years before we received answers. To facilitate communication with home and getting goods regularly from Sydney a small company of five or six I think they were Captn Symonds Dr Johnston Mr Montefiore myself, I forget the others, determined to charter a smart schooner for this purpose and obtained one from Sydney under charter for twelve months. On her rounds she was to call at Wellington. She did so on her first trip and unfortunately for us the Captain brought a few passengers back with him which he obtained in the following way and entirely without instructions from us.

On his arrival at Wellington several mechanics having no work at the time in Wellington went on board and enquired of the Captn what prospect there was of obtaining work in Auckland. He took the hint and thought he could get a full ship in which case he would not continue his voyage but return to Auckland. He advertised his intention to return and brought a few passengers but the Government and no other persons interested in inducing people to leave Wellington had anything to do with the vessel. These circumstances made some of the Wellington people attribute a different motive to the one intended by us but there is much more in connection with this matter and the real cause of mechanics rushing from Wellington as they did that I cannot explain in a letter but I will do so the first time I have an opportunity of talking to you.

You say 'as the name would imply Official Bay was occupied by Govt officers who fairly swarmed &&c.' That you may understand how far this is true I will tell you of whom the swarm consisted. There were Captn Symonds, Dr Johnston M.D. Col Surgeon, Felton Mathew Surveyor General, Mr Shortland Col. Sec, Mr Fisher Attorney Genl and William Mason Colonial Architect, and as to their swallowing up the lion's share of the scanty revenue there was no revenue at this time. Our salaries were then paid by the Sydney Government but the bay was called Official bay because the Governor proposed to give each Govt Officer a section in this bay to build their houses at once and before winter as it would be a long time before any land could be ready for sale. This promise was never carried out but some of the houses were built and the land had to be purchased at the sale afterwards.

You are quite right in what you have said relating the first land sale. I had determined to purchase several lots, had fixed on these lots and instructed a friend to bid for me. I could not bid myself because the Governor had asked me to act as Auctioneer. You may imagine my consternation when I found the sections were selling for four and six times the amount anticipated.

You are misinformed as to Mr G. S. Cooper the present Under-secretary having been a member of the original council. It was his father who was then Colonial Treasurer, Mr G. S. Cooper was then a lad of fifteen or sixteen years of age. Mr Swainson late Attorney General who died a few years ago was the last surviving member of that body.

For your information I will tell you as far as I can remember the names of the first arrivals and the name of the vessels they came in. Capt Hobson Governor, Mr Shortland Col Secretary and I think Mr Cooper the Colonial Treasure[r] came from Sydney in the Herald. They arrived before the signing of the Treaty of Waitangi. Immediately after the Westminster arrived with Felton Mathew Surveyor General, Dr Johnston Col Surgeon Captn Smart in charge of horse police and five or six men (I forget the number) Mr Freeman and Mr Grimstone clerks in the Col Sec office William Mason Col Architect and about 70 mechanics including wives and families and Mr Logie as store keeper who for many years afterwards held the office of collector of customs at Dunedin. I believe I am the only survivor excepting the children.

Yours truly
Wm Mason

P.S.

I could of course say much more on these subjects but as I have nothing to refer to I do not like depending on memory alone – I have spoken of the horse police under Captn Smart. The horses were killed on the passage during a gale of wind and had they arrived at the Bay it would have been impossible to find enough level ground to exercise them on. They were a mistake and the police themselves were soon sent back to Sydney.

APPENDIX III

THE MYTH OF MASON'S WILL

In a Jubilee supplement of the *New Zealand Herald*, issued in 1913, a statement was made that William Mason had been one of the benefactors of Auckland in that he willed a sum approaching £20,000 to the Jubilee Institute for the Blind and sums of £1,000 to the Leys Institute, and £500 to the Salvation Army, the Society for the Prevention of Cruelty to Women and Children, and the Society for the Prevention of Cruelty to Animals. Many subsequent journalists have identified this benefactor with William Mason 'the first Superintendent of Works'. It was in fact another William Mason, a nurseryman, who died in 1905 and whose estate was anyway unable to sustain the provisions of his will – the New Zealand Foundation for the Blind has no record of any benefaction received from that source. He was a brother of James Mason who for many years maintained strawberry gardens in Parnell on the site bought by the Foundation, and of George Mason, also a nurseryman, of Hamilton.

The Dunedin will of the subject of this book was drawn up in 1875 and left a sum of £2,000 to Annie Allison, the sister of his second wife. This provision (unless a division of property was made before his death) was also unfulfilled, for his final estate was sworn for probate at under £100.

BIBLIOGRAPHY

I. LETTERS, PAPERS, DRAWINGS ETC. OF WILLIAM MASON

Mason's diaries for 1877 and 1885 are in the office archives of Mason and Wales, Dunedin, as also are the account books of the practice for 1862 and 1863 and from 1871 onward.

Much of Mason's official correspondence is preserved among the inward letters of the Colonial Secretary and of the Otago Provincial Superintendent, both in the National Archives, Wellington, and among the Auckland Provincial Council papers in the Auckland Public Library. The long letter to Dr Hocken, printed here as an appendix, is among the Hocken autograph letters in the Hocken Library. Of considerable value are the copies of letters from N. Y. A. Wales to Mason and to Mrs Mason, preserved in Wales's personal letter books in the office of Mason and Wales. Also in Mason and Wales's office are a few minor papers such as an undated draft report on the levels of the City of Auckland.

Original drawings are held as follows.

OFFICE OF MASON AND WALES: various pencil and wash drawings from Mason's student days are collected in office scrapbooks. They include details of St Mary [Magdalene?] Church at Oxford, Coldingham (Berwickshire) and Everton (Bedfordshire), Wells, Durham and Lincoln Cathedrals and Westminster Abbey. Also in the scrapbooks are a few preliminary sketches from the Dunedin period, such as the Post Office tower and a chimney-piece for Bishopscourt. The office holds the original drawings for All Saints' Church and George O'Brien's perspective drawing of the Post Office.

MR E. F. MASON, Woodbridge, Suffolk: sketch drawing for the Ipswich Customhouse.

IPSWICH AND EAST SUFFOLK RECORD OFFICE: plans and sketch for the parsonage at Bedingfield.

CHURCH COMMISSIONERS, Millbank, Westminster: Brightlingsea parsonage.

DEAN OF AUCKLAND, Selwyn Court: plans for St Paul's Parochial Office and Schoolroom. Plan and elevation for a Schoolhouse at Auckland, dated 1845.

MR LLOYD VEINT, Arcadia House, Diamond Lake near Queenstown: oil sketches of Bedingfield parsonage and St Lawrence's Church, East Donyland. Line drawings of Bishopscourt, Dunedin, and two unidentified bridges.

MINISTRY OF WORKS, Dunedin: plans and elevations for the Post Office, Dunedin, later the Exchange building.

THE DOMINION MUSEUM, Wellington, holds George O'Brien's perspective drawing for the Colonial Museum at Wellington and the AUCKLAND INSTITUTE AND MUSEUM holds specifications for some minor works at St Paul's Church, Auckland.

William Mason's will is filed at the Supreme Court, Dunedin.

II. PRIMARY SOURCES

A. MANUSCRIPTS, TYPESCRIPTS, MICROFILMS.

ASHWORTH, EDWARD. Journal. Manuscript, Alexander Turnbull Library.

AUCKLAND PROVINCIAL COUNCIL. Miscellaneous papers. Auckland Public Library.

AUCKLAND PROVINCIAL HISTORY INDEX. Auckland Public Library.

BURN, DAVID. Diary. Microfilm, Auckland Institute and Museum.

CAMPBELL, SIR J. L. 'My Autobiography. A Short Sketch of a Long Life.' Manuscript, Auckland Institute and Museum.

COTTON, W. C. Journals, 1841-1848. Photocopy, Alexander Turnbull Library.

DOMINION MUSEUM ARCHIVES. Correspondence, Colonial Museum. Sir James Hector to Mason and Clayton.

DUNEDIN CITY COUNCIL. Ratebook, 1875.

FAIRBURN, ESTHER. 'Reminiscences of Old Days in Auckland.' Typescript, Auckland Institute and Museum.

FRANKLIN, LADY (JANE). Journal, 1841. Photocopy, Auckland Public Library.

GEORGE, JAMES. 'A Few Odds and Ends 1823-1876.' Typescript, Auckland Public Library.

HOBSON, MRS WILLIAM. Mrs Hobson's Scrapbook. Alexander Turnbull Library.

HOCKEN, T. M. Notebooks, 37/11, 37/12, 37/21, 37/40, 37/45. Hocken Library.

HODGKINSON, S. 'Autobiographical Sketch.' Manuscript, Hocken Library.

HOLMAN, ELISABETH A. 'Reminiscences.' Typescript, Auckland Institute and Museum.

KING, GEORGE P. 'St Lawrence Church, East Donyland.' Manuscript in possession of the author.

LANDS AND DEEDS OFFICES, AUCKLAND AND DUNEDIN. Deed Record Book Indexes and Deed Records. Register of Crown Grants, Province of Auckland, (Crawford's Index).

LUSH, VICESIMUS. Journal. Microfilm, Auckland Public Library.

MACKY, THOMAS. Manuscript letter to James Macky, 7 March 1850, in possession of Mr N. L. Macky, Auckland.

MASON, E. F. Family information in letter to the author, 18 February 1962.

MURISON, W. D. Manuscript letter, Dunedin Public Library.

NATIONAL ARCHIVES, Wellington.

——Colonial Secretary, New Zealand. Inwards Letters, I.A.1.

——Colonial Secretary, New Zealand. Outwards Letters (including Colonial Architect's Book), I.A.4.

——Province of Otago, Journals of Proceedings and Papers Laid on the Table of the Provincial Council, 1854-76, O.P.1; Minutes of the Executive Council, 1854-76, O.P.4; Superintendent's General Inwards Correspondence, 1862-77, O.P.7; Superintendent's General Outwards Correspondence, 1853-77, O.P.11; Superintendent's Letters to the General Government, 1856-77, O.P.10; Superintendent's Letters to and Memoranda for Provincial Government Officials, 1862-77, O.P.12.

——Army Department, General Inwards Correspondence, 1863-79, A.D.1.

——New Government House Commission, 1868. Inwards Letters, I.A. 135/1.

PASSENGER LISTS FROM SYDNEY NEWSPAPERS. Typescript, Alexander Turnbull Library.

PREECE, G. A. Diary. Manuscript, Auckland Public Library.

REGISTRAR-GENERAL'S OFFICE, Wellington. Death certificates: William Mason, Sarah Mason, Catherine Mason, John Fenn.

REGISTER OFFICE, Somerset House, London. Marriage certificate: John Fenn to Catherine Allison.

ST PAUL'S VESTRY, Auckland. Minutes, 20 November 1862.

SELWYN, BISHOP G. A. Journal. Typescript, Auckland Institute and Museum.

——Personal Ledger. Auckland Diocesan Office.

ST JOHN'S COLLEGE. Senior Bursar's Abstract Book. Auckland Diocesan Office.

SYDNEY ROAD BOARD. Minutes. Waitaki County Council Office.

SYMONDS, J. J. Journal, 1841-50. Manuscript, Hocken Library.

TAYLOR, RICHARD. Manuscript letter to Mary Taylor, 26 March 1839, Grey papers, Auckland Public Library.

B. PUBLISHED OFFICIAL PAPERS.

GREAT BRITAIN PARLIAMENTARY PAPERS 1841, Vol. XVII No 311. *Copies of Extracts of Correspondence relative to New Zealand.* No 17, Lord John Russell to Governor Hobson, Transmitting Charter . . . and Instructions to the Governor.

——1842, Vol. XXVIII No 569. *Copies of Papers and Despatches Relative to New Zealand, up to the latest date.* Correspondence with Sir G. Gipps and Governor Hobson, No 45, Hobson to Lord John Russell.

——1843, Vol. XXXIII No 134. *Copies of Extracts of any Correspondence relative to the New Zealand Estimates.* No. 1, Hobson to Lord Stanley.

GAZETTES.

Auckland Provincial Government Gazette.

New Zealand Government Gazette.

The Government Gazette of the Province of New Ulster.

Otago Provincial Government Gazette.

Historical Records of Australia. Series 1. Vols. XVII and XIX. Sydney, 1923.

NEW ZEALAND EXHIBITION, 1865. *Official Catalogue of the New Zealand Exhibition, 1865.* Dunedin. 1865.

——*Reports and Awards of the Jurors.* Dunedin, 1866.

NEW ZEALAND. *Parliamentary Debates*. Third Parliament 1861 to 1863. Compiled by Maurice FitzGerald. Wellington, 1886.
——Second Session of the fifth Parliament, Thirtieth day of August to the twenty-fifth day of October 1872. Wellington, 1872.
NEW ZEALAND. *Votes and Proceedings of the House of Representatives.* Session IV, 1856. Report of the Select Committee on the Transfer of Government House, Auckland, 1856.
PROVINCE OF OTAGO, NEW ZEALAND. *Votes and Proceedings of the Provincial Council together with Reports of Select Committees.* Sessions XVIII to XXIV, 1863 to 1868. Dunedin.
SYNOD. *Minutes of the Third General Synod of the Branch of the United Church of England and Ireland in New Zealand Held at Christchurch, April 27th,* 1865. Auckland, 1865.

C. PUBLISHED JOURNALS, LETTERS, REMINISCENCES, ETC.

ACLAND, SIR H. W. AND RUSKIN, J. *The Oxford Museum.* London, 1859.
ARNOLD, THOMAS. *Passages in a Wandering Life.* London, 1904.
BATHGATE, JOHN. *Bathgate Expeditions.* Dunedin, 1952.
BECKETT, R. B. (ed.) *John Constable's Correspondence, The Family at East Bergholt,* 1807-1837. London, 1962.
BUTLER, SAMUEL. *A First Year in Canterbury Settlement.* Oxford, 1964.
CAMPBELL, SIR J. L. *Poenamo.* London, 1881.
COLENSO, WILLIAM. *Fifty Years in New Zealand.* Napier, 1888.
DIEFFENBACH, ERNEST. *Travels in New Zealand.* London, 1843.
ELDER, J. R. (ed.). *Marsden's Lieutenants.* Dunedin, 1934.
ELWELL, E. SIMEON. *The Boy Colonists.* London, 1878.
LARKWORTHY, FALCONER. *Ninety-one Years.* London, 1924.
MARKHAM, EDWARD (E. H. McCormick, ed.). *New Zealand or Recollections of it.* Wellington, 1963.
MUNDY, G. C. *Our Antipodes.* London, 1852.
NEVILL, BISHOP S. T. *A Bishop's Diary . . . with a Short History of S. Paul's Cathedral, Dunedin,* by Canon E. R. Nevill. Dunedin, 1922.
RUTHERFORD, J. (ed.). *The Founding of New Zealand. The Journals of Felton Mathew, first Surveyor-General of New Zealand, and his Wife, 1840-1847.* Auckland. 1940.
ROGERS, L. M. (ed.). *The Early Journals of Henry Williams.* Christchurch, 1961.
SALMOND, J. D. *Hearts of Gold.* Dunedin, 1962.
SELWYN, BISHOP G. A. 'A Letter from the Bishop of New Zealand etc.' *Church in the Colonies, No. XII, New Zealand, Part IV.* London, 1847.
SCHOLEFIELD, G. H. (ed.). *The Richmond-Atkinson Papers.* 2 volumes. Wellington, 1960.
TROLLOPE, ANTHONY. *Australia and New Zealand.* 2 volumes. London, 1873.
WAKEFIELD, E. J. *Adventure in New Zealand.* London, 1845.

D. NEWSPAPERS, PERIODICALS.

Auckland Chronicle. Auckland.

Auckland Times. Auckland.
Bay of Islands Observer. Kororareka.
Builder. London
Building News. London.
Daily Telegraph. Dunedin.
Dunedin Punch. Dunedin.
Evening Star. Dunedin.
Illustrated London News. London
Lake Wakatip Mail. Queenstown.
Mail Coach. Auckland.
New Zealand Advertiser and Bay of Islands Gazette. Kororareka.
New-Zealander. Auckland.
New Zealand Herald. Auckland.
New Zealand Herald and Auckland Gazette. Auckland.
New Zealand Journal. London.
North Otago Daily Times. Oamaru.
Otago Colonist. Dunedin.
Otago Daily Times. Dunedin.
Otago Punch. Dunedin.
Otago Witness. Dunedin.
Southern Cross. Auckland.
Times. London.
Weekly News. Auckland.

III. SECONDARY SOURCES.

A. DICTIONARIES, DIRECTORIES, ETC.

Bryan's Dictionary of Painters and Engravers. G. C.Williamson (ed.).5 vols. London, 1904-9.
Burke's Peerage, Baronetage and Knightage. London, 1967.
A Colonial Directory. Melbourne, 1862.
COLVIN, H. M. *A Biographical Dictionary of English Architects, 1660-1840.* London, 1954.
Cyclopedia of New Zealand. Vol. 2, Auckland. Christchurch, 1902. Vol. 4, Otago and Southland. Christchurch, 1905.
FURKERT, F. W. *Early New Zealand Engineers.* Wellington, 1953.
GRAVES, ALGERNON. *The Royal Academy of Arts. A Complete Dictionary of Contributors and their Work from its foundation in 1769 to 1904.* 8 vols. London, 1905-6.
Harnett's Dunedin Directory. 1863 and 1864.
Mackay's Otago Almanac. 1875.
Roll of Early Settlers and Descendants in the Auckland Province Prior to the End of 1852. Auckland, 1940.
SCHOLEFIELD, G. H. *A Dictionary of New Zealand Biography.* 2 vols. Wellington. 1940.
STEPHEN, LESLIE AND LEE, SIDNEY (eds.). *Dictionary of National Biography.* 57 vols. London, 1885-1912.
VENN, J. A. *Alumni cantabrigienses.* Cambridge, 1922-54.
Wise's Dunedin Directory. 1865.
Wise's New Zealand Directory. 1872-73.

B. BOOKS, PAMPHLETS, ETC.

ALINGTON, MARGARET. *Frederick Thatcher and St. Paul's.* Wellington, 1965.

ANDREWS, WAYNE. *Architecture, Ambition and Americans.* London, 1964.

[BATHGATE, A.] *An Illustrated Guide to Dunedin and its Industries by a Citizen.* Dunedin, 1883.

BATHGATE, ALEX. (ed.). *Picturesque Dunedin.* Dunedin, 1890.

BLORE, EDWARD. *The Monumental Remains of Noble and Eminent Persons.* London, 1824.

BLOXAM, M. H. *The Principles of Gothic Ecclesiastical Architecture.* 8th edition. London, 1846.

BRANCH, LESLEY. *The Sabres of Paradise.* London, 1960.

BRIGGS, ASA. *Victorian Cities.* London, 1963.

CASEY, M., and others. *Early Melbourne Architecture.* Melbourne, 1953.

CASSON, HUGH. *An Introduction to Victorian Architecture.* London, 1948.

CLARK, KENNETH. *The Gothic Revival.* 3rd edition. London, 1962.

CLARKE, B. F. L. *Church Builders of the Nineteenth Century.* London, 1938.

COLLINS AND SON. *A Century of Architecture.* Christchurch, 1965.

COLLINS, PETER. *Concrete: The Vision of a New Architecture.* London, 1959.

——*Changing Ideals in Modern Architecture.* London, 1965.

COTTON, W. C. *A Manual for the New Zealand Beekeeper.* Wellington, 1848.

CRAIG, J. J. *Historical Record of Jubilee Reunion of Old Colonists.* Auckland, 1893.

DAVIS, J. KING. *History of S. John's College.* Auckland, 1911.

DAVIS, TERENCE. *The Architecture of John Nash.* London, 1960.

DIGNAN, F. J., and others. *The Northern Club, Auckland.* Auckland, 1954.

ELLIS, M. H. *Francis Greenway. His Life and Times.* Sydney, 1949.

ELMES, JAMES. *Metropolitan Improvements or London in the Nineteenth Century.* London, 1829.

EVANS, J. H. *Churchman Militant.* London, 1964.

FERRIDAY, P. (ed.). *Victorian Architecture.* London, 1963.

FERGUSSON, J. *History of the Modern Styles of Architecture.* London, 1862.

GILKISON, W. SCOTT. *Earnslaw, Monarch of Wakatipu.* Christchurch, 1957.

GOLDMAN, L. M. *The History of the Jews in New Zealand.* Wellington, 1958.

GOODHART-RENDEL, H. S. *English Architecture since the Regency.* London, 1953.

GRIBBIN, G. A. *The History of the Ara Lodges.* Auckland, 1909.

HALL-JONES, F. G. *John Turnbull Thomson, Surveyor General.* Invercargill, 1963.

HERMAN, MORTON. *The Early Australian Architects and their Work.* Sydney, 1954.

HITCHCOCK, H. R. *Early Victorian Architecture in Great Britain.* London, 1954.

——*Architecture: Nineteenth and Twentieth Centuries.* London, 1958.

HOCKEN, T. M. *Early History of New Zealand.* Dunedin, 1914.

HUSSEY, CHRISTOPHER. *English Country Houses: Late Georgian 1800-1840.* London, 1958.

JORDAN, ROBERT FURNEAUX. *Victorian Architecture.* London, 1966.

LOCKHART, J. G. *Life of Sir Walter Scott.* 10 vols. Edinburgh, 1902.

McCOY, E. J. AND BLACKMAN, J. G. *Victorian City of New Zealand.* Dunedin, 1968.

McDONALD, K. C. *City of Dunedin; a Century of Civic Enterprise.* Dunedin, 1965.

——*The History of North Otago.* Oamaru, 1940.

——*White Stone Country.* Dunedin, 1962.

——*The Way We Came. A Centennial History of St Paul's Presbyterian Church, Oamaru.* Oamaru, 1963.

McKENZIE, FLORENCE. *Wakatipu Pioneers.* Wellington, 1951.

——*The Sparkling Waters of Whakatipua.* Dunedin, 1947.

McLINTOCK, A. H. *Port of Otago.* Dunedin, 1951.

MEIKLEJOHN, G. M. *Early Conflicts of Press and Government.* Auckland, 1953.

MEYER, R. J. *All Aboard.* Wellington, 1963.

MILLER, F. W. G. *Golden Days of Lake County.* Dunedin, 1949.

MOORE, C. W. S. *Northern Approaches.* Dunedin, 1958.

MORLEY, W. *History of Methodism in New Zealand.* Wellington, 1900.

O'BRIEN, DONAGH. *History of the O'Briens from Brian Boroimhe AD 1000 to AD 1945.* London, 1949.

PEVSNER, NIKOLAUS. *The Buildings of England: Essex.* London, 1954.

——*The Buildings of England: South and West Somerset.* 1958.

——*The Buildings of England: Suffolk.* 1961.

PILCHER, D. *The Regency Style, 1800-1830.* London, 1947.

PLATTS, UNA. *Early Identities.* Auckland City Art Gallery Catalogue. 1955.

REED, A. H. *The Story of Early Dunedin.* Wellington, 1956.

ROBERTS, W. H. S. *History of Oamaru and North Otago.* Oamaru, 1890.

——*Place Names and Early History of Otago and Southland.* Invercargill 1913.

ROBERTSON, E. GRAEME AND CRAIG, EDITH N. *Early Houses of Northern Tasmania.* Melbourne, 1964.

ROSS, RUTH M. *New Zealand's First Capital.* Wellington, 1946.

——*A Guide to Pompallier House.* Wellington, 1970.

SAVIDGE, ALAN. *The Parsonage in England.* London, 1964.

SCHOLEFIELD, G. H. *The New Zealand Parliamentary Record.* Wellington, 1913.

——*Captain William Hobson, First Governor of New Zealand.* Oxford, 1934.

SCOTTER, W. H. *Run, Estate and Farm.* Dunedin, 1948.

SELBY, ISAAC. *History of Melbourne.* Melbourne, [1924].

SHAW, M. S. AND FARRANT, E. D. *The Taieri Plain.* Dunedin, 1949.

SHERRIN, R. A. A. AND WALLACE, J. H. *Early History of New Zealand.* Auckland, 1890.

SLOAN, SAMUEL. *Homestead Architecture.* Philadelphia, 1866.

STEPHENSON, P. R. *The History and Description of Sydney Harbour.* Adelaide, 1966.

STEWART, W. DOWNIE. *Brief History of the Dunedin Club.* Dunedin, 1948.

STOCK, EUGENE. *History of the Church Missionary Society.* London, 1899.

SUMMERSON, JOHN. *Georgian London.* London, 1945.

TERRY, CHARLES. *New Zealand, Its Advantages and Prospects as a British Colony.* London, 1842.

WILLIS, F. P. DE L. *A Record of St Andrew's Church and Parish.* Auckland, 1946.

YOUNG, G. M. (ed.). *Early Victorian England.* 2 vols. London, 1934.

C. ARTICLES.

ANON. 'Early Singapore.' *Straits Times Annual.* 1958.

——'Esplanade from Scandal Point, 1851.' *Straits Times Annual.* 1957.

FLEMING, JOHN. 'Robert Adam's Castle Style.' *Country Life.* 30 May 1968.

HANCOCK, T. H. H. 'Coleman of Singapore.' *Architectural Review*, Vol. CXVII, pp. 168-79.

ROCHE, E. H. 'Arthur Guyon Purchas – a New Zealand Pioneer.' *New Zealand Medical Journal.* June 1954.

STACPOOLE, JOHN. 'Bishop Selwyn's Buildings.' *Art and Australia.* June 1967.

WYATT, H. 'Freemasons in Auckland, July 1841.' *Transactions of United Masters Lodge*, No 167. Vol. XV, No 6. Auckland, 1963.

ARCHITECTURAL PLATES

Plate
47. Government House, side elevation. *Ministry of Works drawing.*
48. Government House, the hall. *National Publicity Studios photograph.*
49. Bank of New Zealand, Wellington, 1862. *Alexander Turnbull Library photograph.*
50. Cargill and Company premises, Dunedin, 1863. *Otago Pioneer Settlers Museum photograph.*
51. Bank of New Zealand, Dunedin, 1863. Mason's building for Richmond and Gillies, 1862, is on the left. *Dunedin Public Library photograph.*
52. Bank of New Zealand, Dunedin, public desk. *Photograph by Mr N. Y. A. Wales.*
53. Bank of Australasia, Dunedin, 1863. *From an engraving in the* Otago Witness, *10 June 1864.*
54. Dunedin Public warehouse for William Dalrymple, 1862. *Otago Pioneer Settlers Museum photograph.*
55. Highlawn, Dunedin, 1863. *Watercolour by C. W. Richmond, General Assembly Library.*
56. Highlawn, plan of ground floor. *From a drawing in the Dunedin Public Library.*
57. 104 London Street, 1863, the entrance front.
57. 104 London Street, doorway.
58. 104 London Street, window detail.
59. 104 London Street, corner detail.
60. Exhibition Building, 1864, later the Dunedin Public Hospital. *Alexander Turnbull Library photograph.*
61. Exhibition Building, ground floor plan. *From the exhibition catalogue.*
63. Post Office (later the Colonial Bank and the Exchange Building), 1865, partial plan of ground floor.
64. Post Office. *Auckland Institute and Museum photograph.*
65. Post Office, detail.
66. Bond Store (the Universal Bond) for Cleve and Lazarus, 1865. *Otago Pioneer Settlers Museum photograph.*
67. Provincial Council Chambers and the Bond Store, with the Post Office still under construction. *Dunedin Public Library photograph.*
68. Provincial Council Chambers, 1865. *Ibid.*
69. Provincial Council Chambers, Princes Street front. *Hocken Library photograph.*
70. Colonial Museum, Wellington, 1865. *Watercolour by George O'Brien. Dominion Museum, Wellington.*
71. St Peter's Church, Caversham, 1864. *From a photograph made available by Mr H. R. Walden.*
72. Bank of New South Wales, Dunedin, 1866. *Hocken Library photograph.*
73. St Paul's Church, Oamaru, first stage, 1865. *From* The Way We Came, *K. C. McDonald, 1963.*
74. All Saints' Church, Dunedin, 1864-73, first stage. *Drawing, office of Mason and Wales.*
75. All Saints' Church, street front. *Hocken Library photograph.*
76. All Saints' Church, window detail.
77. Driver house, Driver's Road, Dunedin, c. 1865.
78. Copland house (North Dunedin Manse), 1872.

Plate

Original design for Custom House Ipswich
by J.M. Clark. 1843

23. *Customs House, Ipswich. Competition drawing.*

24. *St Botolph's Church, Colchester.*

25, 26, 27. *St Botolph's.*

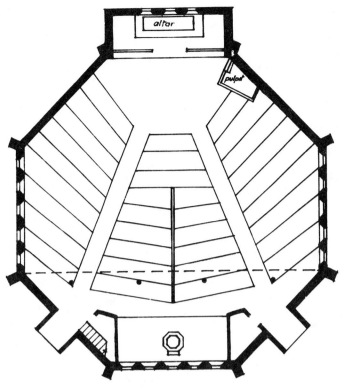

28. *St Lawrence, East Donyland. Plan.*

29. *Oil Sketch.*

30. *St James's, Brightlingsea.*

31, 32. Poorhouse at Epsom.

33, 34. *Poorhouse at Stroud.*

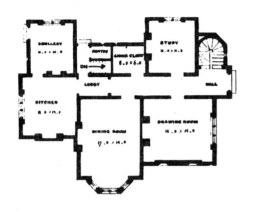

35. *Plans.*

36. *Sketch.*

37. Courthouse at Auckland. (Demolished).

39. *St Paul's Church. (Demolished).*

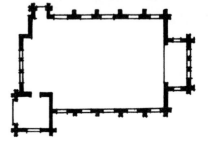

38. *St Paul's Church, Auckland, plan.*

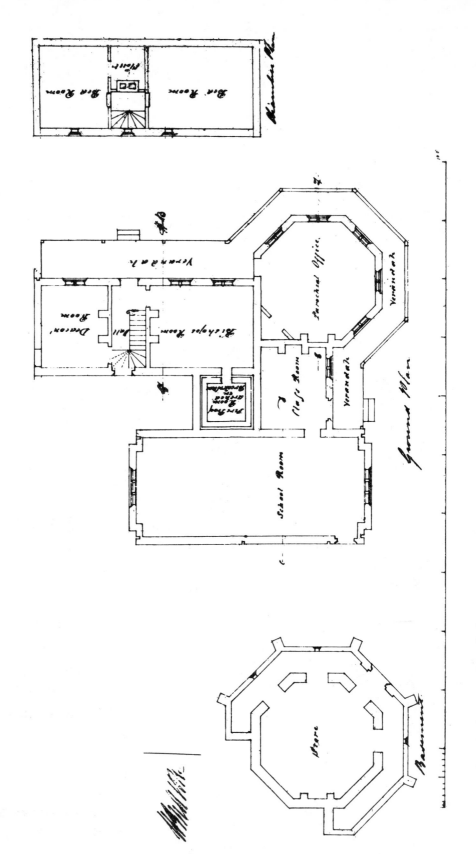

40. *St Paul's schoolroom, proposed plans.*

41, 42.   *Eden Hill, Auckland. (Demolished).*

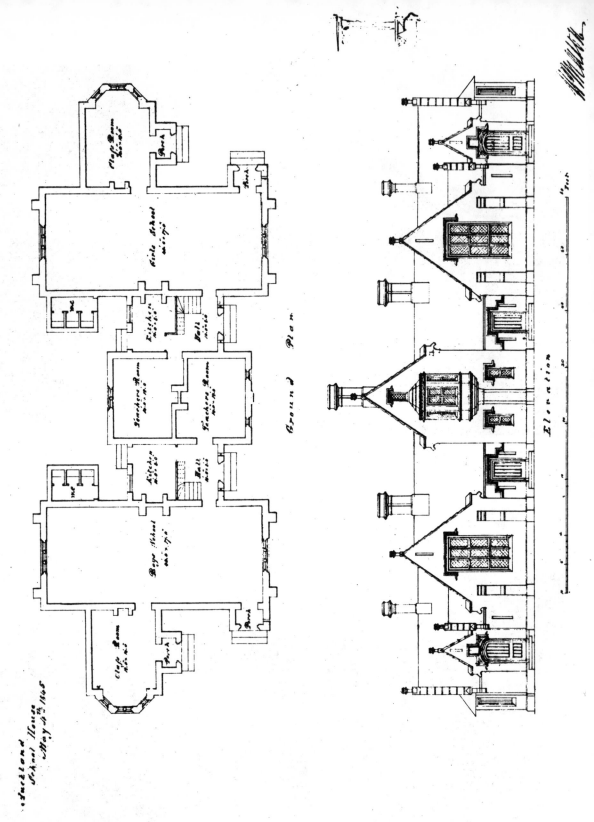

43.   *Proposed School House.*

44. *Second Government House.*

45. *Stairway.*

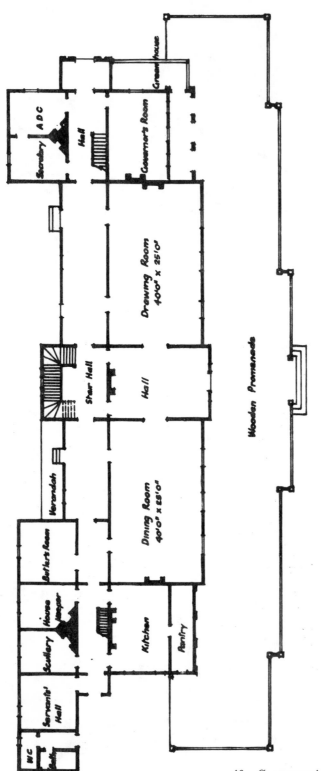

46. *Government House, ground floor plan.*

47. *Government House, west elevation.*

48. *Government House, the hall.*

49. *Bank of New Zealand, Wellington. (Demolished)*

50. *Cargill and Company, Dunedin.*

51. *Bank of New Zealand, Dunedin. (Demolished)*

52. *Desk from the banking chamber.*

THE BANK OF AUSTRALASIA, HIGH-STREET, DUNEDIN.

53. Bank of Australasia, Dunedin. (*Largely demolished*).

54. *Dunedin Public Warehouse.*

55. *Highlawn, Dunedin. (Demolished)*

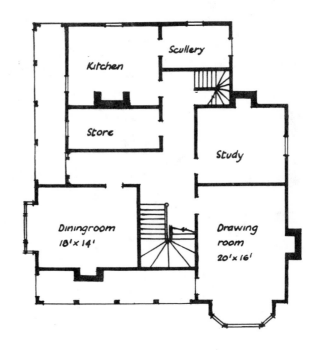

56. *Ground floor plan.*

57, 58, 59, 60. Mason's own house, London Street, Dunedin.

61. *Exhibition building, Dunedin. (Demolished).*

62. *Ground floor plan.*

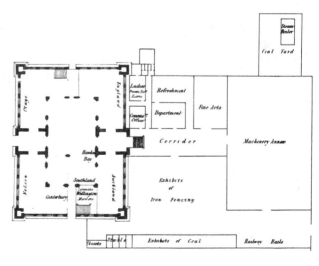

GROUND PLAN

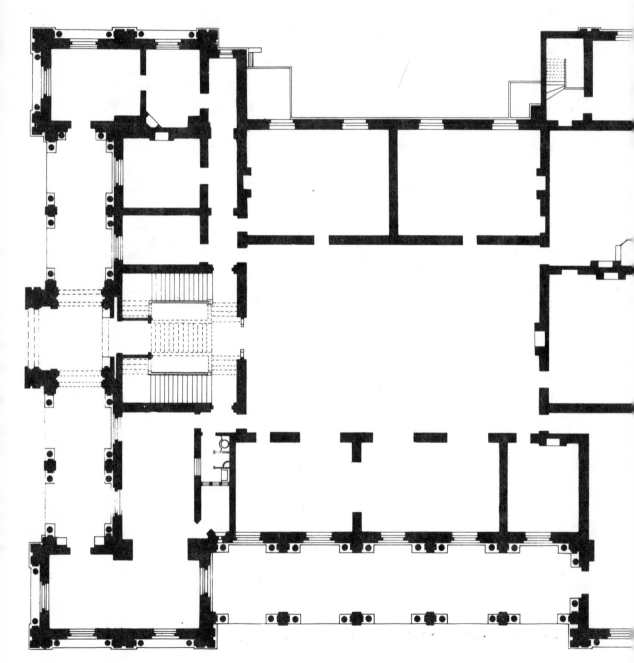

63. *Post Office, Dunedin, part plan.*

64. *Post Office, Dunedin.* (*Demolished*).

65. *Detail.*

66. *Bond store, Dunedin, now the State Advances offices.*

67. *Provincial Council Chambers, Bond store, and Post Office, viewed from the wharf.*

68. *Provincial Council Chambers, Dunedin. (Demolished).*

69. *Council Chambers, Princes Street front.*

70. *Colonial Museum, Wellington. (Demolished).*

71. *St Peter's Church, Caversham, now St Mary's, Mornington.*

72. *Bank of New South Wales, Dunedin.*

73. *St Paul's Church, Oamaru, first stage. (Demolished).*

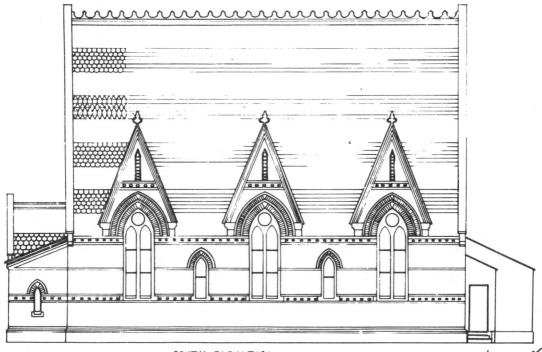

SOUTH ELEVATION

74. *All Saints' Church, Dunedin, first stage.*

75. *All Saints' Church, west end.*

76. *All Saints', side window.*

77. *Driver house.*

78. *Copland house.*

79. Government House, Wellington, sketch proposal.

80. St Matthew's Church, Dunedin.

81. St Matthew's, pulpit.

82. St Matthew's, nave.

83. *Otago Daily Times offices.*
84. *Shops, Princes Street.*

85. Clarion Buildings, Princes Street.

86. Warehouse for Ross and Glendining.

87. *Watsons' Dining Rooms. (Demolished)*.

88. *Choral Hall, Moray Place. (Demolished)*.

89. Bishopscourt, entrance porch.

90. *Bishopscourt, garden front.*

91. *Bishopscourt, stair.*

92. Grendon, Roslyn, Dunedin.

93, 94, 95, 96. Grendon, details.

97. *Keith Hall, East Taieri.*

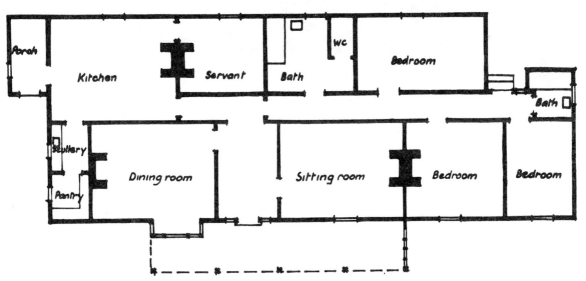

98. *Keith Hall, plan.*

99. Otepopo Presbyterian Church.

INDEX
Italic figures refer to plate numbers